A Search for
the Origins of Human Speech

A Search for the Origins of Human Speech

Auditory and Vocal functions of the Chimpanzee

Shozo Kojima

Kyoto University Press

First published in 2003 jointly by:

Kyoto University Press
Kyodai Kaikan
15-9 Yoshida Kawara-cho
Sakyo-ku, Kyoto 606-8305, Japan
Telephone: +81-75-761-6182
Fax: +81-75-761-6190
Email: sales@kyoto-up.gr.jp
Web: http://www.kyoto-up.gr.jp

Trans Pacific Press
PO Box 120, Rosanna, Melbourne
Victoria 3084, Australia
Telephone: +61 3 9459 3021
Fax: +61 3 9457 5923
Email: info@transpacificpress.com
Web: http://www.transpacificpress.com

Copyright © Kyoto University Press and Trans Pacific Press 2003

Set by digital environs Melbourne: enquiries@digitalenvirons.com

Printed in Melbourne by BPA Print Group

Distributors

Australia
Bushbooks
PO Box 1958, Gosford, NSW 2250
Telephone: (02) 4323-3274
Fax: (02) 9212-2468
Email: bushbook@ozemail.com.au

UK and Europe
Asian Studies Book Services
Nijenrodeplantsoen 104
3554 TT Utrecht, The Netherlands
Telephone: +31 30 289 1240
Fax: +31 30 289 1249
Email: marie.lenstrup@planet.nl
Web: http://www.asianstudiesbooks.com

USA and Canada
International Specialized Book
Services (ISBS)
5824 N. E. Hassalo Street
Portland, Oregon 97213-3644
USA
Telephone: (800) 944-6190
Fax: (503) 280-8832
Email: orders@isbs.com
Web: http://www.isbs.com

All rights reserved. No production of any part of this book may take place without the written permission of Kyoto University Press or Trans Pacific Press.

ISBN 4-87698-455-7 (hardcover)
ISBN 1-87684-347-0 (softcover)

National Library of Australia Cataloging in Publication Data

    Kojima, Shozo, 1943–.
        A search for the origins of human speech : auditory and vocal functions of the chimpanzee.

    Bibliography.
    Includes index.

    ISBN 4 87698 455 7.
    ISBN 1 876843 47 0 (pbk).

    1. Chimpanzees – Physiology. 2. Chimpanzees – Vocalization.
    3. Auditory perception. 4. Speech perception. 5. Speech.
    I. Title.

573.9219885

Contents

Preface	vii
Chapter 1: Introduction	1
Chapter 2: Auditory and vocal functions	5
Chapter 3: Behavioral and acoustical procedures	18
Chapter 4: Basic auditory functions	27
Chapter 5: Perception of human speech sounds	47
Chapter 6: Perception of species-specific vocal sounds	72
Chapter 7: Auditory cognition	94
Chapter 8: Vocal operant	125
Chapter 9: Early vocal development	128
Chapter 10: Vocal communication	143
Chapter 11: Action and language—laterality of the brain	152
Chapter 12: Conclusion	173
Bibliography	176
Index	193

Preface

Understanding the evolution of human speech is one of the primary goals of hominization studies. There have so far been basically two approaches to developing such an understanding: studies of fossil hominids and studies of living apes. Studying the origin and evolution of human speech through fossil hominids presents particular difficulties, as auditory and vocal apparatuses are not usually found in fossils. Consequently, the latter approach may prove more successful and has been adopted for this study. However, investigations of the auditory and vocal functions of apes have not yet proven sufficient to provide a satisfactory understanding of the evolution of human speech.

The first three chapters explain: the scope of the book (Chapter 1); the basic structures and functions of the auditory and vocal system of humans (Chapter 2); and general research methods (Chapter 3). Chapter 4 outlines the basic auditory functions of the chimpanzee, including auditory sensitivity and difference thresholds. Chapter 5 reports on the perception of speech sounds and related perceptual phenomena. The perception of species-specific vocal sounds is examined in Chapter 6.

The auditory cognition of a chimpanzee is reported in Chapter 7. Recognition of vocal sounds by individual chimpanzees was studied with Akihiro Izumi and Miyuki M. Ceugniet (Primate Research Institute, Kyoto University). The human PET (positron emission tomography) study was joint research conducted with Sumiharu Nagumo (Primate Research Institute, Kyoto University), Ryuta Kawashima, Motoaki Sugiura, and Hiroshi Fukuda (Institute of Development, Aging & Cancer, Tohoku University), Kenngo Ito, Takashi Kato, Akinori Nakamura, and Kentaro Hatano (Department of Biofunctional Research, National Institute for Longevity Sciences), and Kayo Asakawa and Shigeru Kiritani (Graduate School of Medicine, University of Tokyo).

The next two chapters examine the plasticity of vocal behaviors, with Chapter 8 focusing on operant conditioning and Chapter 9 on early vocal development. Both of these chapters introduce findings from studies of mother-infant vocal interactions. Chapter 10 reports on the vocal interactions among subgroups of captive chimpanzees discovered through experimentation conducted in collaboration with Naoki Agetsuma and

Kyoko Okamoto (Primate Research Institute, Kyoto University). I express my thanks to these researchers.

Almost all of these studies on the auditory and vocal functions of the chimpanzee were original. I found that there are wide gaps between chimpanzees' auditory and vocal functions and those of humans. Continuities between chimpanzee vocal behavior and human speech are very difficult to establish. While it may be gestures that bridge these communication gaps, I'm also interested in behaviors that are highly developed in humans: imitation, tool-use and right-handedness. My research shows that the left hemisphere of the human brain controls these behaviors, as well as speech. Thus, motor functions of the left hemisphere appear to play important roles in hominization. Chapters 11 and 12 present a tentative scenario of the evolution of human speech from the standpoint of hemispheric lateralization, a scenario I owe to Dr. Doreen Kimura's works.

Publication of this book was supported by Grant-in-Aid for Publication of Scientific Research Results (No. 145196) to Shozo Kojima (S. K.) by the Japan Society for the Promotion of Science (JSPS).

Experiments reported in this book were supported by the Human Frontier Science Program (the principal investigator; Dr. Vittorio Gallese), a Grant-in-Aid for COE Research (No.10CE2005; the principal investigator is Dr. Osamu Takenaka), Grant-in-Aid for Scientific Research on Priority Research (No. 05206109, 09207102), and Grant-in-Aid for Scientific Research (No. 60510059, 63490014, 04610053, 13410025) to S. K. by the Ministry of Education, Culture, Sports, Science and Technology of Japan and by JSPS.

September 2002
Shozo Kojima, Ph.D.

Chapter 1: Introduction

Humans and speech

Of all primates, only humans have language. Research on the learning of 'language' by chimpanzees (Gardner & Gardner, 1969; Premack, 1976; Rumbaugh, 1977) and the vocal behavior of monkeys in the field (Snowdon et al. 1982) suggests that human language is a result of mutations and natural selection. Human language is a spoken language that uses the vocal-auditory channel. Audition has several advantages over other sense modalities: 1) the speed of propagation of auditory stimuli is relatively high, 2) auditory stimuli travel long distances, 3) auditory stimuli are robust against obstacles and darkness, and 4) it is not necessary for listeners to direct attention to auditory sources. However, since auditory stimuli are usually presented successively, it is necessary for listeners to have a high-speed processing system with good working memory for managing complex auditory information. On the other hand, we can 1) produce auditory information by the movements of a small set of musculatures, and 2) the amount of information per unit of time is large (Lieberman, 1975). However, motor skills, i.e., articulation, are required.

Spoken language is unique to humans. It is irrefutable that language characterizes many aspects of human behavior. Without language, humans could not have attained the high level of civilization observed today. It is interesting that the Japanese have long believed in the miraculous power of language (kotodama). When we think about prayers that verbalize wishes, we feel that the prayers appeal to the 'kotodama'.

Chimpanzee 'language' projects

More than 50 years ago, Hayes attempted to train a young female chimpanzee (Viki) to speak a human language (Hayes, 1951). Viki learned four words in 6 years: "mama", "papa", "cup" and "up". She could not master more than four words despite extensive training for 6 years. Thus, researchers who followed this research gave up on the auditory and vocal channels. Researchers used sign languages (Gardner & Gardner, 1969), plastic plates of different colors and shapes (Premack, 1976), and lexigrams (Rumbaugh, 1977). In other words, they adopted the visual channel. Except for the sign language study, the required motor responses were very simple.

These studies clearly showed that chimpanzees have concepts and that they can label signs, color plates or lexigrams to these concepts. That is, they acquired the use of *symbols*. They could also combine symbols. For example, they labeled "red" "key" or "blue" "ball". However, there are many controversies over whether they have true syntax. The language chimpanzees acquired may be a 'proto language' (Bickerton, 1990).

These findings clearly suggested that the cognitive abilities of apes are more advanced than previously considered. Chimpanzee 'language' studies caused considerable controversy in comparative psychology, anthropology and linguistics. Together with observations of tool-using behavior in the field (Goodall, 1964) and the realization of a close similarity in genes (King & Wilson, 1975; Chen & Li, 2001), these new findings suggested that the genetic and cognitive differences between humans and chimpanzees are small.

However, it was humans that invented these symbols, not chimpanzees themselves. These studies do not clarify how human *speech* evolved. We may assume that the hearing of early hominids was not very different from that of living great apes. Hence, it is important to examine the hearing ability of great apes and to compare it with that of humans to understand the evolution of the vocal-auditory and speech functions of humans.

Psycholinguistic analyses of vocal behaviors in the monkey

In 1975, Green published a monograph on the vocal behavior of the Japanese macaque in the field (Green, 1975). In this monograph, he reported a variation in coo calls and their relationship to social contexts. He found that there were seven coo types and that the coo vocal patterns were correlated with social contexts. That is, a specific coo call pattern was vocalized in a specific social context more often than other patterns.

This was the start of a new research trend (Snowdon et al. 1982). The traditional ethological view poses a dichotomy between human and animal communication. That is, animal communication is regarded as simple, stereotyped, fixed and affective, whereas human communication is highly complex, variant, open and semantic. However, recent research has provided evidence against this dichotomy. Primate communication is not simple, and subtle differences in acoustic structure convey important information. There are individual, population and localization differences in many of the calls of primates (Snowdon, 1982). Monkeys can identify an individual caller, the population or subspecies the caller belongs to, and their distance from the caller based on such differences. Moreover, the alarm calls of the vervet monkey are 'semantic': three specific alarm calls refer to three different predators (Struhsaker, 1967). Such correspondences are acquired through experience (Seyfarth & Cheney, 1980).

Researchers adopted psycholinguistic approaches to the understanding of vocal communication in primates. Adoption of these approaches can be very fruitful, since they provide tools for analyzing the acoustic structure of primate calls, i.e., distinctive feature analysis. Computer-synthesized vocal sounds are indispensable in investigating the categorical perception of voices in primates. A rule or 'syntactic system' is found in the sequences within calls and in exchanges between monkeys (Cleveland & Snowdon, 1982). In laboratories, researchers found that monkeys also showed categorical perception of human speech sounds (Kuhl & Padden, 1982; 1983).

Studies on auditory and vocal functions in the chimpanzee: scope of this book

Despite their obvious importance, there have been only a few studies of the hearing and vocal behaviors of apes (Elder, 1934, 1935 for basic hearing, Lieberman, 1968; Marler & Tenaza, 1977 for basic vocal behavior). In this book, I report on studies of the auditory and vocal functions of the chimpanzee. In Chapter 2, I will describe basic findings on the structures and functions of the auditory and vocal apparatus. In Chapter 3, behavioral procedures for studying vocal and auditory functions, and acoustic measurements of auditory stimuli will be described.

It is widely recognized that animals have an auditory system that matches the spectrum of sounds emitted by the animals themselves (Hopkins, 1982; Lieberman, 1975, 1984). Hearing of humans may be adapted to the sounds of human speech and that of apes to their vocal sounds. In Chapter 4, the basic auditory functions, auditory sensitivity and difference thresholds will be described. In Chapter 5, the perception of human speech sounds, vowels and consonants, and related speech perception phenomena will be examined. In Chapter 6, the production and perception of species-specific vocal sounds in the chimpanzee will be described.

To study auditory cognition in nonhuman primates is difficult, for they often fail to acquire tasks. For example, for monkeys and even for chimpanzees, it was difficult for them to match auditory sample stimuli to visual test stimuli in an audio-visual matching to sample task. Cross-modal or intermodal abilities are necessary for the evolution and development of spoken language. In Chapter 7, I will describe recognition of environmental sounds, identification of individuals by vocal sounds, and auditory working memory in the chimpanzee.

The plasticity of vocal behavior is prominent in humans. However, it is not easy for nonhuman primates to differentiate voices according to different visual stimuli, as Viki showed (Hayes, 1951). In Chapter 8, an attempt to condition vocal behavior in a chimpanzee infant and its later influences will be described. Human infants develop their vocal behavior in steps leading to the emergence of the first language (Oller, 1980). Chimpanzee infants without a spoken language show different vocal development. In Chapter 9, early vocal development will be described in chimpanzee infants and will be compared with that of human infants. Infant-mother vocal interactions will be also described.

Recent studies of the vocal communication of monkeys in the field suggest that there may be continuity between vocal communication in nonhuman primates and spoken language in humans (Snowdon et al. 1982). Although the vocal sounds of chimpanzees convey little information compared with human speech sounds, they actually communicate with voices. In Chapter 10, vocal exchange between two parties (subgroups) of a captive chimpanzee group will be described. I will focus our attention on the functions of pant hoots.

In general, languages are processed in the left hemisphere of the human brain. There are several other types of behavior that are unique to or highly developed in humans, e.g., bipedal walking, tool-using and -making, manipulation, imitation, pantomime gestures and handedness. Except for bipedal walking, these types of behavior (actions) are controlled mainly by the left hemisphere of the brain. Aphasia is a language disorder, and apraxia is a disorder of actions (Kolb & Whishaw, 1980), and both may result from damage to the left hemisphere. In Chapter 11, we will discuss laterality from broader perspectives, and discuss the origins of speech and spoken language from this standpoint. Special attention will be paid to mirror neurons in the monkey ventral premotor cortex and the mirror system (Gallese et al., 1996). In these chapters, I often present data of macaque monkeys and humans for comparison.

In the last chapter, I present a tentative scenario for the origins of speech and its evolution.

Chapter 2: Auditory and vocal functions

Structures and functions of the auditory system

The functions of the auditory system are to perceive and recognize auditory stimuli, and to identify the position of the source. The auditory system consists of four parts, the external (outer) ear, the middle ear, the inner ear (Figure 2-1), and the auditory nervous system. I will briefly describe the structure of each and their functions. The external ear consists of the pinna (the auricle) and the external ear canal (the external auditory meatus). At the end of the canal is the ear drum (the tympanic membrane). The pinna gathers sounds, and the external ear canal is a closed tube resonator. The resonance frequencies are about 3 kHz for the human ear. At these

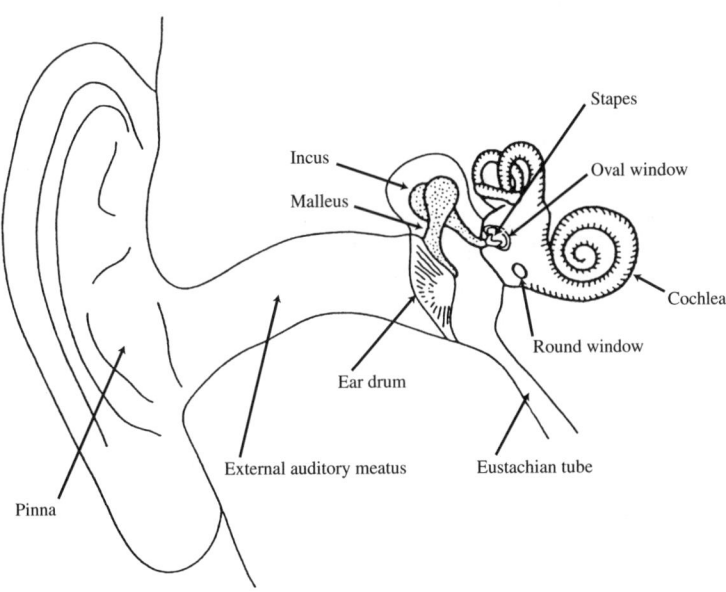

Figure 2-1
The peripheral auditory system. See text for details.

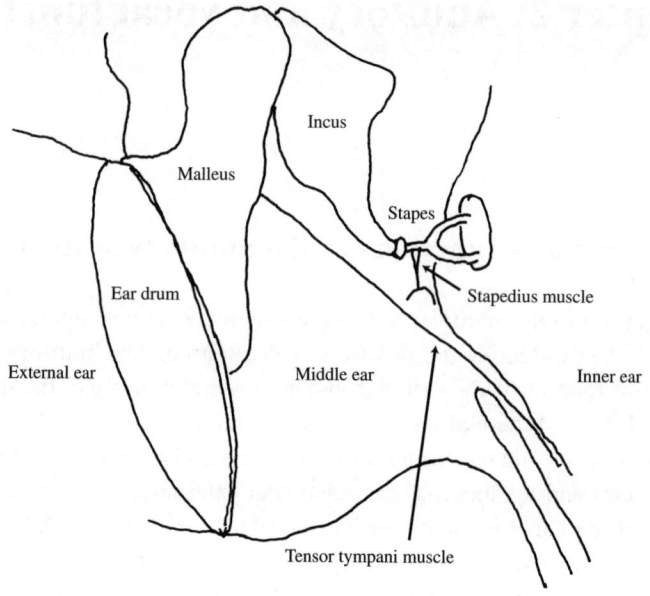

Figure 2-2
The ossicular chain and middle ear muscles.

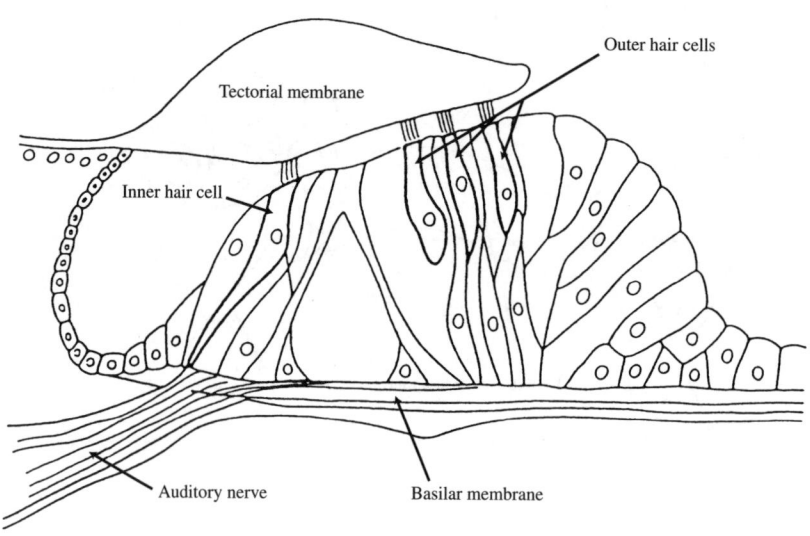

Figure 2-3
The organ of Corti.

frequencies, the sound pressure inside the meatus is greater than that at the entrance of the canal. At the ear drum, changes in air pressure are converted to mechanical movements of the body.

In the middle ear, the auditory ossicles (the ossicular chain) connect the ear drum with the inner ear (Figure 2-2). The ossicles are three tiny bones, namely, the malleus, the incus, and the stapes. The malleus is attached to the ear drum and the stapes to the oval windows of the cochlea of the inner ear. The ossicular chain transmits mechanical movements of the ear drum to the cochlea. Two middle ear muscles are attached to the bones. The tensor tympani muscle is attached to the malleus, and the stapedius muscle to the stapes. When a loud sound reaches the ear drum, these muscles contract to reduce the movements of the ossicles. This is the middle ear muscle reflex that protects the auditory system from intense sounds. The middle ear is an impedance transformer that matches the impedance of the eardrum to the higher impedance of the cochlea. The diameter of the ear drum is larger than that of the oval window. Thus, sound pressure is also amplified in the middle ear.

The cochlea is in the inner ear. There are three scalae in the cochlea, namely, scala vestibuli, scala media, and scala tympani. The Reissners membrane separates the scala vestibuli and the scala media. The basilar membrane separates the scala media and the scala tympani. Scalae are filled with lymph. The organ of Corti is on the basilar membrane (Figure 2-3). The organ of Corti contains four rows of hair cells (three rows of outer hair cells and one row of inner hair cells) which are receptor cells. They transform mechanical movement of hair cells to electrical activity of the nervous system. The vibration of the ear drum is transmitted to the oval window of the cochlea via the ossicular chain. The movements of the oval window produce traveling waves of the basilar membrane and the lymph through the scala media. The organ of Corti, and thus the hair cells, are deflected. The deflection produces electrical activity in hair cells that travels to the central nervous system.

The cochlea can be described as a frequency analyzer. In the cochlea, each part of the basilar membrane (and hair cells) responds to specific frequencies. For example, hair cells near the oval window respond to high frequencies and hair cells at the apex of the cochlea respond to low frequencies (tonotopy, see Figure 2-4). Thus, each frequency of the sound wave is represented on different parts of the cochlea.

Electrical activity from hair cells travels to the cerebral cortex via subcortical relay nuclei (Figure 2-5). Hair cells in each ear send information mainly to the opposite hemisphere. Thus, the left hemisphere

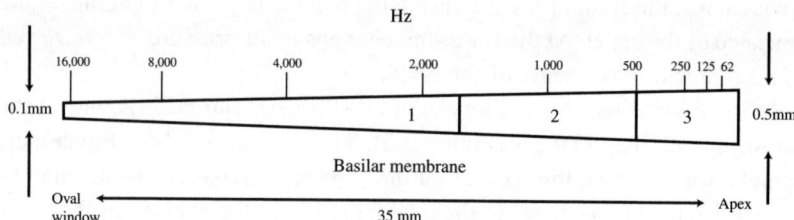

Figure 2-4
The tonotopy in the human cochlea. The basilar membrane is straightened. Each number in the basilar membrane indicates the turn.

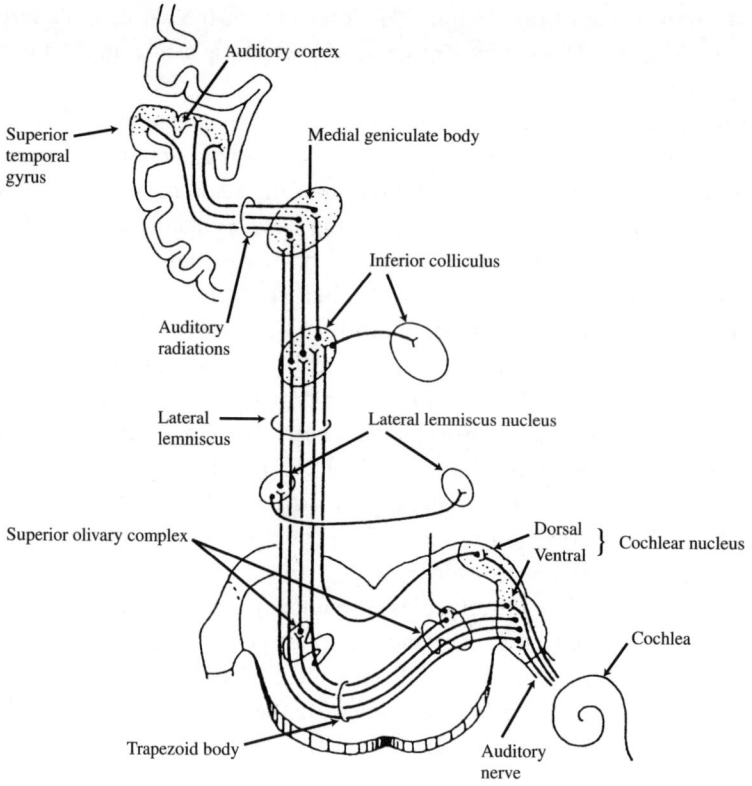

Figure 2-5
The auditory nervous system.

receives input mainly from the right ear. The cerebral cortex interprets the meaning of auditory stimuli.

Structures and functions of the vocal system

Production of vowels

There are two factors required for the production of vocal sounds: the source and the filter (Figure 2-6). The vibration of the vocal cords in the larynx produces the source of vocal sounds. The spectral pattern of the source sound is shown in Figure 2-6. It consists of the fundamental tone

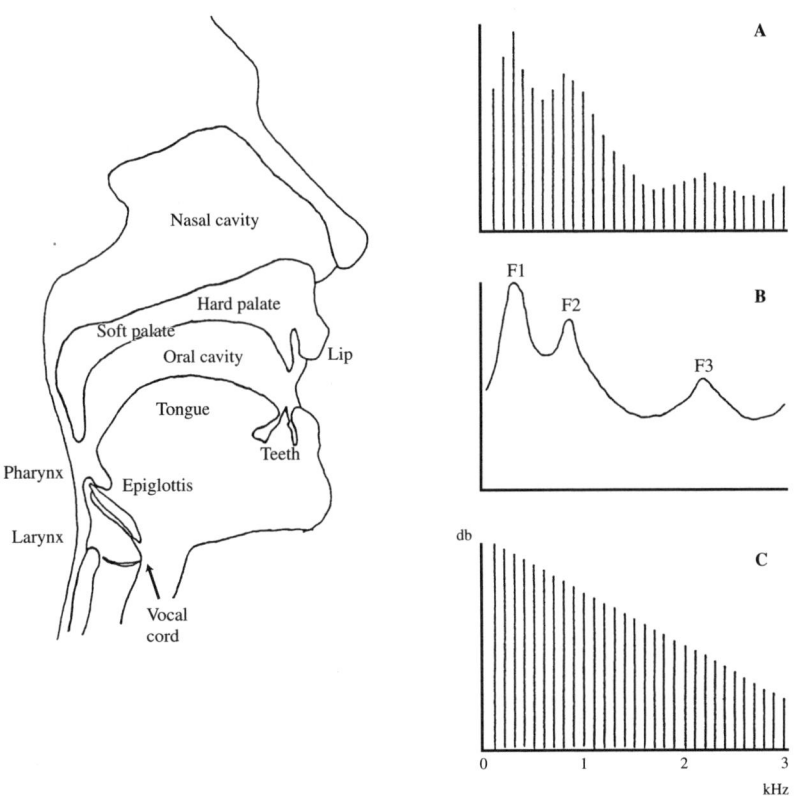

Figure 2-6
Left: The human vocal system. Right: The spectral pattern of vocal sound (A). The filter function of the supralaryngeal vocal tract (B). The spectral pattern of the laryngeal source sounds (C). F1, F2 and F3 indicate the first formant, second formant and third formant, respectively.

and harmonics. The fundamental tone has the strongest energy, and the power decreases as the harmonics become higher. The frequencies of the fundamental tone (the fundamental frequency, F0; pitch) are about 100 Hz and 200 Hz for adult males and adult females, respectively. Infants have a much higher F0 than adults.

The laryngeal source waves are modified by the filter function of the supralaryngeal vocal tract, as shown in Figure 2-6. The shape of the supralaryngeal vocal tract determines its filter function. The positions of the tongue and the lips form the shape of the vocal tract. The filter consists of band-pass filters. Thus, there are frequency bands (formants) that pass the energy of the laryngeal source, and these formants determine vowels. That is, each vowel has a specific shape of the vocal tract and specific formants. The vowel [i] needs a wide space in the back of the vocal tract. A wide space in the front of the vocal tract must be realized for uttering the vowel [a]. The vowel [u] uses both the front and back part of the vocal tract. The first two formants (F1 and F2) largely determine vowels. Figure 2-7 indicates vowels on the first and second formant (F1-F2) plane with the position of the tongue. Table 2-1 shows frequencies of the first and second formant of five Japanese vowels. Table 2-2 shows classification of vowels based on the position of the tongue. Figure 2-8 indicates sound spectrograms of the five Japanese vowels.

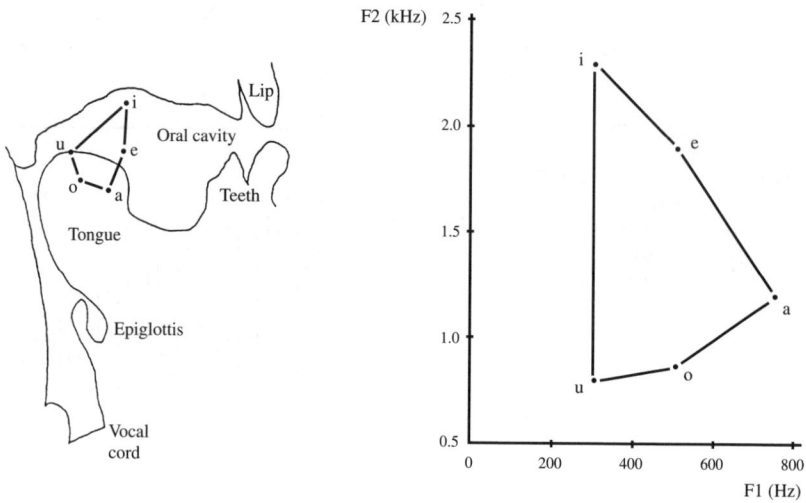

Figure 2-7
Left: The position of the tongue for each English vowel. Right: Five English vowels on the first (F1) and second (F2) formant plane.

Table 2-1 The frequency of the first two formants of Japanese vowels

	a	i	u	e	o
F1(Hz)	741	305	344	496	459
F2 (Hz)	1302	2132	1472	1863	702

Table 2-2 Vowel categories[a]

Front		Central		Back		
i	ü	ɨ	ʉ	ɯ	u	high
I	Ü	ɪ	ʊ̇	Ï	U	lower-high
e	ö	ė	ȯ	ë	o	higher-mid
E	Ö	ə	Ȯ	Ë	O	mid
ɛ	ɔ̈	ɛ̇		ʌ	ɔ	lower-mid
æ		æ̇			ɒ	higher-low
ä		a	ȧ	ɑ	ɑ̈	low

a From Crothers (1978).

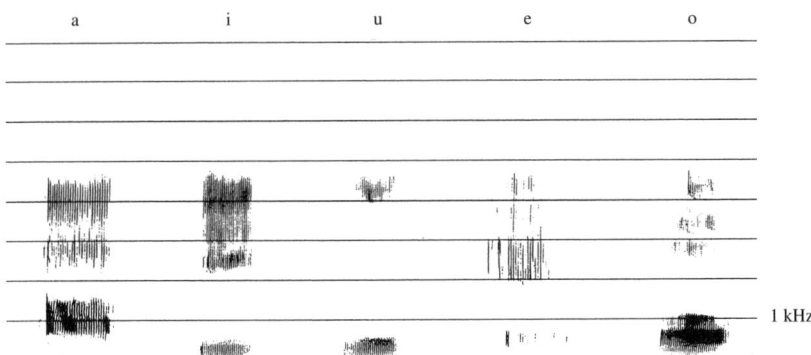

Figure 2-8
Sound spectrograms of the five Japanese vowels.

Production of consonants

The classification of consonants is presented in Table 2-3. There are three dimensions: the manner of articulation, the place of articulation and the voiced-voiceless distinction. Stop or plosive consonants (e.g., [p]) are produced by a complete stop of air passing through the vocal tract and then

Table 2-3 Classification of English consonants by place and manner of articulation

Place of articulation	Stops Voiceless	Stops Voiced	Fricatives Voiceless	Fricatives Voiced	Nasals Voiceless	Nasals Voiced	Glides & liquids Voiceless	Glides & liquids Voiced
Labial	[p]	[b]				[m]	[hw]	[w]
Labiodental			[f]	[v]				
Dental			[θ]	[ð]				
Alveolar	[t]	[d]	[s]	[z]		[n]		[l]
Palatal	[tʃ]	[dʒ]	[ʃ]	[ʒ]				[j] [r]
Velar	[k]	[g]				[ŋ]		
Glottal			[h]					

its abrupt release. Fricative consonants (e.g., [s]) are produced by a partial constriction of the vocal tract and its relatively gradual release. Acoustic analyses of stop and fricative consonants (e.g., [pa] and [sa]) are shown in Figure 2-9. Stops and fricatives are characterized by click and noise sounds, respectively. The stop consonants [p], [t] and [k] are produced at the lips, the alveolar ridge and the velum, respectively. The difference in the place of articulation is characterized by the starting frequencies of the transition of the second and third formants. Figure 2-10 shows sound spectrograms of [ba], [da] and [ga]. Although the first formant is similar for these three syllables, the starting frequency is lower for [ba] than for [da], and for [da]

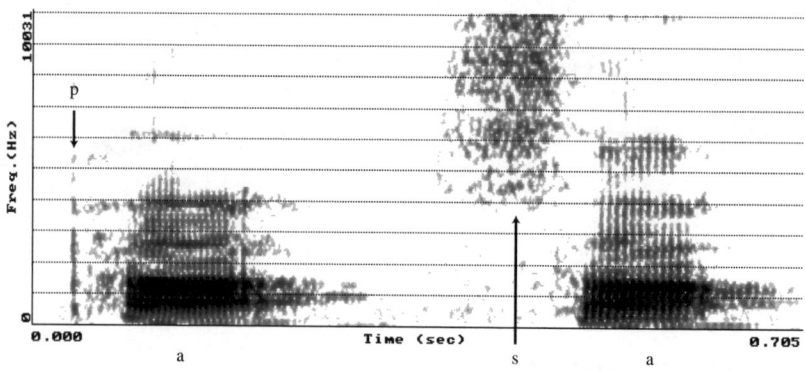

Figure 2-9
Acoustic analysis of stop (left, [pa]) and fricative (right, [sa]) consonants, showing sound spectrograms of these consonants. The left arrow indicates a click sound [p], and the right arrow indicates a noise sound [s].

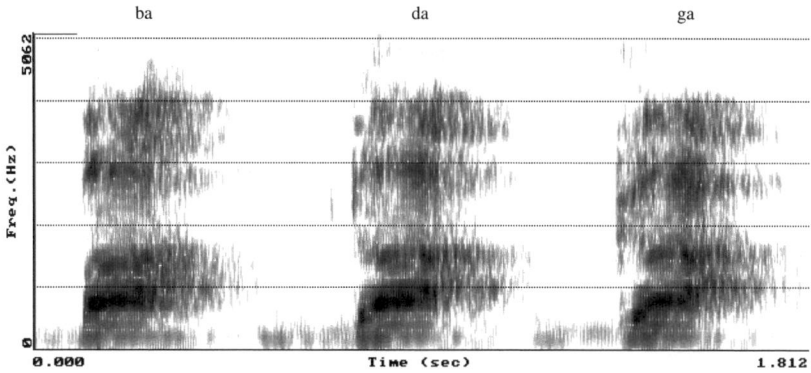

Figure 2-10
Sound spectrogram for each stop consonant (left: [ba], center: [da], and right: [ga]).

than for [ga]. The voiced-voiceless (e.g., [pa] and [ba]) distinction is characterized by the time interval between the plosive and the vibration of the vocal folds (voice onset time [VOT], see Figure 2-9). That is, when VOT is about 0 ms, we hear the syllable [ba] (voiced sound). When VOT is about 50 ms, it is [pa] (voiceless sound).

Topics in speech perception

In this section, I describe several phenomena of speech perception. Some researchers assert that there may be a special mode for the processing of speech sounds (e.g., Liberman et al., 1967; Repp, 1982). Other auditory stimuli may be processed through a different mode. Only humans have spoken language. Therefore, the speech mode may be specific to humans. The following four phenomena of speech perception are related to these topics. These speech perception phenomena will be examined later in the chimpanzee (see Chapter 5).

Vocal tract normalization
Vowels, such as [a], when pronounced by different speakers, have different acoustic properties. For example, the fundamental frequency (pitch) and formant frequencies of vowels are higher in females and children than in males (Lieberman, 1984; 1986; see Figure 2-11). However, humans can perceive these speech sounds as the same vowel. This phenomenon has been called vocal tract normalization, talker

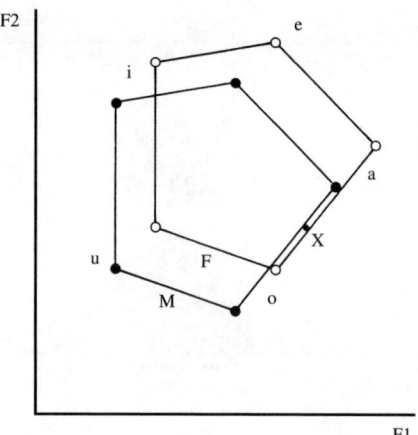

Figure 2-11
Five Japanese vowels uttered by female (open circles) and male (filled circles) speakers on the F1-F2 plane. If we are unable to normalize the size of the vocal tract, we hear the vowel X on the F1-F2 plane as [a] when it is uttered by a male speaker and as [o] when it is uttered by a female speaker.

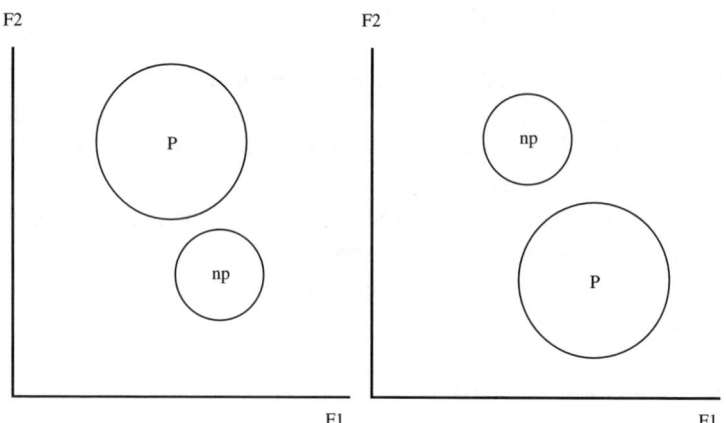

Figure 2-12
Prototypic (p) and nonprototypic (np) vowels on the F1-F2 plane. The vowel [i] is a prototype, but [y] is a nonprototype for English (left). The vowel [y] is a prototype and [i] is a nonprototype for Swedish (right). Vowels within each circle are perceived as the same vowel. A prototypic vowel occupies a wide area.

normalization or perceptual constancy, and it has been suggested that the pitch and the third and fourth formants serve as cues for the normalization (Fujisaki & Kawashima, 1968). Vocal tract normalization has been considered to be an important aspect of speech perception and one of the prerequisites for human spoken language (Lieberman, 1984; 1986). Infants of about 6 month old have the ability to perform vocal tract normalization (Kuhl, 1979). It is of interest to examine whether chimpanzees normalize the size of the vocal tract (see Chapter 5).

Prototype or magnet effect

Each language has prototypic vowels. On the F1-F2 plane, and compared with a nonprototypic vowel, a prototypic vowel usually occupies a wide area (see Figure 2-12). Vowels that fall in this area are perceived as the same vowel. For example, the vowel [i] is a prototype and [y] is a nonprototype for English. On the other hand, the vowel [y] is a prototype and [i] is a nonprototype for Swedish. At about 6 months of age, infants were observed to adapt their perception of these vowels to the language environment (Kuhl, 1991). Macaque monkeys did not show the prototype or magnet effect on these vowels. It is not known whether chimpanzees exhibit the prototype or magnet effect. We will test this possibility in Chapter 5. The repertoire of vowel-like sounds of the chimpanzee may be an important contributing factor.

Categorical perception or the phoneme boundary effect

Humans discriminate the voicing and place-of-articulation features categorically (Lisker & Abramson, 1964; Mattingly et al., 1971). Human listeners demonstrate good discrimination at the boundaries between phonetic categories (see Figure 2-13). This phoneme boundary effect has been thought to be specific to the sounds of human speech, to require speech-specific mechanisms for processing, and thus to be unique to humans. However, nonhuman animals, including chinchillas and macaque monkeys, have demonstrated the phoneme boundary effect (Morse & Snowdon, 1975; Waters & Wilson, 1976; Kuhl & Miller, 1978; Kuhl,1981; Kuhl & Padden, 1982; 1983). These results in animals have had a significant impact on the theories of speech perception. No data is available on categorical perception in chimpanzees. We will examine this phoneme boundary effect on the distinction between voiced and voiceless ([ga-ka]) stop consonants and on that between place-of-articulation ([ba-da]) features of stop consonants in Chapter 5.

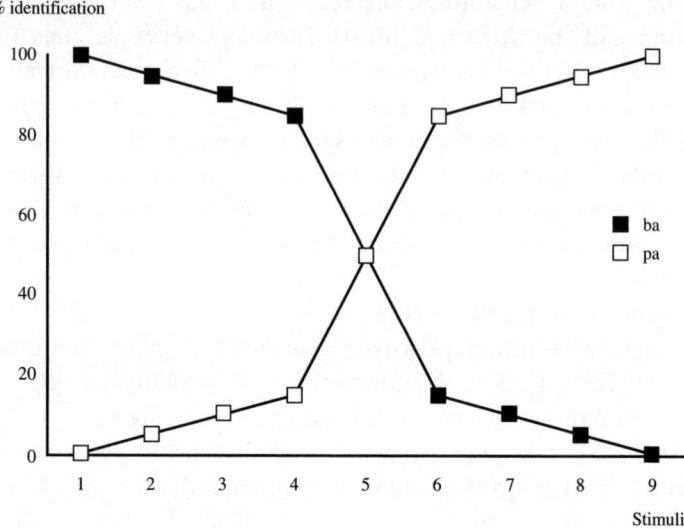

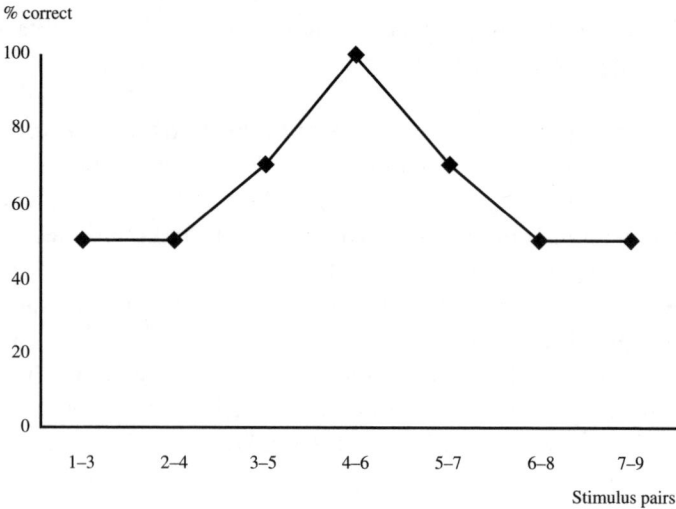

Figure 2-13
Categorical perception between voiced and voiceless stop consonants (for example, between [ba]-Stimulus 1 and [pa]-Stimulus 9). Humans label the voicing feature categorically (upper), and demonstrate good discrimination at the boundary (Stimulus 5) between phonetic categories (lower).

Context effect or rate normalization

Acoustically, the duration of the formant transition determines the difference between the syllables [ba] and [wa]: it is shorter for the syllable [ba] than [wa]. However, the duration of the syllable as a whole has effects on the position of the boundary of these two syllables (Miller & Liberman, 1979). This is an example of the context effect and is called rate normalization. Thus, even if the duration of the formant transition is the same, the syllable is perceived as [ba] or as [wa] depending on the duration of the syllable. Usually, the boundary moves to the [wa] side, when the duration of the syllable becomes long (see Figure 2-14). In Chapter 5, we will examine this phenomenon in the chimpanzee.

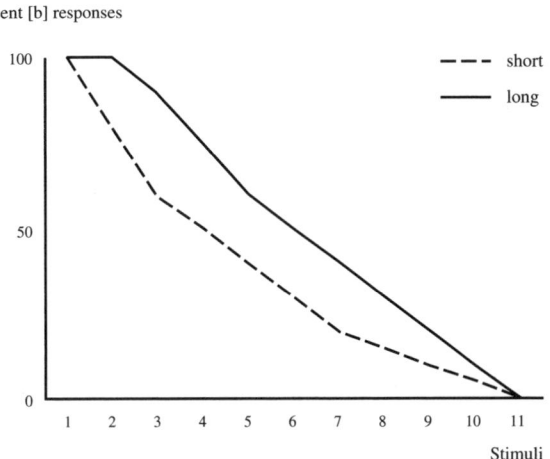

Figure 2-14

The perception of syllables on the [ba]–[wa] continuum (stimulus No. 1–No. 11). The duration of the formant transition is different between the syllable [ba] and [wa]. The duration of the syllable has effects on the perception of the boundary between these two syllables. When the duration of the syllable is long, the boundary moves to the [wa] side.

Chapter 3: Behavioral and acoustical procedures

Subjects

The subjects used in the following experiments were three female chimpanzees (Pendesa [Pen], Popo, and Pan). Pan has a female infant, Pal. Usually, they were not deprived of food or water. The chimpanzees spontaneously joined in the experiments and the incentive value of rewards maintained their performance. Figure 3-1 shows a picture of each subject, and Table 3-1 shows the profiles of the chimpanzees in the Primate Research Institute, Kyoto University.

The use of the subjects followed the *Guide for the care and use of laboratory primates* (Primate Research Institute, Kyoto University, 1986).

Apparatus

Figure 3-2 shows a diagram of the apparatuses used in the auditory experiments that will be described in Chapters 4, 5, and 6. A personal

Table 3-1 Chimpanzees (sex, month and year of birth)

Subjects of the experiments			Other chimpanzees			
Pendesa	♀	Feb. 1977	Reiko	♀	1966	*
Popo	♀	Mar. 1982	Gon	♂	1966	*
Pan	♀	Dec. 1983	Puchi	♀	1966	*
			Akira	♂	Jun. 1976	*
			Mari	♀	Jun. 1976	*
			Ai	♀	Oct. 1976	*
			Kuroe	♀	Feb. 1980	
			Reo	♂	May 1982	
			Ayumu	♂	Apr. 2000	
			Kureo	♀	Jun. 2000	
			Pal	♀	Aug. 2000	

* estimated (captured from the wild).

Figure 3-1
Chimpanzee subjects used in the experiments. Upper: Pen, middle: Popo and lower: Pan.

computer (PC) controlled the presentation of auditory stimuli, detected responses, and measured reaction times. An analog data processor (ADP; Mark-1, NCC) contained AD/DA converters and digital memories. A

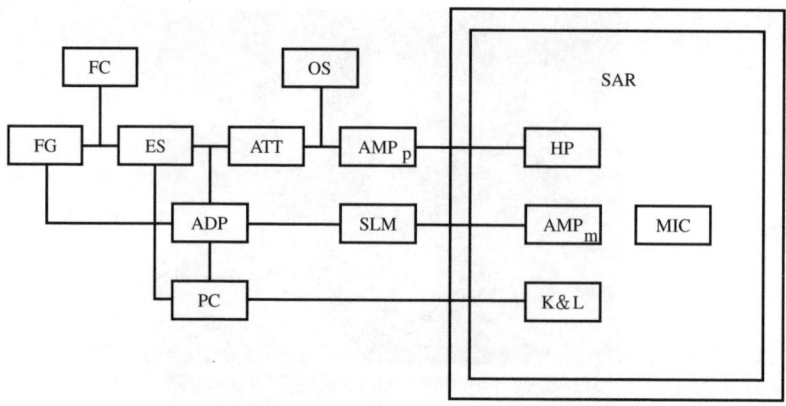

Figure 3-2
A diagram of apparatuses used in the auditory experiments.

Figure 3-3
Pan with earphones.

function generator (FG; FG-350, Iwatsu) produced pure tones. The FG had VCA (voltage controlled amplitude) and VCF (voltage controlled frequency) inputs. Thus, the intensity and frequency of a pure tone were controlled by the PC through the DA converter of the ADP. A frequency counter (FC) measured the frequency of pure tones. An electroswitch (ES; SB-10A, Rion) produced rise and fall times of pure tones, and the ES was controlled by the PC. A manual attenuator (ATT; LAT-45, Leader) controlled the intensity of pure tones. An oscilloscope (OS) monitored the waveform of pure tones. A power amplifier (AMPp) presented pure tones through earphones (HP; TDH-39 with MX-41/AR ear cushions).

The intensity of auditory stimuli was measured through a microphone (MIC; VC-29, Rion). The output of the MIC was amplified by another amplifier (AMPm), which in turn fed into a sound level meter (SLM; Na-72, Rion). The SLM was connected to the ADP, and it sent analog outputs to the ADP. The PC received outputs from the AD converter of the SLM. The earphones were calibrated using a 6-cc coupler with a 450-g weight, the condenser microphone (MIC) and the SLM.

Experiments were conducted in a double-walled sound-attenuating room (SAR; RE-246A, Tracoustics). The subject wore earphones facing a panel that contained a key and a lamp (K & L). Figure 3-3 shows Pan with the earphones in the SAR.

Figure 3-4 shows an experimental booth used for studying auditory cognition (auditory-visual intermodal matching to sample) that will be described in Chapter 7. In these experiments, a different testing system was used. A personal computer that had an auditory input/output system and a color monitor with a touch panel system were used to control the experiments. In the early part of the experiments, a laser disc player was used for recording, storing, and presenting visual stimuli. Later in the experiments, visual stimuli were stored in the hard disk and presented directly from the computer.

Auditory stimuli and acoustical procedures

In the following experiments described in Chapters 4, 5, and 6, pure tones, natural and synthetic human speech sounds, and species-specific vocal sounds of the chimpanzee were used. The vocal sounds were digitized and stored in the memory of the ADP or in the hard disk of the computer. In the experiments described in Chapter 7, environmental sounds, such as those of artifacts and vocal sounds of animals, were used. These sounds were digitized and stored in the computer.

Figure 3-4
The experimental booth used for audio-visual matching experiments. Upper: a picture from the outside, lower: from the inside.

In Chapter 9, early vocal development is described. Vocal sounds and situations in which the chimpanzee vocalized were described in notebooks, and were taped (TC-D5M, Sony). Vocalizations recorded on a tape recorder were analyzed by sound spectrographs (Digital Sona-Graph, Model 7800, Kay and SA-70, Rion). Vowel-like sounds of the chimpanzee infant were recorded and analyzed by an LPC (linear predictive coding) program (Siga I, Western Village) to measure formant frequencies. The frequency range of the analysis was 8 kHz and the sampling rate was 16.67 kHz (12 bits). The analyzing resolution was 105 Hz. The order of prediction of the LPC analysis was 10. The overlap ratio was 0.5. The frequency of peak positions (formants) of a spectrum envelope was measured.

In the experiments described in Chapter 7, a vocal sound (grunt, whimper or squeak) was manipulated with a filter. A harmonic sound or combinations of harmonic sounds of a grunt, whimper or squeak were deleted by a digital filter (-100 dB; SDF, Western Village), and the subjects were required to discriminate filtered vocal sounds from the original sound.

The synthetic vowels were synthesized by a computer program which was similar to that described by Klatt (1980).

Tasks

Reaction Time Tasks

The subjects faced a panel containing a lamp and a telegraph key. Two types of reaction time tasks were used (AX procedure). The following is the first type of reaction time task (RT I, see Figure 3-5). This task measures auditory sensitivity. A trial was started by illumination of the lamp. The subjects were required to press the key until a pure tone was presented. The time between key press and onset of the tone (lag period) was varied between 2 and 6 s. The subjects were extensively trained to release the key as quickly as possible when they detected the tone. Key release during the 1-s tone presentation produced a reward (a piece of fruit), turned off the light and terminated the trial. The latency of key release (reaction time) after the tone onset was measured. In general, the reaction time decreased as the intensity of the tone increased. If the subject did not release the key within 1 s after the tone onset, or if the subject released the key during the lag period, the stimuli were turned off and the trial was terminated.

In the second type of reaction time task (RT II, see Figure 3-6), used for measuring difference thresholds, speech perception, and voice discrimination, pressing the key in the presence of the light initiated

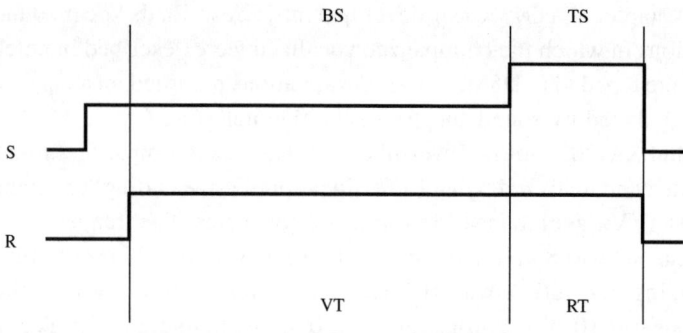

Figure 3-5
A time chart of reaction time task I (RT I). S: stimuli, R: responses. BS: background stimulus (light), TS: target stimulus (pure tone). VT: variable time, RT: reaction time.

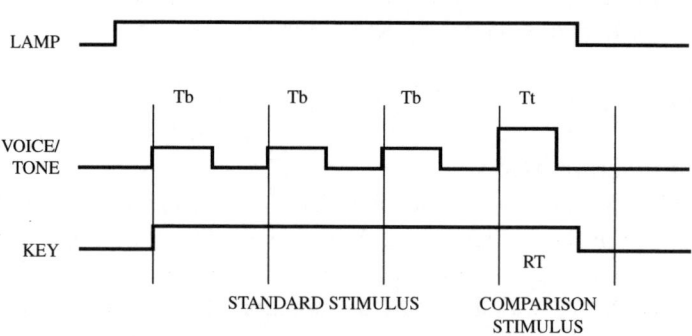

Figure 3-6
A time chart of reaction time task II (RT II). Tb: background tone or voice (standard stimulus), Tt: target tone or voice (comparison stimulus). RT: reaction time.

repeated presentation of a background (standard) stimulus with a 1-s or 1.5-s interstimulus interval. The background sound stimulus was repeated 2–8 times and then changed to another target (comparison) stimulus. The subjects were trained to release the key when they detected the change in stimulus. Key release within 1 s or 1.5 s after the change produced a reward (a piece of fruit), turned off the light and terminated the trial. The latency of key release (reaction time) after the occurrence of the change was measured. In general, reaction time decreased as the differences between the background and the target auditory stimuli increased. Thus, reaction time data are a kind of similarity index. If the subject did not release the key within 1 s or 1.5 s after the change, or if the subject released the key during the presentation of the background stimulus, all stimuli were turned off and the trial was terminated.

A non-metric multidimensional scaling method (MDSCAL) and cluster analyses were applied to data on reaction times, which are an index of similarity between vowels.

Audio-visual matching to sample task

As described above, a touch panel system was used in this task. In the first part of training, the sound of a real object was presented as the sample. After the subject acquired the task, sounds recorded and stored in the computer were used. The test stimulus consisted of pictures of the objects presented side by side. The position of the pictures was counterbalanced. A correct response was to touch the picture of the objects that matched the auditory sample stimuli and was reinforced with a piece of fruit. An incorrect response was to choose the other picture. Both correct and error responses terminated both sample and test stimuli. In a typical experiment, after the intertrial interval, the auditory sample stimulus was presented for 4 s, and the visual test stimulus was presented 2 s after the onset of the sample (simultaneous matching), or in another experiment, it was presented 2 s after the offset of the sample (delayed matching).

Go/No Go auditory delayed matching to sample task

There were an auditory sample and test stimuli in this task. Following a 10-s intertrial interval, the sample stimulus was presented at 1-s intervals. The sample was presented 10 times, followed by the delay interval (for example, 2 s). After the delay interval, the test stimulus was presented at 1-s intervals. When the sample stimulus and the test stimulus were identical, a key press after the 10-s test stimulus presentation was reinforced by a piece of fruit (GO trials, a fixed-interval schedule of 10 s) and immediately extinguished the test stimulus. On the other hand, if the test stimulus was different from the sample stimulus, pressing the key was not reinforced (NO GO trials, extinction) and the test stimulus was turned off automatically after 10 s. A discrimination index was calculated using the following equation:

Discrimination index = $100 \times N[GO] / (N[GO] + N[NO\ GO])$
where,
  N[GO]: total responses during GO trials
  N[NO GO]: total responses during NO GO trials

Chapter 4: Basic auditory functions

Auditory sensitivity and loudness

In this chapter, basic auditory functions of the chimpanzee will be described (see Kojima, 1990 for details). Previous reports have demonstrated that many Old and New World monkeys have W-shaped audibility functions: although they are sensitive to 1-kHz and 8-kHz tones, they show a low sensitivity to 2- to 4-kHz tones (Beecher, 1974; Fay, 1988; Stebbins, 1973; see Figures 4-1 and 4-2). Monkeys are more sensitive to higher frequencies (>16 kHz) than are humans. Normal humans do not show a low sensitivity to 2- to 4-kHz tones; in fact, they are most sensitive to tones in this frequency range. We must, therefore,

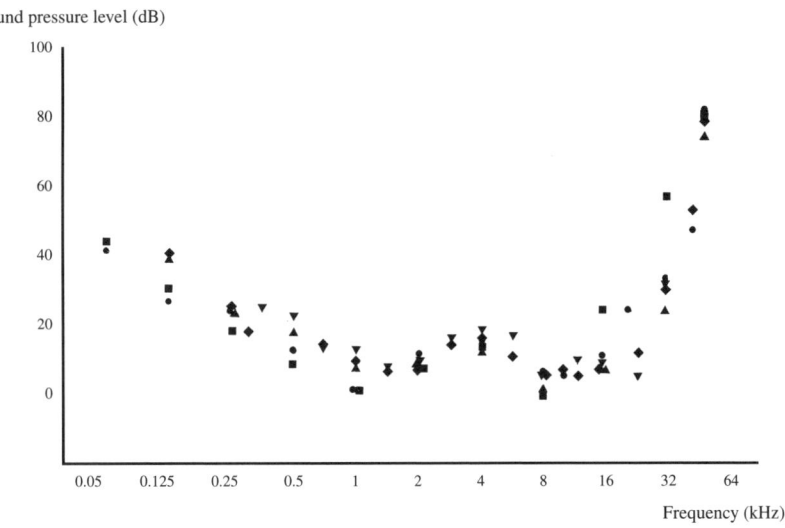

Figure 4-1
Auditory sensitivity functions of several species of the Old World monkey from different laboratories. The data of this figure are taken from Fay (1988).

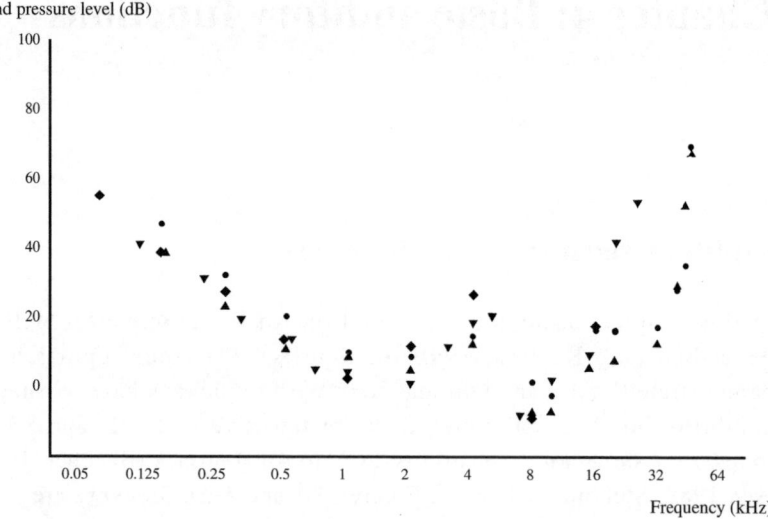

Figure 4-2
Auditory sensitivity functions of several species of the New World monkey from different laboratories. The data of this figure are taken from Fay (1988).

determine whether great apes have human-type or monkey-type hearing. There have been only a few studies on the hearing of great apes (Elder, 1934; 1935; Farrer & Prim, 1965).

The hearing ability (absolute thresholds and loudness) of chimpanzees was measured at various frequencies and compared directly with that of humans using the same apparatus and procedures. If chimpanzees show a low sensitivity to 2- to 4-kHz tones, then only humans have specialized hearing, which may in turn be related to the development of human speech and spoken languages. The subjects were Pen and Popo (see Chapter 3). The subjects were tested for two sessions (eight trials each). Reaction time task I (RT I) was employed because reaction times for detection of tones have been suggested to reflect loudness (Pfingst et al., 1975a, b). Pure tones from 125 Hz to 32 kHz were used.

Figure 4-3 shows intensity-reaction time functions at 1 kHz for one of the chimpanzee subjects. It is clear that reaction times became shorter as the intensity of the tone increased and that there were only small differences in reaction times between the two sessions. A curvilinear regression line was fitted to intensity-reaction time functions and equal

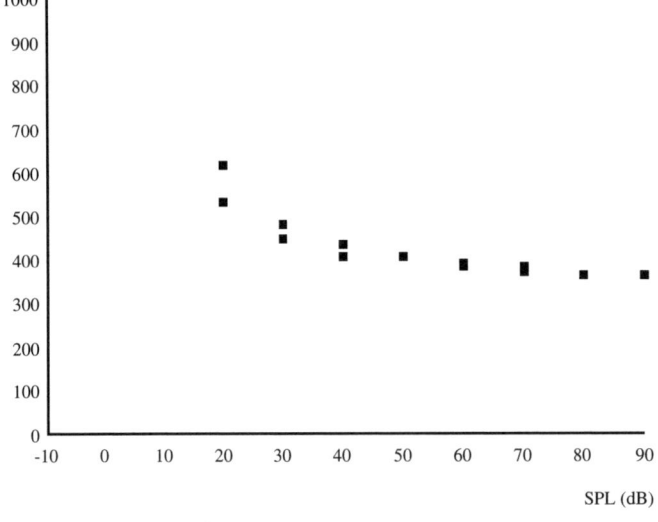

Basic auditory functions

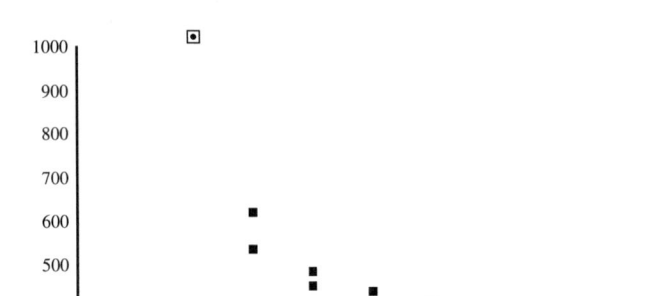

Figure 4-3
Intensity-reaction time functions at 1 kHz for one of the chimpanzees (Pen). Each filled square indicates a median reaction time of 8 trials. An open square with a dot indicates that the reaction time was the same for two sessions. Reaction times at 50, 60, 80 and 90 dB were similar between the sessions. SPL: sound pressure level.

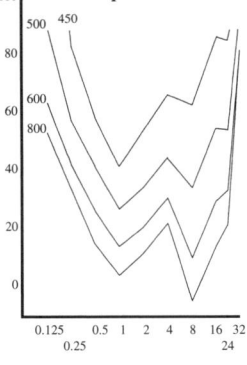

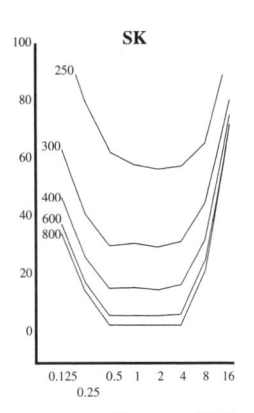

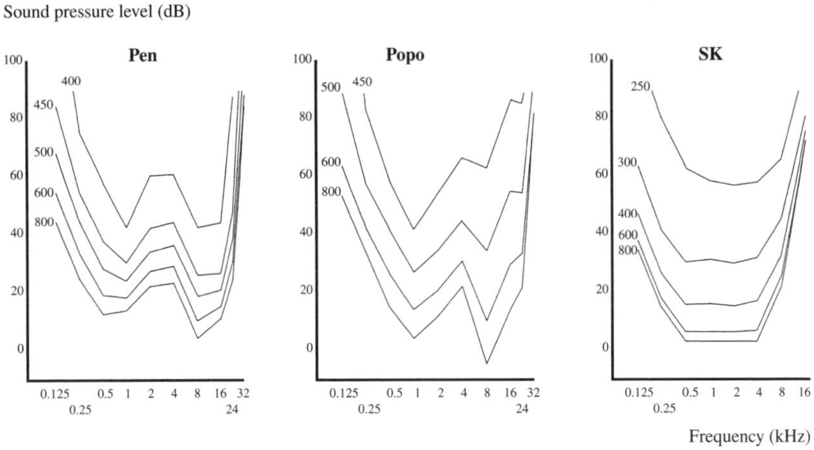

Figure 4-4
Equal reaction time contours for the chimpanzees (Pen and Popo) and the human subject (SK). Numbers within each graph are reaction times in ms.

reaction time (equal loudness) contours were derived from them for the chimpanzee and human subjects (see Figure 4-4). The absolute threshold at any frequency was defined as the intensity associated with a median reaction time of 800 ms. Both chimpanzees were sensitive to 1-kHz and 8-kHz tones. The best frequency was 8 kHz. They could detect 32-kHz tones when their intensity was 90 dB. It is noteworthy that the chimpanzees showed a 10- to 20-dB loss of auditory sensitivity to 2- to 4-kHz tones at the threshold level. Thus, the chimpanzee subjects showed a W-shaped auditory sensitivity function. In contrast, the human subject, tested using the same apparatus and procedures, showed U-shaped sensitivity and was most sensitive to middle frequencies of 0.5- to 4-kHz. In addition, although the human subject was less sensitive to higher frequencies (higher than 8 kHz), he was more sensitive to lower frequencies (lower than 250 Hz) than were the chimpanzees.

The chimpanzee showed a loss in auditory sensitivity to 2-to 4-kHz tones and showed a W-shaped auditory sensitivity function. This is similar to that of Old and New World monkeys but different from that of humans, who have a U-shaped sensitivity function. Monkeys can hear tones higher than 32 kHz (e.g., Masterton et al., 1969). Thus, chimpanzees appear to be more sensitive than humans, but less sensitive than monkeys to higher frequencies. Chimpanzees and monkeys are less sensitive than humans to lower frequencies (lower than 250 Hz),. Thus, humans have acquired high sensitivity to low and middle frequencies as a specialization of auditory function during their evolution.

Data on the hearing of chimpanzees were first reported by Elder in 1934 (Elder, 1934). Because threshold data of chimpanzees were presented in contrast with those of humans, it is not easy to compare his data with those of the present study. However, his chimpanzees showed a '4-kHz dip' and high sensitivity to 8 kHz. Thus, although there are some differences, the results of the present study support his main observations. In experiments on Old World monkeys (Brown & Waser, 1984; Jackson et al., 1999), a W-shaped auditory sensitivity function was not observed. Monkeys in these studies were tested in a free-field situation. However, a W-shaped sensitivity function was obtained with earphones (Beecher, 1974; Stebbins, 1973). This procedural difference may be responsible for the discrepancy between the results of these studies. Therefore, it is clearly necessary to use the same apparatus and the same procedure for studying differences in hearing between species, as in the present study. It is also necessary to compare auditory sensitivity both in a free field and in the case of using earphones.

A high sensitivity to higher frequencies in monkeys and apes is correlated with the distance between the left and the right ears and has been suggested to be related to auditory localization (Masterton et al., 1969). Sounds with frequencies of less than 4 kHz are often used in human speech (Fant, 1959), and only humans have spoken languages. Therefore, a higher sensitivity to middle-frequency (2- to 4-kHz) and lower-frequency tones in humans may be associated with perception of human speech sounds. This will be discussed in the next chapter.

Difference thresholds

The frequency and intensity difference thresholds for pure tones were also measured in chimpanzees and in a human using the same apparatus and procedures. Frequency and intensity difference thresholds for monkeys have been previously reported (Sinnott et al., 1985). According to this study, only the thresholds of intensity increments overlapped with those of humans. Thresholds of intensity decrements in monkeys were about four times larger than those in humans. With respect to discrimination of increments and decrements in frequency, difference thresholds of monkeys were about seven times larger than those of humans. There is no published information available concerning difference thresholds in chimpanzees. Thus, this is the first report. It is important to study auditory difference thresholds, because the sounds of human speech often change in frequency and intensity.

Pure tones between 500 Hz and 4 kHz were used for measuring frequency difference thresholds. The intensity of these stimuli were 70 dB SPL. Pure tones of 1 kHz between 60 dB and 90 dB SPL were used for measuring intensity difference thresholds. The subjects were Pan and Popo. The task used was reaction time task II (RT II). A human subject was also used.

Figure 4-5 shows the results of frequency discrimination (detection rates) by one chimpanzee subject at each frequency. Values for the difference threshold (defined as the difference in frequency between the standard and comparison stimuli that is accompanied by a detection rate of 50%) for chimpanzee and human subjects are presented in Figure 4-6. Difference thresholds for frequency were about 10–15 Hz and were relatively low between .5 kHz and 2 kHz, but they rose abruptly to 35–40 Hz at 4 kHz in both chimpanzees. The difference thresholds for the human subject showed a similar tendency, but they were lower than those of the chimpanzees. In one of the chimpanzees, thresholds for frequency increments were lower than those for frequency decrements at three of the four frequencies tested.

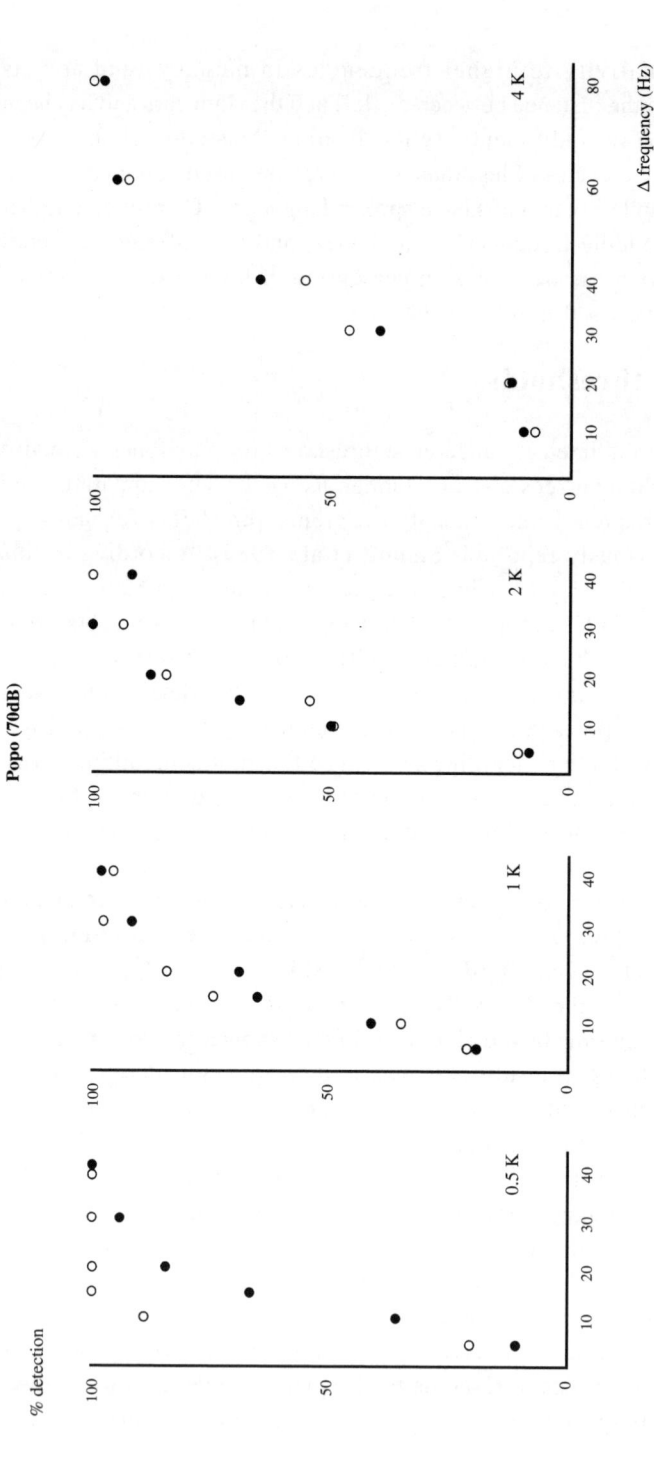

Figure 4-5
Frequency discrimination for one of the chimpanzees (Popo) at each frequency. Filled circles indicate rates of detection of frequency increments and open circles indicate those for frequency decrements. Δ frequency: frequency difference between the standard and comparison stimuli.

Basic auditory functions 33

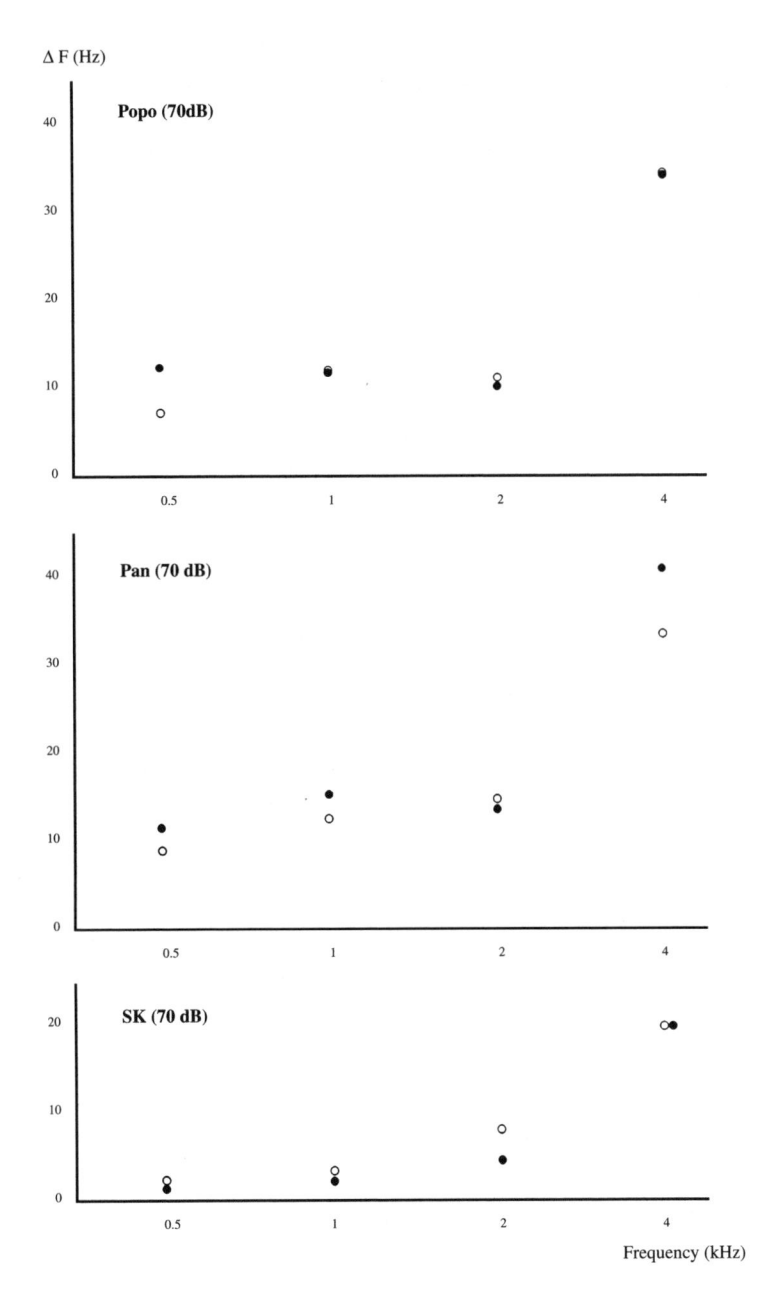

Figure 4-6
Difference thresholds for frequency increments (filled circles) and for frequency decrements (open circles) at each frequency for the chimpanzees and the human subject. ΔF: difference threshold for frequency.

Figure 4-7 shows discrimination of intensity differences for one of the chimpanzees. Figure 4-8 shows the intensity difference threshold at each intensity for the chimpanzees and for the human subject. In general, the chimpanzee subjects showed U-shaped intensity-threshold functions. Intensity difference thresholds decreased as the intensity of the pure tone increased. However, at the highest intensity (90 dB, SPL), difference thresholds increased again, particularly for intensity increment thresholds. Thresholds for discrimination of intensity increments were usually smaller than those for intensity decrements when the intensity of the tones was low, that is, when the stimulus intensity was lower than 70 dB SPL for Popo and lower than 80 dB SPL for Pan. In the human subject, intensity difference thresholds decreased as the stimulus intensity increased and the lowest thresholds were observed at the highest intensity. At lower intensities, thresholds for intensity increments were lower than those for intensity decrements, as in the chimpanzees. Variation in intensity difference thresholds between species ranged from 0.81 dB to 1.74 dB (mean 1.25 dB).

These results indicate that difference thresholds for frequency and intensity of auditory stimuli in chimpanzees were larger than those in humans. Differences in frequency difference thresholds between chimpanzees and humans may influence perception of speech sounds. This subject will be discussed further in the next chapter. Differences in intensity difference thresholds between the chimpanzees and the human subject were relatively small at 1 kHz, 70–80 dB (SPL). Chimpanzees may be sensitive to the prosodic aspects, for example stress accents, of speech sounds.

The present experiments were not designed to test neural mechanisms that underlie discrimination of frequency and intensity. Two codes have been proposed for frequency discrimination, that is, the 'place' and the 'temporal' codes (Pickles, 1982). According to the place code theory, subjects discriminate two frequencies based on two places of maximum excitation in the cochlea. In the temporal code theory, subjects discriminate two frequencies based on two time intervals of phase-locked firings of the auditory nerve. The temporal codes operate for frequencies less than 4 kHz. The abrupt increase in difference thresholds at 4 kHz in the present study may suggest the importance of the temporal codes. It is necessary to measure frequency difference thresholds at higher frequencies to test this possibility in more detail.

Subjects discriminate differences in intensity by monitoring differences in the rate of firing of the auditory nerve (Pickles, 1982). Chimpanzees in

Basic auditory functions

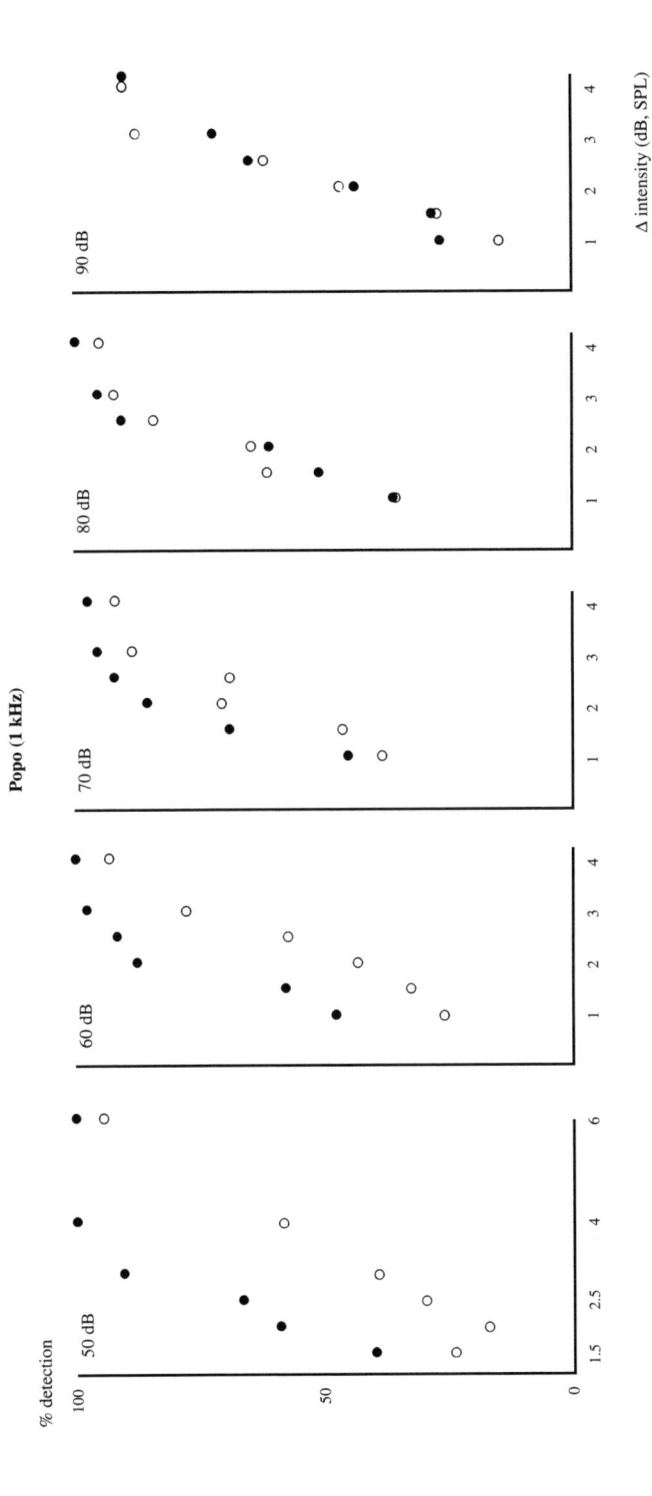

Figure 4-7

Intensity discrimination for one of the chimpanzee subjects (Popo) at each intensity. Filled circles indicate results for intensity increments and open circles those for intensity decrements. Δ intensity: intensity differences between the standard and comparison stimuli.

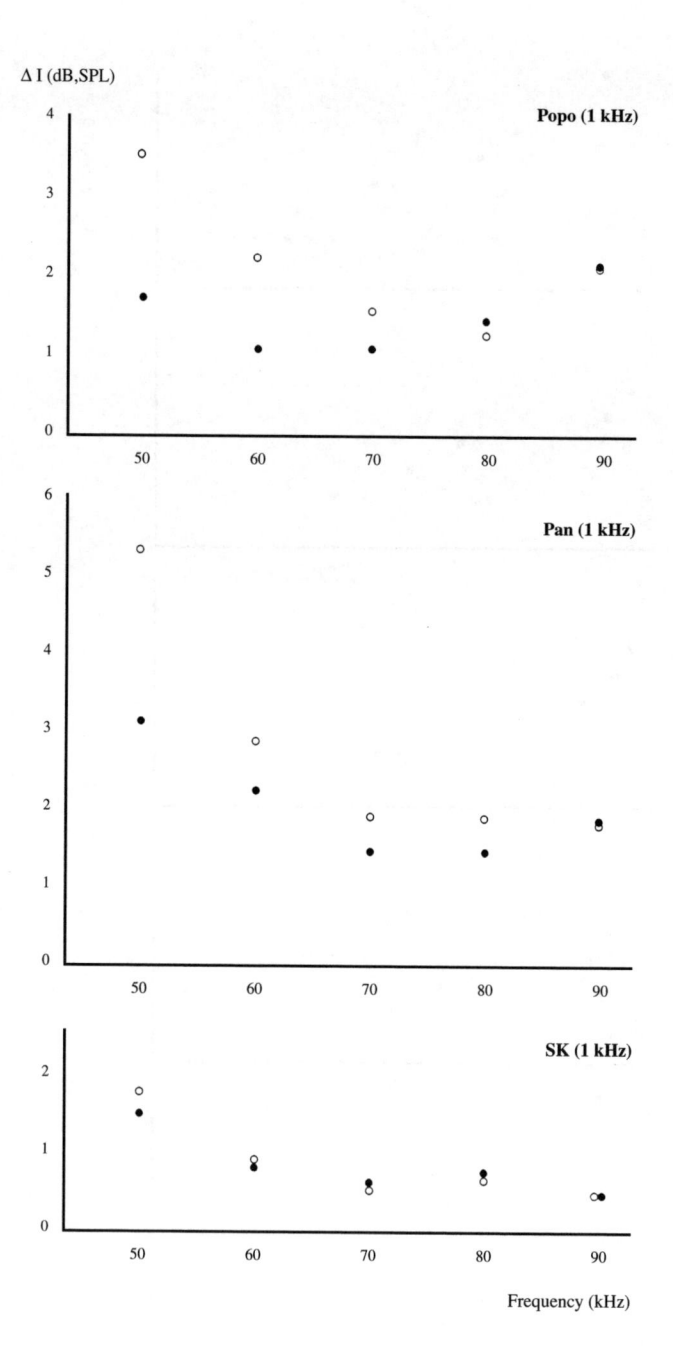

Figure 4-8
Intensity difference thresholds (ΔI) for each subject. Filled circles indicate thresholds for intensity increments and open circles indicate those for intensity decrements.

the present study showed a U-shaped intensity-difference threshold function. The elevated difference thresholds at the highest frequency in the present experiment may reflect saturation of firing of the auditory nerve at this intensity. There are only excitatory processes in peripheral auditory neurons which may account for the differences in thresholds between intensity increments and decrements (Sinnott et al., 1985). Further experiments are necessary to clarify this issue.

Resonance of the external auditory meatus

The origins of hearing loss for 2- to 4-kHz tones were investigated by measuring the resonance of the external auditory meatus in a cadaver of the chimpanzee and three humans. The resonance of the external auditory meatus, which produces a sound pressure gain of about 20 dB (SPL) for 2- to 5-kHz tones, contributes to hearing in humans (Shaw, 1974). It is of interest to measure the resonance of the chimpanzee external ear, as such measurements might explain differences in hearing between the two species. No reports on the resonance of the external auditory meatus in chimpanzees were available.

For measuring the resonance of the external auditory meatus, three humans and a formaldehyde-preserved chimpanzee cadaver were used. The resonance of the external auditory meatus was measured with Eartron equipment (Horag, Switzerland). The probe tube of a microphone was inserted into the external auditory meatus of the subjects and that of a reference microphone was placed at the tip of the nose. Pure tones from 0 to 10-kHz at 80 dB SPL were presented.

Figure 4-9 shows the resonance of the external ear of the subjects. In the cadaver of the chimpanzee, a peak of about 20 dB SPL at 2.5 kHz in sound pressure gain was observed. The frequency and the magnitude of the gain were about the same as those of the humans.

The auditory system is divided into four parts: the external ear, the eardrum and middle ear, the inner ear, and the auditory nervous system, as described in Chapter 2. Loss of hearing for 2- to 4-kHz tones may be localized in some part of the auditory system. Resonance of the external ear contributes to human auditory sensitivity (Shaw, 1974). We might therefore expect a decrease in resonance at 2- to 4-kHz in the chimpanzee. However, our measurements showed that the resonance frequency of the external ear of the chimpanzee was 2.5 kHz, a frequency at which chimpanzees show a loss in sensitivity. The resonance frequency of the external ear in Japanese macaques is about 6 kHz (Fukuda, 1959), and

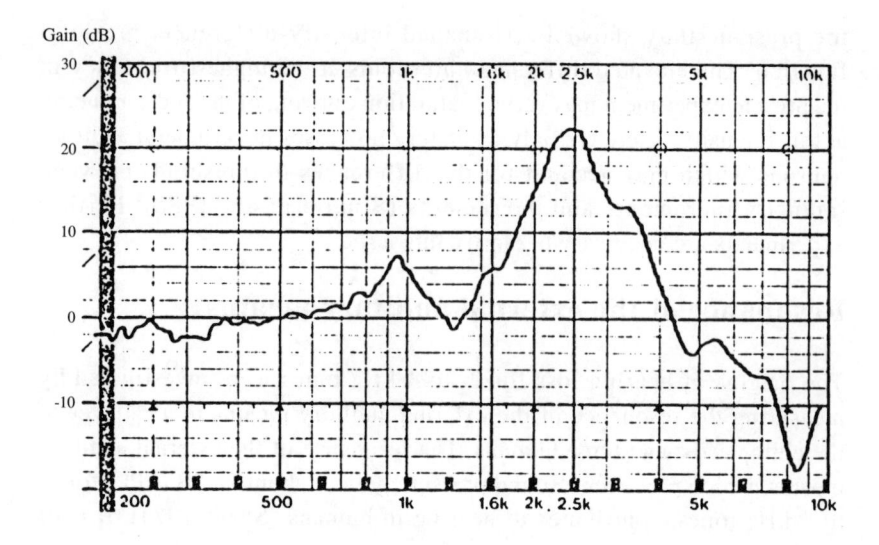

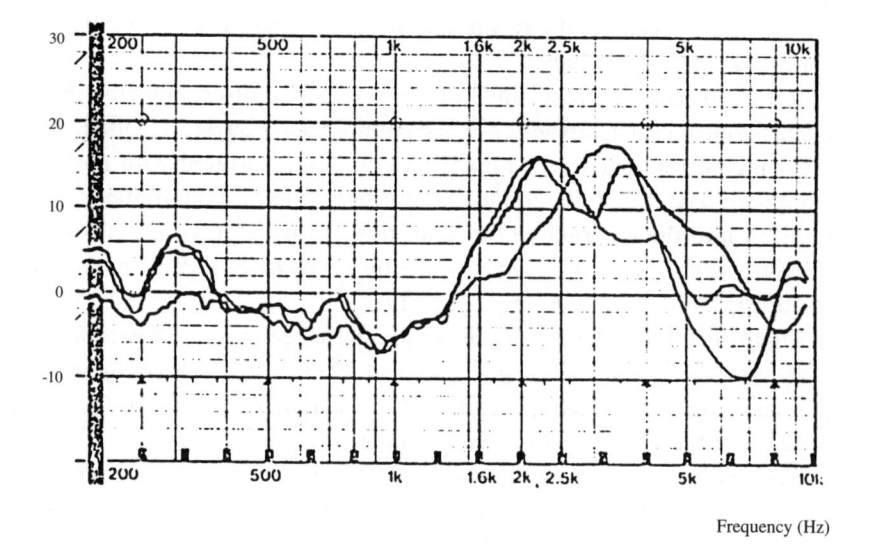

Figure 4-9
Resonance of the external auditory meatus of the formaldehyde-preserved cadaver of a chimpanzee (upper panel) and of the three humans (lower panel).

Japanese macaques also show a loss in sensitivity to this frequency. Thus, the resonance of the external ear does not contribute to auditory

Basic auditory functions 39

sensitivity in chimpanzees or in Japanese macaques. Rather, it is possible that resonance of the external ear may itself be an indirect cause of the loss of sensitivity. In contrast to humans, chimpanzees and Japanese monkeys often use loud calls, such as pant-hoots and screams, in everyday life. These loud calls, which are amplified by the external ear, may affect auditory transmission in the middle and the inner ear. Histological and electrophysiological examinations of these structures are necessary to clarify this issue (see Appendix B). Human speech might have evolved from the short-distance, relatively calm calls of monkeys (Itani, 1963). The evolution of human hearing may accordingly have some relation to the evolution of human speech.

Appendix A: Comparison of difference thresholds between Japanese macaques, chimpanzees and humans

Figure 4-10 shows frequency and intensity difference thresholds measured by the same procedures for Japanese macaques, chimpanzees and a human. Incremental and decremental thresholds are combined and averaged. It is clear that frequency and intensity difference thresholds in chimpanzees fall between those of Japanese macaques and humans.

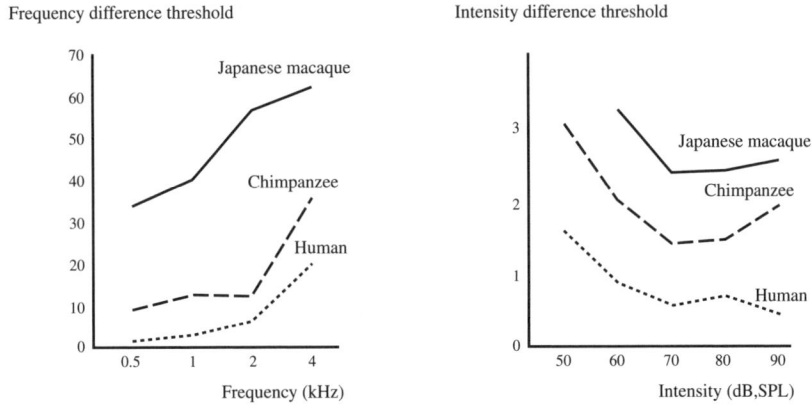

Figure 4-10
Comparison of frequency (left) and intensity (right) difference thresholds among the Japanese macaque, chimpanzee and human.

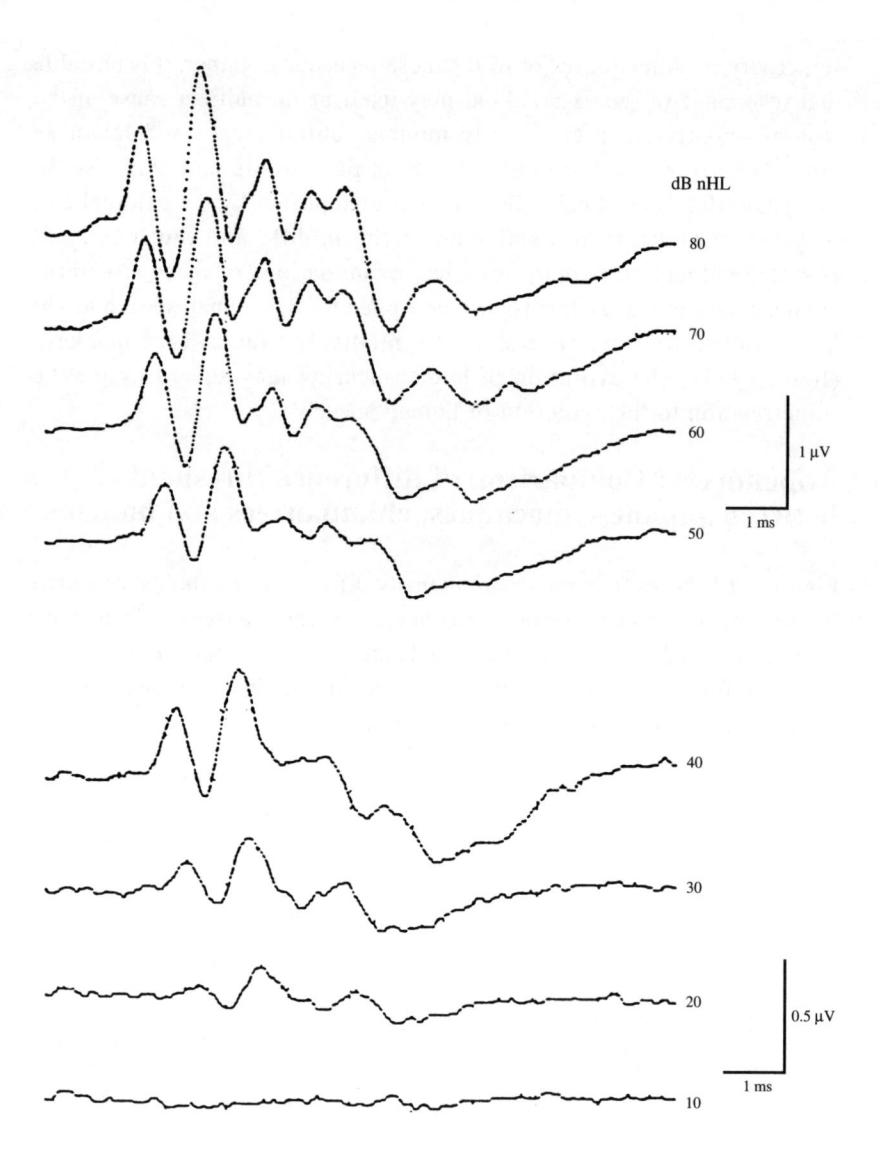

Figure 4-11
The ABR waves to clicks at each stimulus intensity.

Appendix B: Auditory evoked potentials in the Japanese macaque

In this part, the origin of the sensitivity loss at middle frequencies (2–6 kHz) was examined in the auditory system (see Kamada et al., 1991 for details). We recorded auditory brainstem responses (ABR), whole nerve action potentials (AP) and cochlear microphonics (CM) in the Japanese macaque. We determined the absolute threshold at each frequency based on these evoked potentials. Each wave of the ABR reflects the activity of the auditory central nervous system at each level. The AP reflects the activity level of the auditory nerve. The origin of the CM is the activity of the hair cells in the cochlea and the CM reflects the activity level of the middle and the inner ear. We compared physiologically and behaviorally determined thresholds and tried to identify the origin of the sensitivity loss at middle frequencies in the Japanese macaque.

ABR

Three Japanese macaques were anesthetized with sodium pentobarbital at 25–35 mg/kg body weight and studied in a sound-attenuating chamber.

The ABR was recorded by a skin electrode placed on the vertex. The click and the sine wave tone bursts were presented at a rate of 10/s. The frequencies of the tone bursts usually ranged between 1 and 8 kHz in octave intervals and at 6 kHz, and in one monkey 0.5 kHz was also used.

Figure 4-11 shows the ABR waveforms at each intensity of clicks; five waves (I–V) are distinguishable at 50 dB nHL or higher. Figure 4-12 shows the ABR to 1 kHz tone bursts at each intensity. As shown, there are two peaks. The latencies of these two peaks were 5.3 and 6.5 ms, respectively, at 90 dB SPL, which roughly corresponded to those of the fifth wave of the ABR to clicks at 60 dB nHL. Figure 4-13 shows frequency-threshold (auditory sensitivity) functions for all three monkeys. The best frequency was 8 kHz and an increase in the threshold occurred at 6 kHz.

Based on latencies, the ABR to tone bursts reflects the activity of the auditory nervous system particularly in the midbrain or the diencephalon. The W-shaped auditory sensitivity function based on the ABR to tone bursts is similar to that determined by behavioral procedures, although we did not record the ABR at frequencies higher than 8 kHz. The sensitivity decreased at 6 kHz in the present ABR study. The auditory sensitivity determined based on the ABR suggests that the origin of the sensitivity

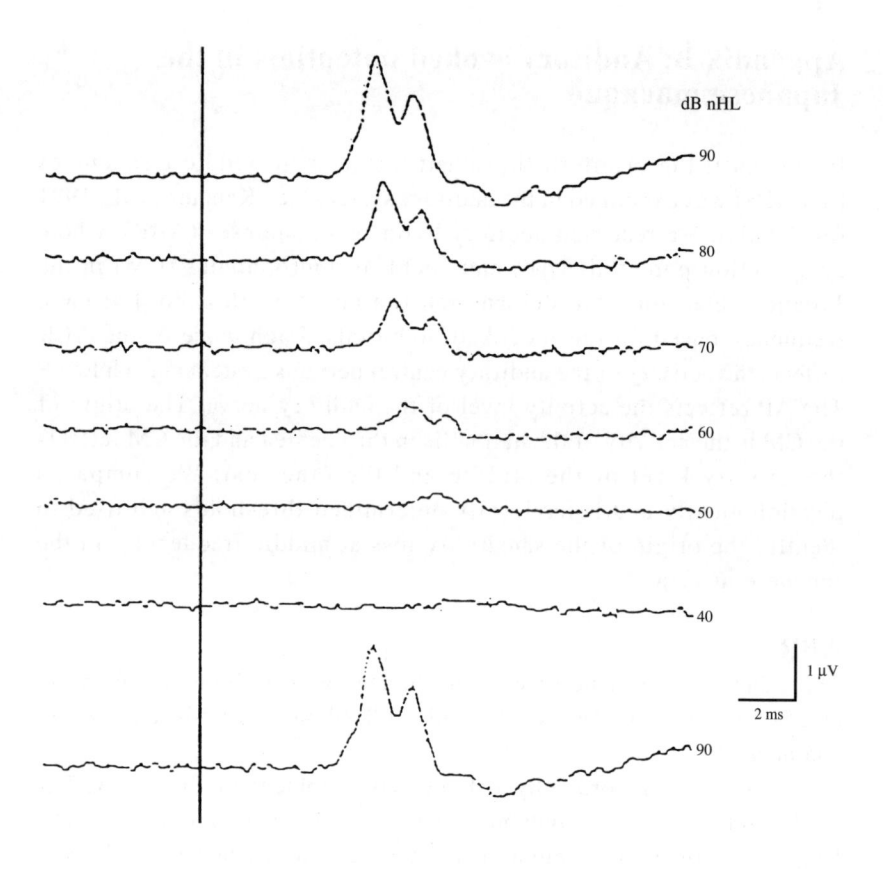

Figure 4-12
The ABR waves to 1-kHz tone bursts at each sound pressure level. The vertical line indicates the onset of tone.

loss exists in the auditory system peripheral to the midbrain or the diencephalon.

AP and CM

Two additional Japanese macaques served as subjects. The subjects were anesthetized with sodium pentobarbital at 25–35 mg/kg body weight and studied in the same sound-attenuating chamber.

The CM and the AP were recorded by a silver ball electrode attached to the wall of the external auditory meatus near the ear drum using electrode paste. The stimuli were sine wave tone bursts. The frequencies used were

Basic auditory functions

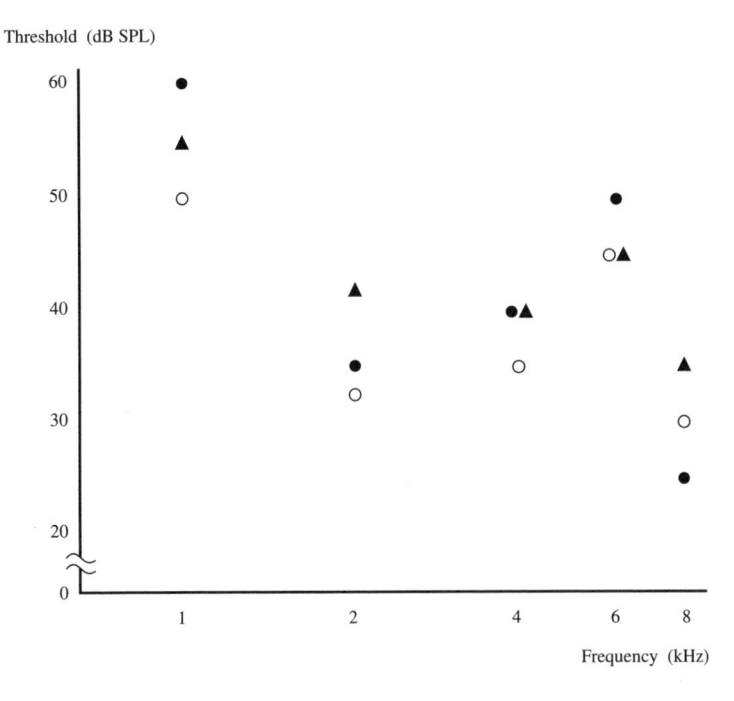

Figure 4-13
Frequency-threshold (auditory sensitivity) functions of the ABR waves to tone bursts for the three monkeys.

0.5, 1, 2, 4, 6 and 8 kHz. The tone bursts were presented at a rate of 10/s through a loud speaker

Figure 4-14 shows the AP waves for 1-kHz tone bursts at each intensity. Figure 4-15 shows the auditory sensitivity (absolute threshold at each frequency) function based on the AP for each monkey. The best frequency was 2 kHz and an increase in the threshold occurred at 6 kHz, as in the case of the ABR.

Figure 4-16 shows examples of the CM for 500-Hz tone bursts at each intensity. Figure 4-17 shows an auditory sensitivity function based on the CM for each monkey. These functions were similar to those of the AP. The best frequency was 2 kHz and a decrease in sensitivity was observed at 6 kHz.

The increase in auditory threshold at 6 kHz was observed in the AP and the CM recordings, as in the case of the ABR. As stated above, the resonance of the external ear canal is not the direct cause of the sensitivity loss at middle frequencies. Thus, the origin of the sensitivity

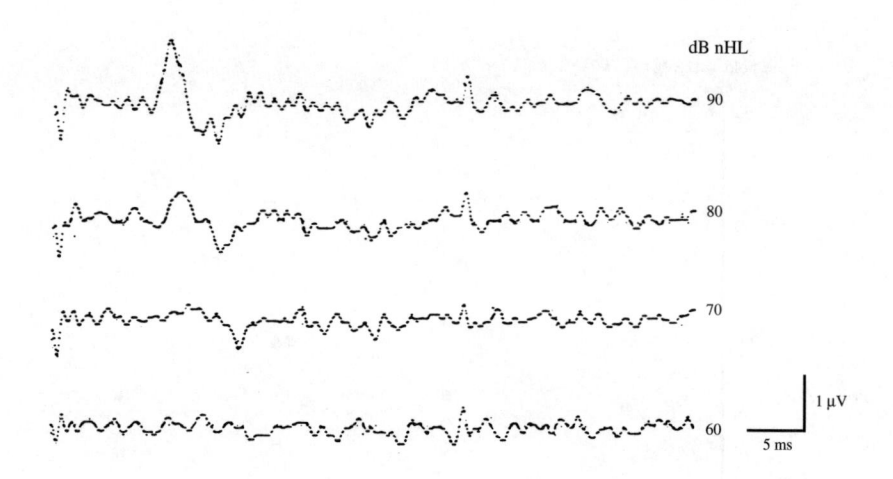

Figure 4-14
The AP waves to 1-kHz tone bursts at each sound pressure level.

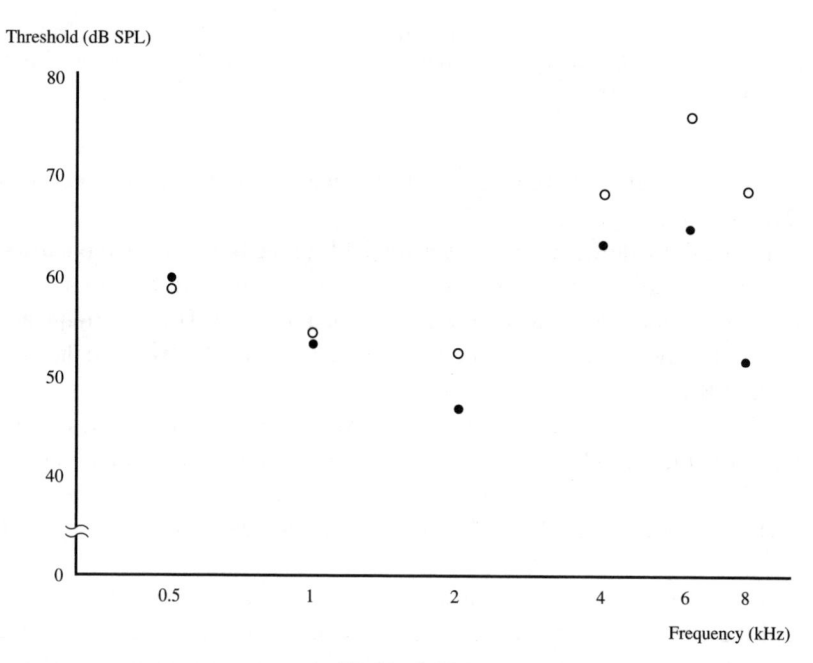

Figure 4-15
Auditory sensitivity functions of the AP responses to tone bursts for the two monkeys.

Basic auditory functions 45

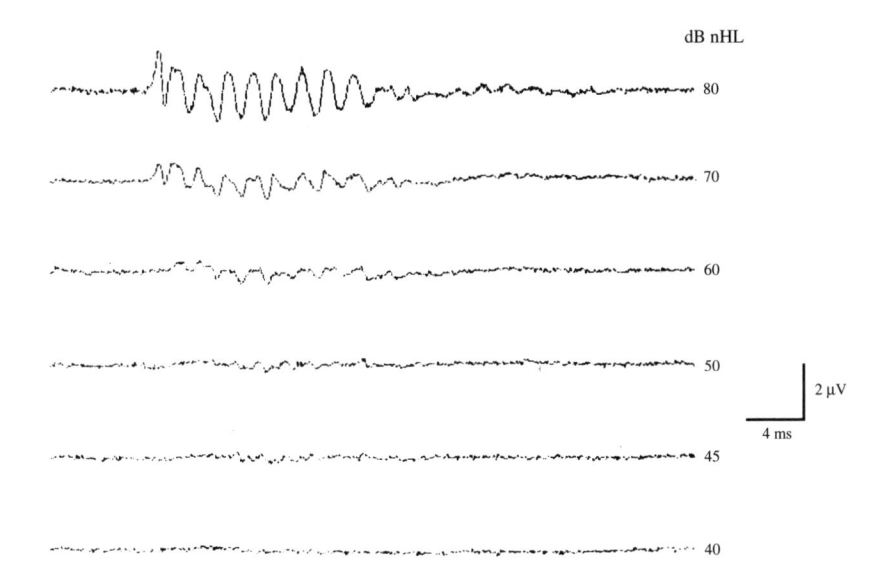

Figure 4-16
The CM waves to 0.5-kHz tone bursts at each sound pressure level.

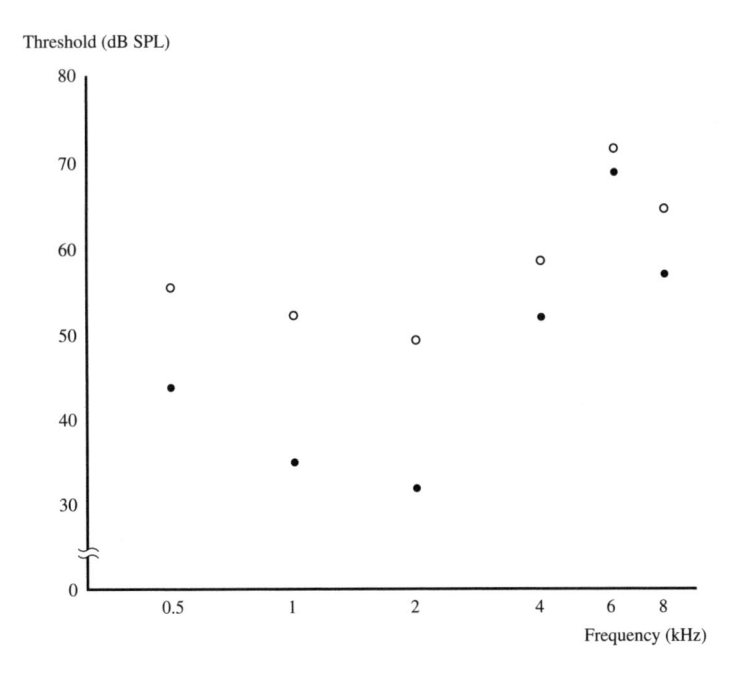

Figure 4-17
Auditory sensitivity functions of the CM responses to tone bursts for the two monkeys.

loss exists in the middle and/or inner ear. It is necessary to determine in the future the cause of the sensitivity loss at middle frequencies by histological, electrophysiological and otological procedures.

Chapter 5: Perception of human speech sounds

Vowel perception

As shown in the previous chapter, chimpanzees and humans have different auditory functions; that is, different auditory sensitivity and difference thresholds. These differences in basic auditory functions may have lead to a difference in speech perception between these two species. In this chapter, the perception of human speech sounds is examined in chimpanzees and humans. See Kojima and Kiritani (1989) and Kojima et al. (1989) for details.

In the first part, the perception of three kinds of vowels was examined. Vowels used were five synthetic and natural Japanese vowels pronounced by a male speaker and eight natural basic French vowels pronounced by a female speaker. The fundamental frequency and the frequencies of the first two formants are presented in Table 5-1. A vowel in a vowel set was paired with all other members of the set. Reaction times for discrimination between vowels were taken as an index of similarity between vowels (e.g., Mohr & Wang, 1968). The subjects were three female chimpanzees (Pen, 9 years old; Popo, 5 years old; and Pan, 3 years old when the experiment was conducted) and three normal humans (MR, NH and SK). The task employed was reaction time task II (RT II).

Figure 5-1 shows the perception of synthetic Japanese vowels by the chimpanzees and one of the human subjects (MR). The upper figures show the results of the cluster analysis (dendrograms) and the lower figures show those of the MDSCAL analysis. Numbers above the dendrograms are similarity indexes (reaction times in seconds). It is clear that longer reaction times were necessary for discrimination of [i] from [u] and of [e] from [o] by all the chimpanzee subjects, which suggests that the vowels in each pair were perceptually similar for chimpanzees. The human subject discriminated between these vowels with short reaction times, as shown by the similarity index. Although differences in reaction times were small between vowel pairs, the human subject required longer

Table 5-1 *The frequencies of the first (F1) and second (F2) formant of the vowels used in the present experiments*

	Synthetic Japanese vowels				
	[i]	[e]	[a]	[o]	[u]
F1	230	500	750	550	300
F2	2100	1900	1300	950	1500

	Natural Japanese vowels				
	[I]	[e]	[a]	[o]	[u]
F1	390	651	911	520	390
F2	2604	2213	1367	911	1302

	Natural French vowels						
	[i]	[e]	[ɛ]	[a]	[ɑ]	[ɔ]	[o]	[u]
F1	260	520	716	911	911	911	455	325
F2	2734	2473	2213	1367	1236	2148	846	781

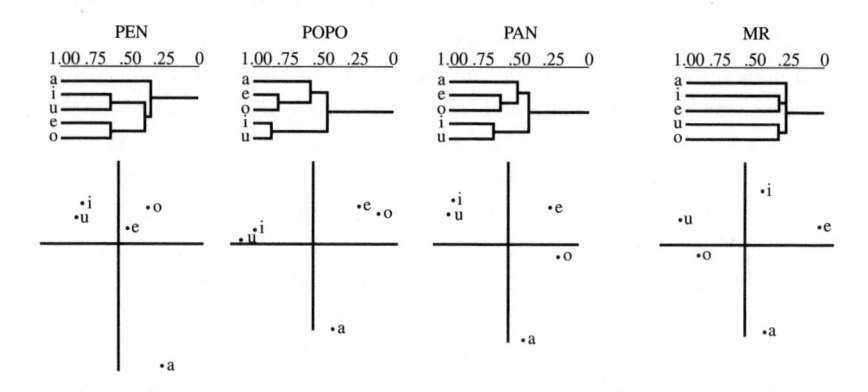

Figure 5-1
Discrimination between synthetic Japanese vowels by the chimpanzee and human subjects. Upper panels are the results of the cluster analysis (dendrograms) and lower panels are those of MDSCAL. Numbers above each dendrogram are similarity indices (reaction times in second).

latencies for discrimination of [u] from [o] and of [i] from [e]. Another human subject (SK) showed the same pattern of vowel perception.

Figure 5-2 shows discrimination of natural Japanese vowels by the three chimpanzees and a human subject (SK). These chimpanzees discriminated

Perception of human speech sounds 49

[i] from [u] with the longest reaction time. The next vowel pair which required long reaction times for discrimination was that of [a] and [e] for Pen and Popo and that of [a] and [o] for Pan. The human subject required the longest latency for discrimination between [i] and [e]. Another human subject (NH) showed the same tendency in the perception of these vowels.

Figure 5-3 shows discrimination of natural French vowels by the chimpanzees and a human subject (NH). For the chimpanzees, the French vowels were classified into two groups, that is, the group of [i], [u] and [e] and the group of [a] and [o]. It is noteworthy that for the human subject, who is Japanese, the eight French vowels were grouped into five Japanese vowels [u, o, a, e and i].

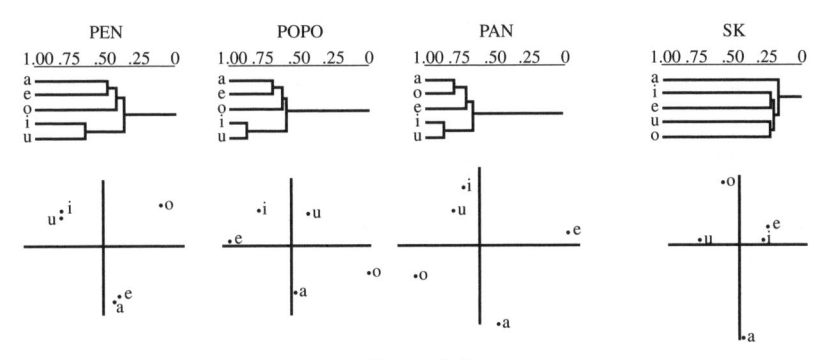

Figure 5-2
Discrimination between the natural Japanese vowels by each subject.

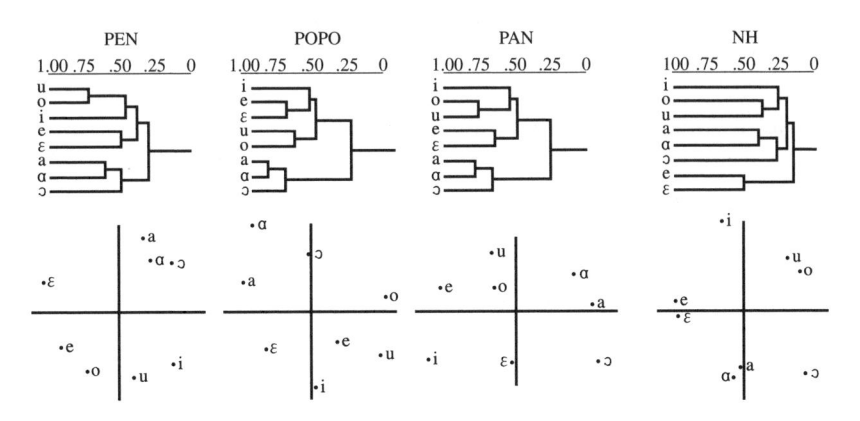

Figure 5-3
Discrimination between the natural French vowels by each subject.

The results showed that the chimpanzees required long reaction times for discrimination of [i] from [u] in the two Japanese vowel sets and also for discrimination of [e] from [o] in the synthetic vowels. Although it was less clear, a similar tendency was observed in the perception of the French vowels [i] and [u] by the chimpanzees. Because the intensity and duration of the synthetic vowels were well controlled, the following discussion is based on the perception of the synthetic Japanese vowels.

Although the frequencies of the second formant were different for the vowels [i] and [u] and for the vowels [e] and [o], the frequencies of the first formant of these vowels in each vowel pair were similar and were about 300 Hz or lower and 500 Hz, respectively (see Table 5-1). Thus, the chimpanzees required long reaction times to discriminate between vowels based on differences in the frequency of the second formant. In other words, it was difficult for chimpanzees to discriminate vowels when these vowels have a similar first formant frequency. The human subject discriminated between the members of each vowel pair with short reaction times. He required long reaction times for discrimination of [i] from [e] and [u] from [o]. Thus, long latencies were necessary for discrimination of vowels along the first formant axis by the human subject.

There may be two separate but related explanations of these results. One explanation is related to differences in auditory sensitivity between chimpanzees and humans. Humans with a hearing loss at middle frequencies show the same pattern of vowel perception as chimpanzees (e.g., Fukuda et al., 1976). Thus, differences in hearing may be related to the difference between species in vowel perception. Kojima (1990, and in the previous chapter) reported that chimpanzees were less sensitive to 2- to 4-kHz tones than to 1 kHz and 8 kHz tones; therefore, they have a W-shaped auditory sensitivity function that is similar to that of Old and New World monkeys. In contrast, humans have a U-shaped auditory sensitivity function and are most sensitive to 2- to 4-kHz tones. As shown in the previous chapter, the human subject was more sensitive to frequencies lower than 250 Hz than were the chimpanzees. Thus, compared with humans, chimpanzees may have difficulty in hearing the first formant of [i] and [u]. Chimpanzees may also have difficulty in hearing the second formant of [i] and [e], because the frequency of the second formant of these vowels is higher than 2 kHz. This suggests that the perception of these vowels may be different for chimpanzees and humans. Thus, the differences in the auditory sensitivity function between these two species may explain the results of our vowel perception experiment.

It is of interest that, in contrast to the results for chimpanzees, [i] and [u] are the vowels that are least confused with other vowels by human listeners (Peterson & Barney, 1952). Lieberman (1984) suggested that vowels [i] and [u] are the best calibrators of the size and shape of the speaker's vocal tract. Thus, the vowels that are least confused with other vowels by humans are perceptually most similar for chimpanzees.

The position of the human tongue for each vowel matches the position of each vowel in the F1-F2 plane. The results of the MDSCAL analysis of the perception of vowels matched the position of vowels in the F1-F2 plane, as shown in the case of perception of synthetic Japanese and natural French vowels by the human listeners (see Figures 5-1 and 5-3). Thus, the production of vowels matches the perception of vowels, a result that suggests that these two processes are intimately related. The other explanation of the results of the present vowel perception experiment is that of the motor theory of speech perception (Liberman et. al., 1967).

It is of interest to examine what kinds of vowel-like sounds the chimpanzees utter, because there is an intimate relationship between the perception and production of speech sounds, as stated in the motor theory. Kojima (2001 and Chapters 6 and 9 in this book) studied the early development of vocal behavior in a chimpanzee infant. The chimpanzee uttered vowel-like sounds (grunts) which were heard by the author as one of the Japanese vowels [u], [o] or [a]. The chimpanzee did not pronounce vowel-like sounds which were heard as the vowels [i] and [e]. Thus, it may be difficult for the chimpanzee both to produce and to perceive the vowels [i] and [e]. The high position of the larynx and the small pharynx of the chimpanzee may be responsible for the limited repertoire of vowel-like sounds (Lieberman, 1975). It is known that a large pharynx is necessary for production of the vowels [i] and [e] (Chiba & Kajiyama, 1941). Thus, during the course of hominization, the larynx moved downward and this change enabled humans to pronounce these vowels. In other words, these vowels, particularly the vowel [i], may be those that were acquired most recently in human speech. In this context, it is interesting that the vowel [i] plays an important role in the perception of speech sounds, as discussed above.

These two explanations are not mutually exclusive. With regard to hearing, humans have acquired a sensitivity to low and midrange frequencies which improves the perception of the vowels [i], [e] and [u]. With regard to the production of vocal sounds, the larynx of humans moved downward which enables humans to pronounce the vowels [i] and [e]. This may also improve the perception of these vowels. Thus, the evolution of

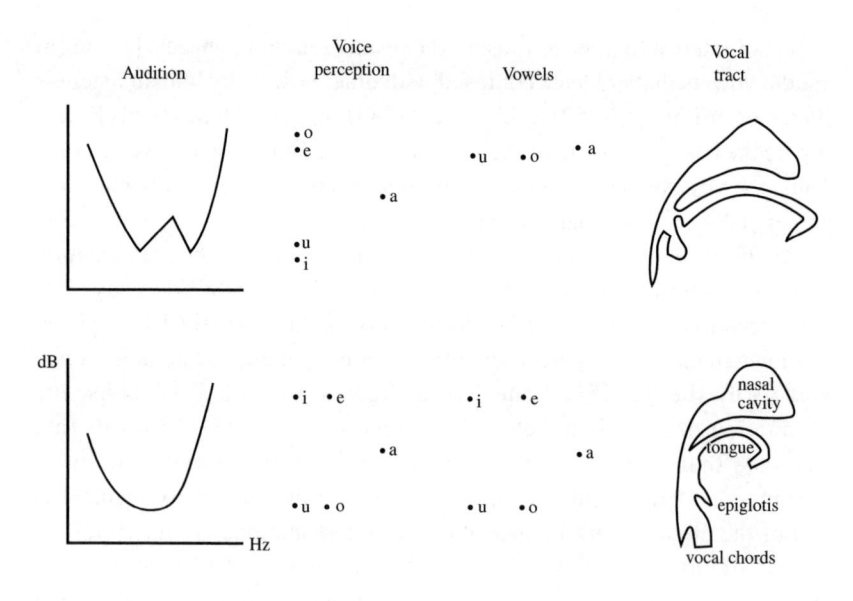

Figure 5-4
Auditory sensitivity (audition), vowel perception (voice perception), vowel production (vowels), and the vocal tract of the chimpanzee (upper panels) and the human (lower panels).

hearing and speech perception appears to match that of speech production. Figure 5-4 summarizes hearing, vowel perception, vowel production and the vocal tract of chimpanzees and humans.

Vocal tract normalization

Vowels, for example [a], when pronounced by different speakers, have different acoustic properties. However, humans can perceive these speech sounds as the same vowel (see Chapter 2). In the second part of this chapter, we examined whether chimpanzees can ignore differences in the sex of speakers and can normalize the effects of the size of the vocal tract.

The subjects were two chimpanzees (Popo and Pan) used in the first part of this study and a human subject (SK). Three tests were conducted. In the first test, we examined whether the chimpanzees could ignore the sex of speakers who pronounced the same vowel. The task employed was the same reaction time task (RT II). The vowels used were three Japanese vowels [a], [i] and [u] uttered by a female and a male speaker. For background vowels of the task, the vowel uttered by the female and the same vowel by the male speaker were mixed. The subjects were trained to ignore the change in the sex of the speaker of the background vowels. Other conditions were the same as those in the first part of this study.

In the second and the third tests, the difference in the [o]-[a] boundary between male and female voices, that is, vocal tract normalization, was examined. For this purpose, two sets of eight vowels on the [o]–[a] continuum were synthesized (Fujisaki & Kawashima, 1968. See Figure 5-5). The two sets of synthetic vowels had the same first and second formant

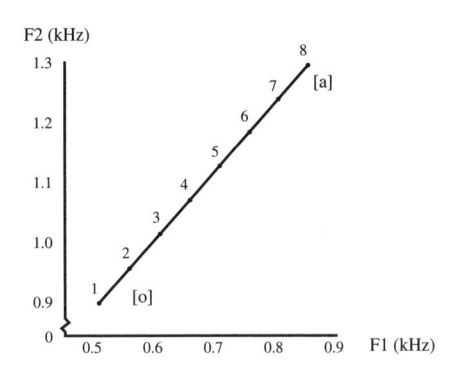

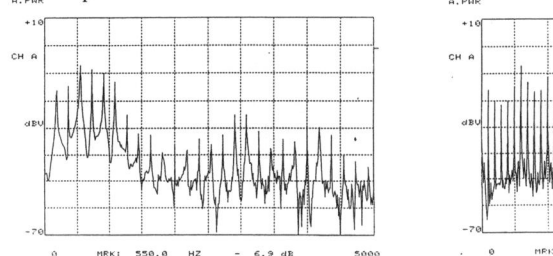

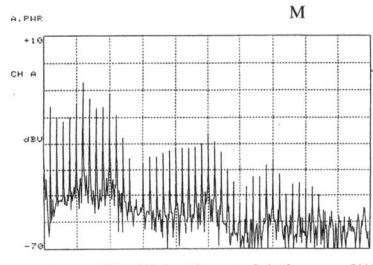

Figure 5-5
Upper: Synthetic [o]–[a] continuum in the first formant-second formant (F1-F2) plane. Frequencies of F1 and F2 are determined by the following equations: $F1 = 500 + 50(i - 1)$; $F2 = 1.1F1 + 350$, $i = 1$ to 8. The fundamental frequency of one of the sets is 180 Hz and it is heard as female voices. The other set has a fundamental frequency of 100 Hz and is heard as male voices. The frequencies of the third and fourth formants of female voices are 3 kHz and 4.2 kHz, respectively, while those of male voices are 2.5 kHz and 3.5 kHz, respectively. Numbers in the upper panel are Stimulus No. The duration of each synthetic vowel is 300 ms and the rise and fall times are 10 ms and 20 ms, respectively.

Lower: Power spectra of the typical [o] of female (left; F) and male (right; M) speakers.

frequencies but differed in the frequencies of the pitch and the third and fourth formants (Fujisaki & Kawashima, 1968). One set of synthetic vowels with a higher pitch, and higher third and fourth formant frequencies, was heard as female voices and the other as male voices. In the second, the identification test, these vowels were presented randomly to the human subject. The subject was required to give one of four numbers [1–4] corresponding to each synthetic vowel (ratings), in which 1 corresponded to a typical [a] and 4 to a typical [o] while 2 and 3 fell between them. Then

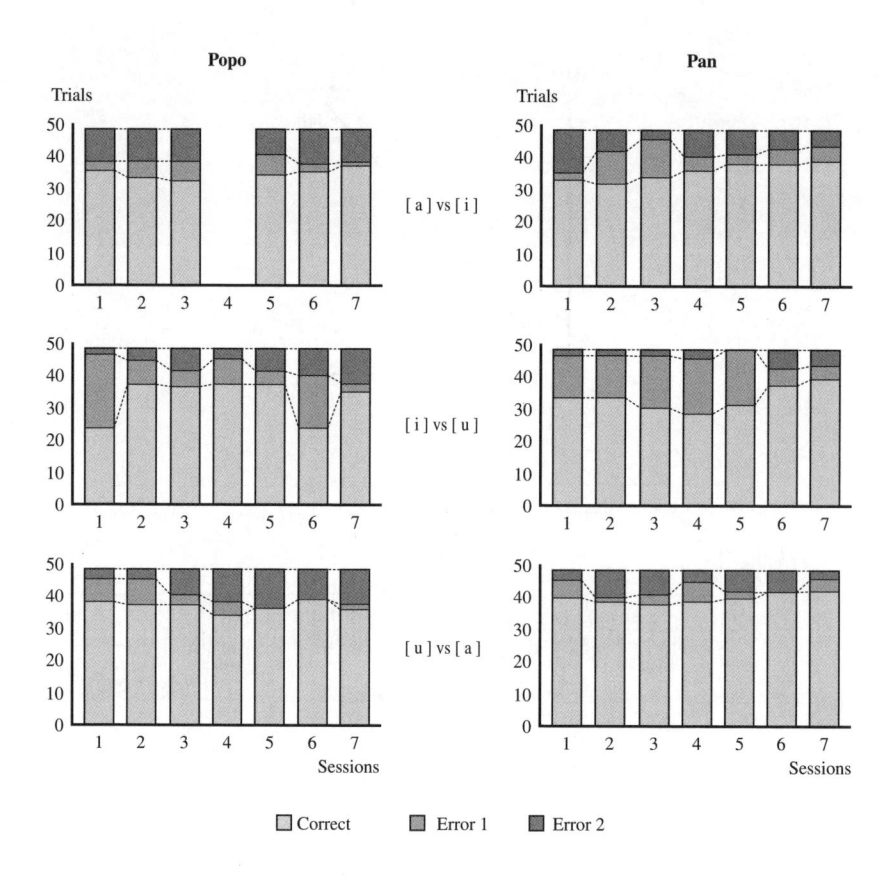

Figure 5-6
Discrimination of the three vowel pairs ([a] vs. [i], [i] vs. [u] and [u] vs. [a]) uttered by different speakers, i.e., the results of the perceptual constancy experiment with the chimpanzees. Error 1 indicates errors in which there was no response to changes in vowels (miss) and Error 2 indicates errors in the response to changes in the sex of the speaker of the background vowel (false alarm). The data of Popo from the fourth session of the [a]–[i] pair were lost by accident.

the third, the discrimination test, using a similar reaction time task (RT II), was administered to the chimpanzees and the human subject. The background vowel was a typical [o] (Stimulus No.1 in Figure 5-5) or [a] (Stimulus No.8) in each vowel set and was paired with all other members of the set.

Figure 5-6 shows the results of the first test. The chimpanzees discriminated between vowels with 70–83% correct responses, and incorrect responses to the difference in the sex of the speakers (Error 2 in Figure 5-6) occurred in 15–16% of the trials in the last two sessions. Thus, the chimpanzees could perceive vowels as the same vowel irrespective of the speaker. Figure 5-7 shows the result of the second identification test. The boundaries between [o] and [a], which were defined as a rating of 2.5, were between Stimulus No.3 and No.4 for male voices and were between No.4 and No.5 for female voices. Thus, the boundary for the female vowel set had higher first and second formant frequencies than those for the male vowel set, suggesting that the human subject normalized the effects of the vocal tract size of the speakers. From Figure 5-7, longer reaction times were expected for the female vowel set than for the male vowel set when the background vowel was a typical [o], if the subjects normalized the vocal tract size of the speaker in the third discrimination test. However, when the background vowel was a typical [a], a longer reaction time was expected for discrimination of male vowels

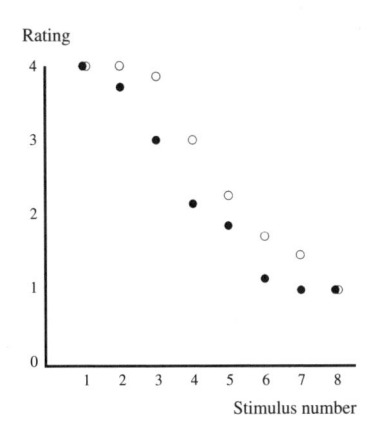

Figure 5-7
The ratings of vowels in the synthetic [o]–[a] continuum by the human subject (the identification test). Open circles are the results for female voices and filled circles are those for male voices.

than for that of female vowels. Figure 5-8 shows the results of the third test of discrimination for the chimpanzees and the human subject. Note that the reaction times were longer for female than for male voices when Stimulus No.1 was paired with No.3 or 4 (Popo) or when it was paired with Stimulus No.3 (Pan and SK). However, when Stimulus No.8 was paired with No.7 (Popo) or with No.6 or 7 (Pan and SK), a longer reaction time was required for discrimination of male voices than of female voices. Thus, these results support the assumption described above and suggest that the chimpanzees, similar to the human subject, may have the capacity for vocal tract normalization.

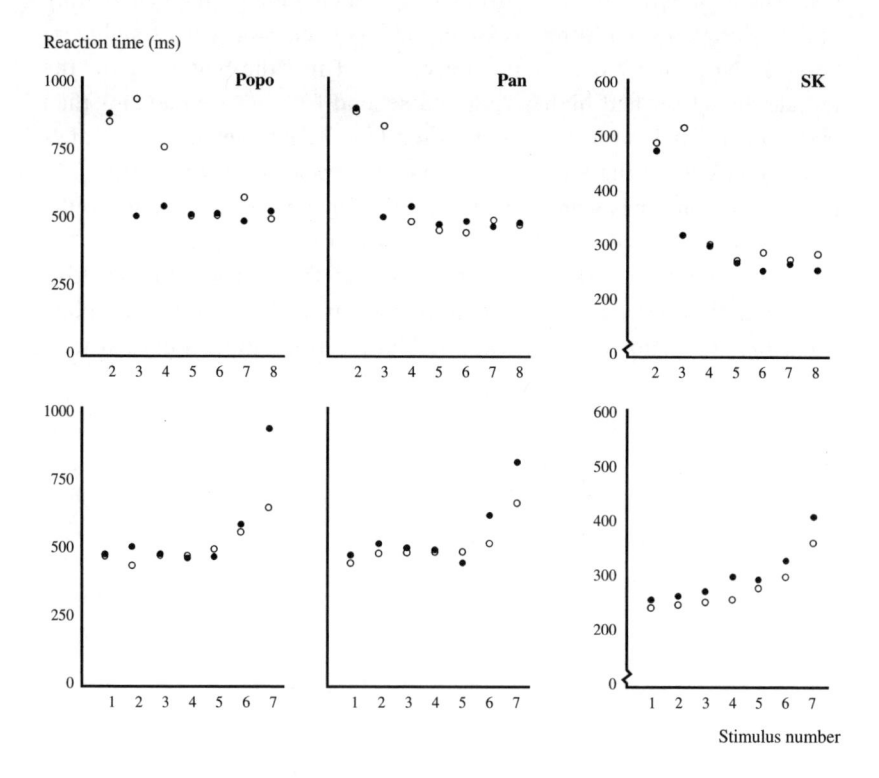

Figure 5-8
Reaction times for discrimination of vowels in the synthetic [o]–[a] continuum by the chimpanzees (the left two panels) and human (the right panels) subjects. The upper panel in each figure indicates the results of trials in which the background vowel was a typical [o] (Stimulus No.1), and the lower panel indicates those of trials in which the background vowel was a typical [a] (Stimulus No.8). Open circles correspond to female voices and filled circles to male voices.

The results of the second part indicate that chimpanzees can perceive a vowel uttered by different speakers as the same vowel, and provide the first evidence that chimpanzees have the capacity for vocal tract normalization. In the present experiment, only the human subject performed the identification task. The identification or labeling task should be administered to chimpanzees in the future to confirm the present results.

It has been reported that human infants can ignore the sex of speakers, suggesting that human infants can normalize the effects of the size of the vocal tract of speakers (Kuhl, 1979). The present study suggests that the capacity for normalization can be traced back at least to the ape. Chimpanzees pronounce vowel-like sounds which are heard as [u], [o] or [a]. Chimpanzees may utilize their capacity for vocal tract normalization for the identification of the age and/or sex of vocalizers in the field. Lieberman (1984, 1986) suggested that vocal tract normalization may be one of the prerequisites for the evolution of human speech. However, it now appears that chimpanzees are similarly endowed with the ability to normalize the effects of the size of the vocal tract (but see Appendix).

As described earlier, the vowels [i] and [u] are the best calibrators of the shape and size of the vocal tract for humans. The chimpanzees had difficulty in discriminating these vowels, as shown in the first part of this chapter. Therefore, different normalization processes may occur for these two species.

Prototype or magnet effect

In the third part of this chapter, I will examine the prototype effect (or the magnet effect) in a chimpanzee. It is known that each language has prototypic vowels (see Chapter 2). In the previous section (and in Chapter 9), the repertoire of chimpanzee vowel-like sounds was reported. It was difficult for chimpanzees to utter vowel-like sounds [i] and [e]. The vowel-like sound [u] is a prototype and [i] is a non-prototype for the chimpanzee. Thus, it is expected that the perception of vowels [i] and [u] by the chimpanzee may be different.

The subject was Pen. A set of eight vowels on the [u]–[i] continuum was synthesized (see Figure 5-9). The task used was RT II. The background vowel was the typical [u] (Stimulus 1) or the typical [i] (Stimulus 8). Other vowels on the continuum became the target vowels.

Figure 5-10 shows that reaction times increased when the typical [u] (Stimulus No. 1) was paired with Stimuli No. 2–No. 4. When the typical

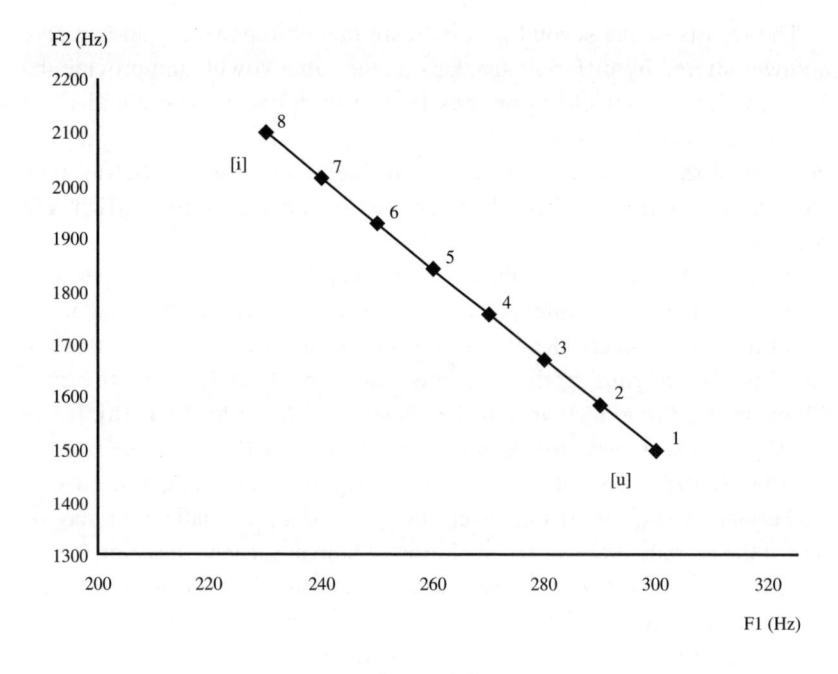

Figure 5-9
Synthetic [u]–[i] continuum (Stimulus No. 1–No. 8) in the F1-F2 plane. Frequencies of F1 and F2 are determined by the following equations: $F1 = 300 - 10(i - 1)$; $F2 = 1500 + 85.7(i - 1)$; $i = 1$ to 8. The fundamental frequency is 100 Hz.

[i] (Stimulus No. 8) was paired with Stimulus No. 7, reaction times decreased abruptly. Thus, Stimuli 1–4 were perceived as the same vowel [u]. On the other hand, Stimulus 7 was perceived as different from Stimulus 8 (a typical human [i]). These results are consistent with the results of human infants (Kuhl, 1991) and suggest that the chimpanzee has the prototype (magnet) effect. In Kuhl's experiments, macaque monkeys did not show the prototype effect for vowels [i] and [y]. If we choose the stimuli appropriately, however, we may be able to demonstrate the prototype or magnet effect in animals.

Perception of consonants: 20 natural french consonants

In the following sections, various aspects of perception of consonants are discussed. In experiments with humans, the structure of the perception of consonants and its relation to feature systems was investigated in terms of the similarity or confusion between consonants (e.g., Miller & Nicely,

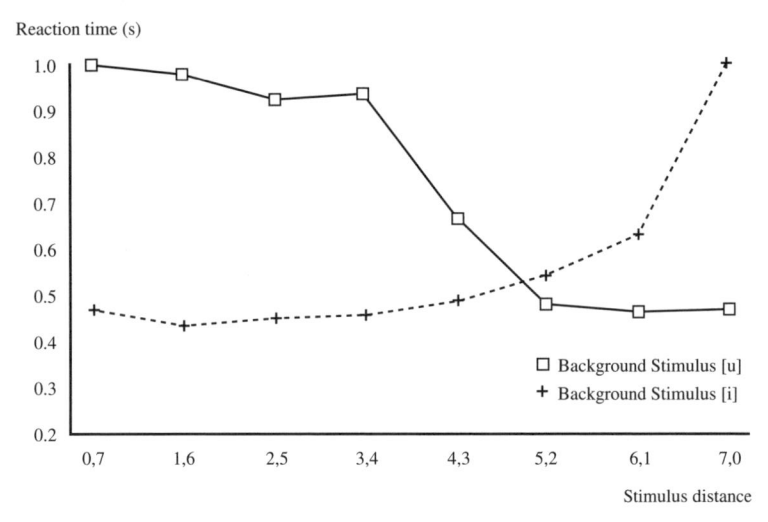

Figure 5-10
Results of the magnet effect experiment. Reaction times increased when the typical [u] (Stimulus No. 1) was paired with Stimuli No. 2-No. 4. When the typical [i] (Stimulus No. 8) was paired with Stimulus No. 7, reaction times decreased abruptly. The x-axis indicates the stimulus distance between the background and target stimuli. Left numbers indicate the stimulus distances when Stimulus No. 1 was the background; the right numbers indicate the stimulus distances when Stimulus No.8 was the background.

1955; Peters, 1963; Wilson, 1963; Singh et al., 1972). In the first part of the study, perception of 20 French consonants by chimpanzees was investigated.

The subjects were female chimpanzees (Pen, 9 years old and Popo, 5 years old when the experiment was conducted). Consonant-vowel (CV) syllables used were 20 natural French consonants followed by the vowel [a] pronounced by a female speaker. The task was Reaction time task II (RT II). All syllables were paired with each other.

Figure 5-11 shows the results of the perception of 20 French consonants by the chimpanzees. The left panel in each pair shows the results of the cluster analysis and the right panel shows those of the MDSCAL analysis. In the case of Pen, the stop consonants constituted one cluster and were located in the right part of the two-dimensional MDSCAL space, while the fricatives constituted another cluster and were situated mainly in the left part. The nasal consonants, semivowels and others constituted another cluster and were located between the stops and the fricatives. In the case of Popo, the stop consonants again constituted a cluster, although

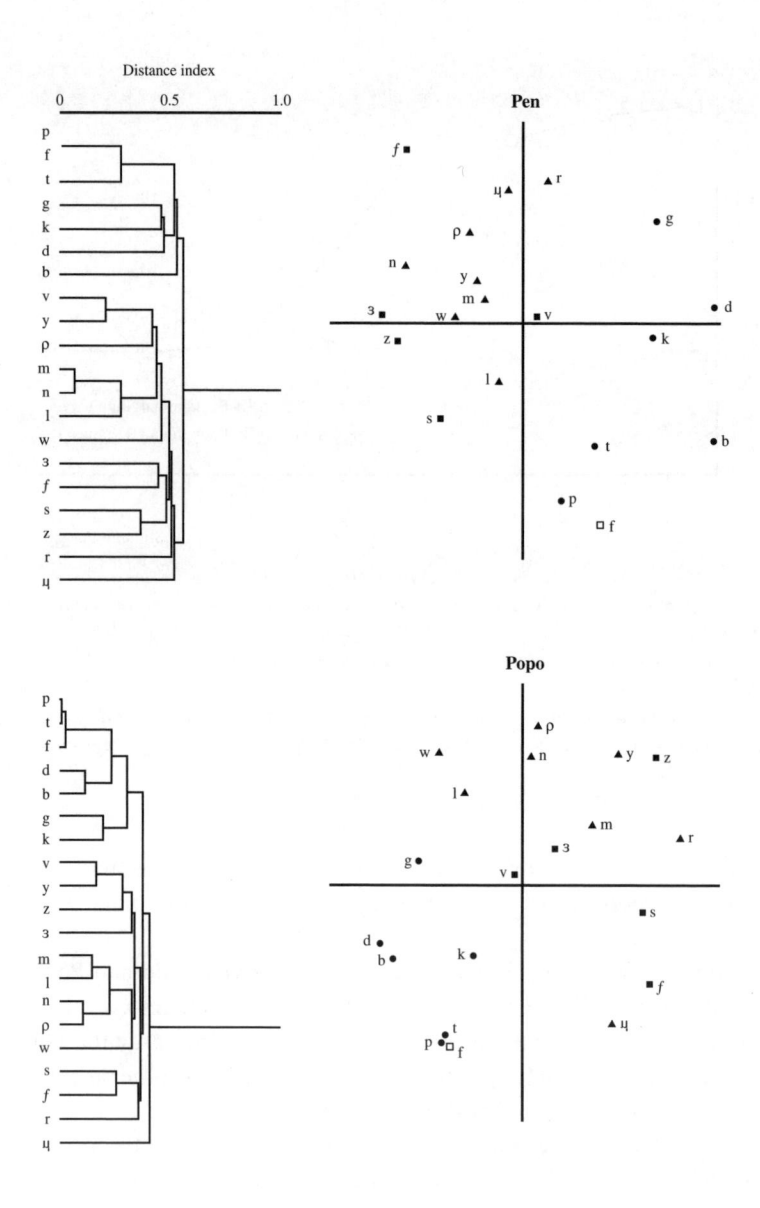

Figure 5-11
The perceptual structure of the 20 French consonants by chimpanzees(Pen and Popo). The left panels are the results of the cluster analysis (dendrograms) and the right panels are those of MDSCAL. Circles are stop consonants, squares are fricatives and triangles are other consonants. Due to a mistake in digitizing, the consonant [f] was indistinguishable from the consonant [p].

differentiation between other consonants was not clear. Figure 5-11 suggests that the place-of-articulation and voicing features determined the structure of perception of the stop consonants by both chimpanzees. That is, for Pen, the voiced stops ([b], [d] and [g]) were located towards the upper right and the voiceless or unvoiced stops ([p], [t] and [k]) were located towards the lower left part of the stop consonants in the two dimensional MDSCAL space. In the case of Popo, the stop consonants of the same place of articulation were located close together in the two-dimensional MDSCAL space.

The results of the first part of this study suggest that the manner of articulation may be the major determinant of the structure of perception of consonants by chimpanzees. Voicing and place of articulation appear to play some role in the perception of the stop consonants, as shown in this analysis. Human listeners have been reported to show a similar structure of perception of consonants. For example, Peters (1963) reported that the major grouping of the consonants was based on the manner of articulation, with either the place-of-articulation or voicing feature represented as a within-group dimension. Walden et al. (1980) reported that manner of articulation was also important in the perception of consonants by hearing-impaired listeners. The present results indicate that although chimpanzees do not have spoken languages, their perception of human consonants is similar to that of humans.

Perception of stop consonants

As shown in the perception of French consonants, the voicing and place-of-articulation features may be factors that determine the structure of the perception of stop consonants. In the second and third parts of the consonant studies, the perception of stop consonants was examined in detail.

The subjects were three female chimpanzees (Pen and Popo, who were used in the first test, and Pan, 3 years old, when the experiment was conducted) and two humans. The CV syllables used were natural and synthetic stop consonants ([p], [b], [t], [d], [k] and [g]) articulated by a male, followed by the vowel [a]. Synthetic speech stimuli were prepared using a computer simulation with a terminal analog synthesizer that contained a noise source, a buzz source, formant circuits, and a radiation circuit. The interval between the onset of the noise burst in a stop consonant and of glottal pulsing (voice onset time, VOT) was 0 ms ([ga]) or 56 ms ([ka]). Each syllable was paired with each member of the group.

Figure 5-12 shows the results of the test on perception of the natural Japanese stops by two of the chimpanzees (Pen and Popo) and a human (SK). For both chimpanzees, one of the two dimensions was that for the voicing feature. That is, voiceless (unvoiced) stop consonants [p, t, k] were located on the left side of each panel whereas voiced stop consonants [b, d, g] were located in the right side of each panel. The other dimension did not represent the place-of-articulation feature. The place of articulation from the lips to the velum was reproduced only in the perception of the voiceless stops by Popo in the two-dimensional MDSCAL space. The human subject showed perception of the stops similar to that shown by the chimpanzees, although reaction times of the human subject were shorter than those of the chimpanzee subjects.

Figure 5-13 shows the results of the test on perception of the synthetic Japanese stops by the three chimpanzees and another human subject (NH). As in the case of the natural Japanese stops, one of the two dimensions separates the voiced from voiceless stops both in the chimpanzee and the human subjects. The place of articulation of the voiceless stop consonants from the lips to the velum was reproduced in all the chimpanzees in the two-dimensional MDSCAL space. However, with regard to the voiced stops, there was an inversion in the order of [da] and [ga] in two of the three chimpanzees (Pen and Pan).

Figure 5-14 compares reaction times for discrimination of the voicing (for example, [pa] vs. [ba]) and the place-of-articulation features (for example, [pa] vs. [ta]) of the synthetic stop consonants. For all the three

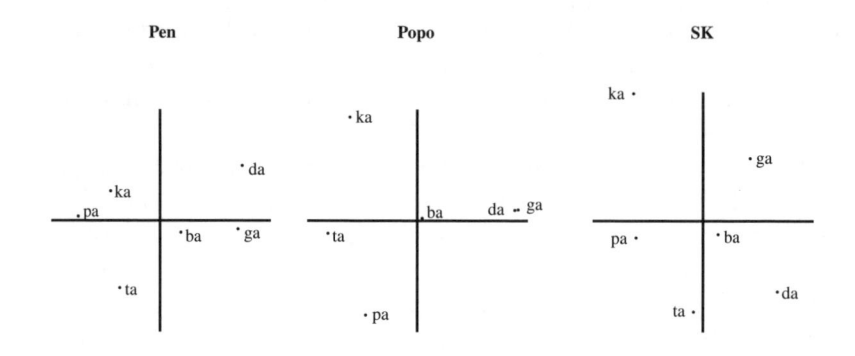

Figure 5-12
MDSCAL analyses of the perception of natural stop consonants by the chimpanzees (Pen and Popo) and a human (SK).

Figure 5-13
MDSCAL analyses of the perception of synthetic stop consonants by the chimpanzees (Pen, Popo and Pan) and a human (NH).

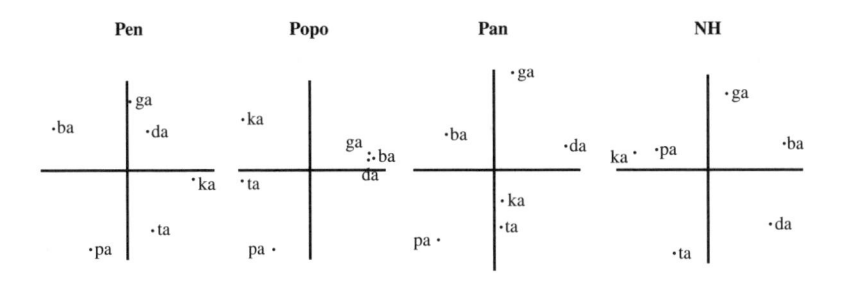

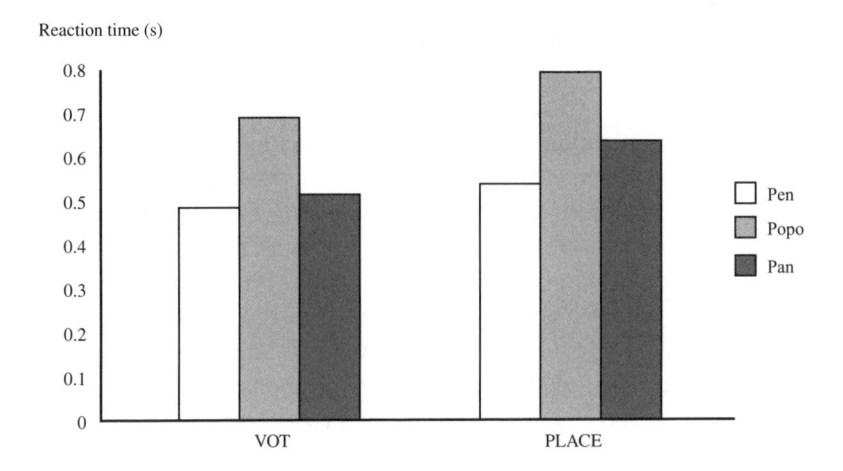

Figure 5-14
Mean reaction times for discrimination of the voicing (VOT) and the place of articulation (PLACE) features of the stop consonants by the three chimpanzees. All the subjects showed shorter reaction times for the voicing feature.

chimpanzees, longer reaction times were necessary for discrimination of the stops based on the place feature than for discrimination of stops based on the voicing feature.

The results of the second part of the consonant studies suggest that the major grouping of the stop consonants was based on the voicing feature in the chimpanzees. Human listeners exhibit a similar structure in perception of stop consonants (Miller & Nicely, 1955; Wilson, 1963), as shown in the present experiment. Thus, the basic strategy for the identification of stops in chimpanzees may be similar to that in humans.

Stop consonants are classified based on two features, namely, the voicing and place-of-articulation features. For the chimpanzees, discrimination between voiced and voiceless stops was easier than discrimination of stops based on differences in the place of articulation. One of the main acoustic cues which differentiates voiced from voiceless stop consonants is voice onset time (VOT), that is, the time interval between the onset of laryngeal vibration (voicing) and the release of the constriction in the supra-laryngeal musculature (Lisker & Abramson, 1964). In voiced stops, the onset of voicing precedes the release of the constriction, while, in voiceless stops, the release of the articulatory constriction precedes the onset of voicing. One of the acoustic cues that differentiates each place of articulation is the starting frequencies of the second and third formant transitions, that is, an abrupt change in the resonance of the vocal tract (Mattingly et al., 1971). Thus, discrimination between voiced and voiceless stops is related to discrimination of time intervals. Discrimination of the place-of-articulation feature is related to discrimination of frequencies and frequency modulation.

Frequency difference thresholds in chimpanzees are higher than those in humans (Kojima, 1990). Thresholds for detecting frequency modulation are also higher in monkeys than in humans (Moody et al., 1986). In addition, the chimpanzee is less sensitive to the second (and third) formants, as shown in the perception of vowels. These data may explain the difficulty experienced by and the longer reaction times of chimpanzees during discrimination between stops based on the place-of-articulation cue in the present study. With respect to the temporal resolution ability in chimpanzees, which is important for discrimination of voice onset time, no data are available. Sinnott et al. (1987) reported that difference thresholds for auditory duration in humans are smaller than those in Old World monkeys. Chimpanzees may be less sensitive to temporal discrimination than humans, which explains their longer reaction times when discriminating between stops with different VOTs.

Categorical perception or the phoneme boundary effect of stop consonants

The results of the second part of the consonant studies showed that the chimpanzees discriminated stop consonants in the same way as humans.

Humans discriminate the voicing and place-of-articulation features categorically (categorical perception or phoneme boundary effect, see Chapter 2). In this section, the phoneme boundary effect for the voicing ([ga-ka]) and place-of-articulation features ([ba-da]) of stop consonants was examined in the chimpanzees. No data are available on the categorical perception in this species.

To study the categorical perception between voiced and voiceless stop consonants, eight stop consonants on a [ga]–[ka] continuum with a VOT of 8-msec steps were synthesized, as described above (see Figure 5-15A). For studies of the categorical perception between stops with different places of articulation, eight stop consonants on a [ba]–[da] continuum were synthesized, which differed in the starting frequency of the transition of the second and third formants (see Figure 5-15B). The starting frequencies of the second and third formant transitions of the voiced, bilabial stop consonant ([ba]) were 1100 Hz and 2250 Hz, respectively. Those for the alveolar stop consonant ([da]) were 1800 Hz and 2819 Hz, respectively.

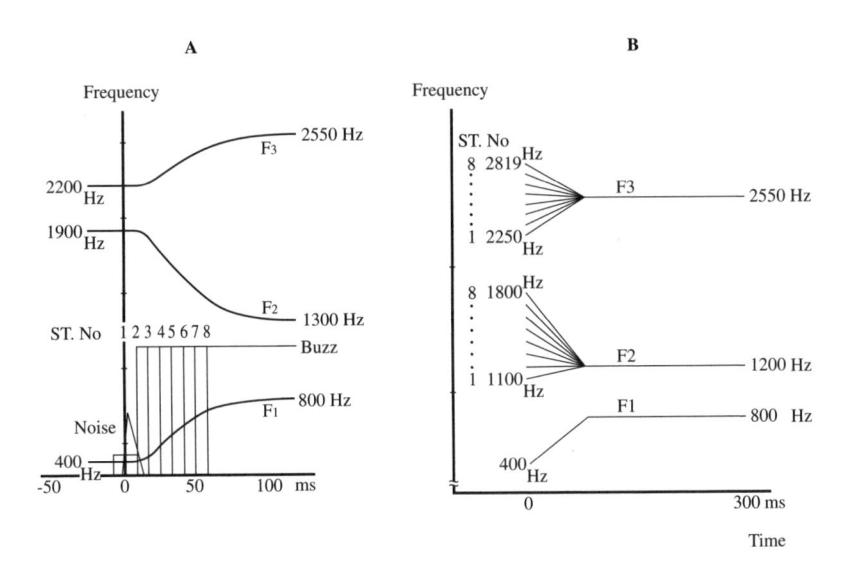

Figure 5-15
A: Eight synthetic stop consonants on a [ga]–[ka] continuum (Stimulus No. 1–8) with VOT of 8-ms steps used to study the phoneme boundary effect between voiced and voiceless stop consonants.
B: Eight synthetic stop consonants on a [ba]–[da] continuum (Stimulus No. 1–8) used to study the phoneme boundary effect between stops with different places of articulation. The starting frequency of the second and third formant transition was different between the consonants.

Each stimulus on the [ba]–[da] continuum was separated by 100 Hz and 81.3 Hz for the second and third formant, respectively.

The subjects were one of the chimpanzees used in the first and the second parts (Pen) and one of the human subjects used in the second part of the consonant studies (SK). In this task, stimulus pairs separated by two steps in each continuum ([ga]–[ka] and [ba]–[da]) were used. That is, Stimulus No. 1 was paired with No. 3, Stimulus No. 2 was paired with No. 4, and so on. Thus, the difference in VOT was 16 ms in each pair for the voicing feature, and the starting frequencies of the second and third formant transition of each pair, for the place-of-articulation feature, were 200 Hz and 162.6 Hz apart, respectively.

Figure 5-16 shows the results of discrimination of stimulus pairs based on VOT differences. The chimpanzee detected the VOT difference with the highest rate of success (approximately 50 %) when Stimulus No. 3 (16 msec VOT) was paired with Stimulus No. 5 (32 msec VOT). Thus, the chimpanzee showed the phoneme boundary effect for discrimination of [ga] from [ka],

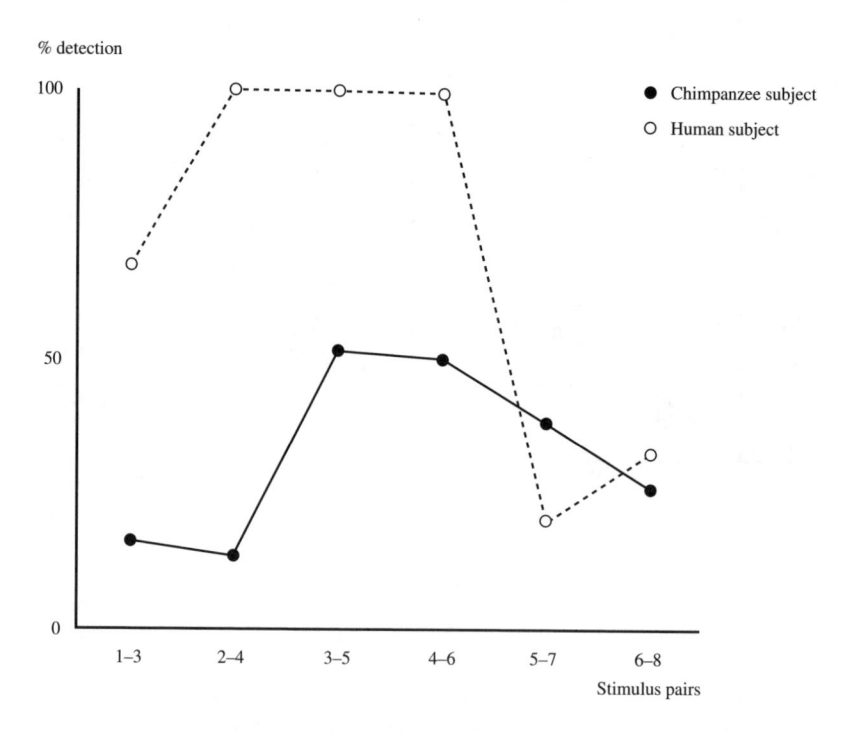

Figure 5-16
Discrimination of stimulus pairs based on VOT differences.

Perception of human speech sounds

and the VOT of the [ka]-[ga] boundary was 24 msec. The human subject also showed a similar phoneme boundary effect and the VOT of the boundary was the same as that in the case of the chimpanzee, although the human subject discriminated stimulus pairs more accurately and with shorter reaction times than did the chimpanzee subject.

Figure 5-17 shows the results of discrimination of voiced stops ([ba] from [da]) based on the difference in the starting frequencies of the second and third formants, that is, the place of articulation. The highest success in detection occurred with the Stimulus No.5-No.7 pair. Thus, the chimpanzee showed the phoneme-boundary effect for discrimination of the place-of-articulation feature ([ba]-[da]) when the starting frequencies of the boundary were 1600 Hz and 2656.5 Hz for the second and third formants, respectively. The human subject also showed the phoneme-boundary effect, although the position of the boundary of the [ba]–[da] continuum was slightly different from that in the case of the chimpanzee.

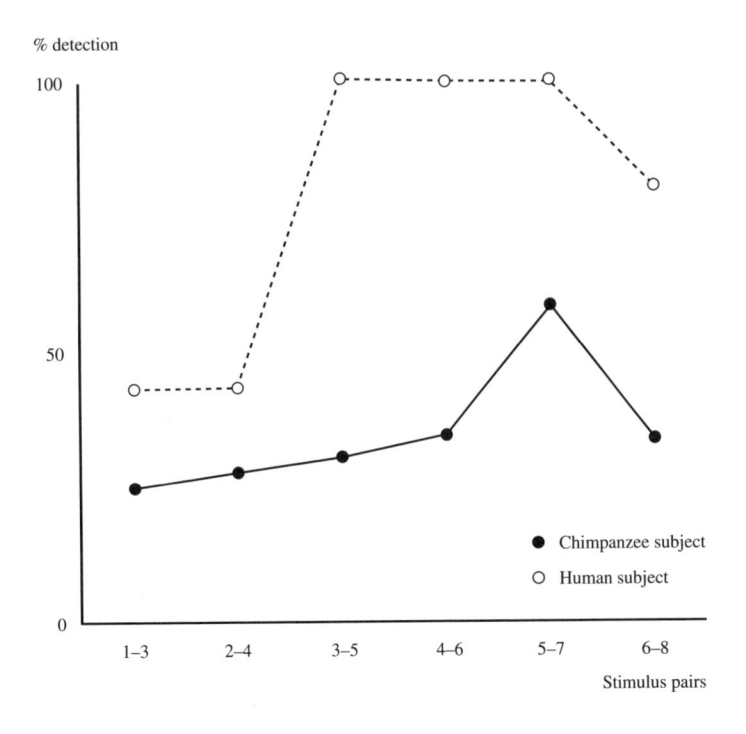

Figure 5-17
Discrimination of stimulus pairs based on differences in the starting frequency of the second and third formant transition (place of articulation).

The third part of this study showed that the chimpanzee displayed good discrimination at boundaries between the voiced and voiceless ([ga]-[ka]) stop consonants and between stops with different places of articulation, that is, between the bilabial and alveolar stops ([ba]-[da]), as has also been shown for the chinchilla and macaque monkeys (Kuhl, 1981; Kuhl & Miller, 1978; Kuhl & Padden, 1982, 1983; Morse & Snowdon, 1975; Waters & Wilson, 1976). Thus, although identification or labeling tests were not imposed on the subjects, the phoneme-boundary effect for the voicing and place-of-articulation features of stop consonants is not unique to humans and is, in fact, common to many species. These results, together with results obtained with other animals, suggest that a higher, phonetic level of processing, which is specific to humans (e.g., Liberman et al., 1967), may not be necessary, and a lower, auditory level of processing, which is common to many species, may be sufficient to account for some examples of categorical perception, as Kuhl (1986) suggested.

Kuhl and Padden (1983) described three possibilities with regard to the role of audition in the evolution of the acoustics of language: (1) audition does not provide a strong selective pressure on the choice of a phonetic inventory; (2) audition provides an independent pressure, but one that

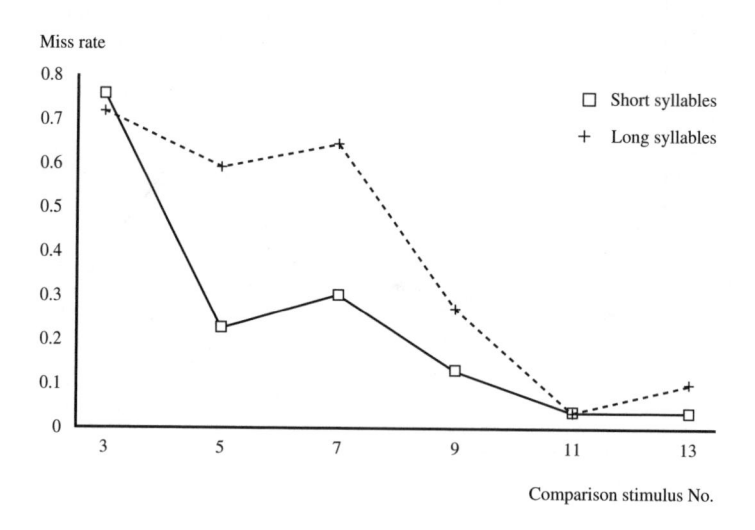

Figure 5-18

Discrimination (miss rates) of consonants on the [ba]–[wa] continuum (Stimulus No. 1–13). The background (standard) stimulus was typical [ba] (Stimulus No.1). Open squares: results for the short syllables, plus signs: those for the long syllables.

serves to initially structure rather than solely determine the selection of the inventory; or (3) audition per se directs the selection of the inventory by providing a set of "natural classes" for auditory stimuli that the articulatory mechanism evolved to achieve. Although the present experiments were not designed to test these possibilities, the results of the present study, together with those of other studies that demonstrated the boundary effects, suggest that at least the first possibility is not plausible, as suggested by Kuhl and Padden (1983).

The results of the third part of the consonant studies, together with those of the first and the second parts, suggest that the basic strategy for the identification of consonants in chimpanzees may be similar to that in humans, although chimpanzees are less accurate than humans in discriminating consonants.

Context effect or rate normalization

The fourth part of consonant perception is related to the context effect (see Chapter 2 for details). Discrimination between [ba] and [wa] was examined by varying the duration of these syllables (context). This is also the first report of the context effect in the chimpanzee.

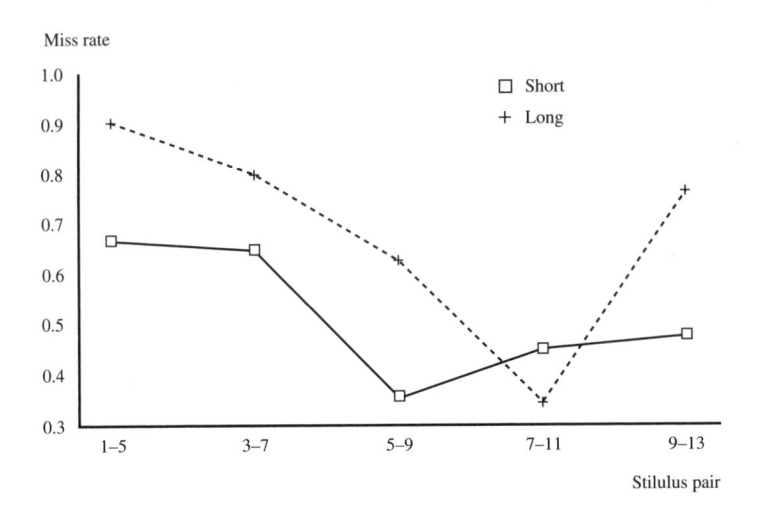

Figure 5-19
Discrimination (miss rates) of consonant pairs on the [ba]–[wa] continuum. The best performance was shown at Stimulus pair of No.5 and No.9 for the short syllables and Stimulus pair of No. 7 and No. 11 for the long syllables.

The subject used was Pan. The stimuli were two sets of 13 syllables on the [ba]–[wa] continuum. The duration of the syllable was 80 ms (short) or 296 ms (long). The task used was RT II. In the first test, the background syllable was the typical [ba] (Stimulus No. 1), and the target was one of odd-numbered stimuli on the continuum. In the second test, the odd-numbered stimuli separated by 4 steps were paired to find the boundary of the syllables. That is, Stimulus No.1 was paired with No. 5, and No. 3 was paired with No. 7, and so on.

Figure 5-18 shows the results of the first test in which miss rate decreases abruptly when the duration of the syllable was short, compared with the long syllable. As shown in Figure 5-19, the boundary (the pair showing the lowest miss rate) moved to the [ba] side when the syllable duration was short. These results are consistent with those for humans (Miller & Liberman, 1979). Thus, the chimpanzee shows the context effect.

Appendix: Vocal tract normalization in the Japanese macaque

In the appendix two Japanese macaques (Gon and Obie) were examined to determine whether or not they show the ability to perform normalization of the effect of the vocal tract size, using the same synthetic stimuli, apparatus, and procedures.

Fig. 5-20 shows that the general pattern of reaction times for discrimination was similar for the human and the monkey subjects.

The present study suggests that the capacity for normalization can be traced back to the macaque monkey. Japanese macaques may make use of their capacity for vocal tract normalization for the identification of the age and/or gender of vocalizers in the field. The chinchilla (Burdick & Miller, 1975) and dog (Baru, 1975) also show the ability to perform vocal tract normalization. These results suggest that vocal tract normalization or perceptual constancy may be common to many species.

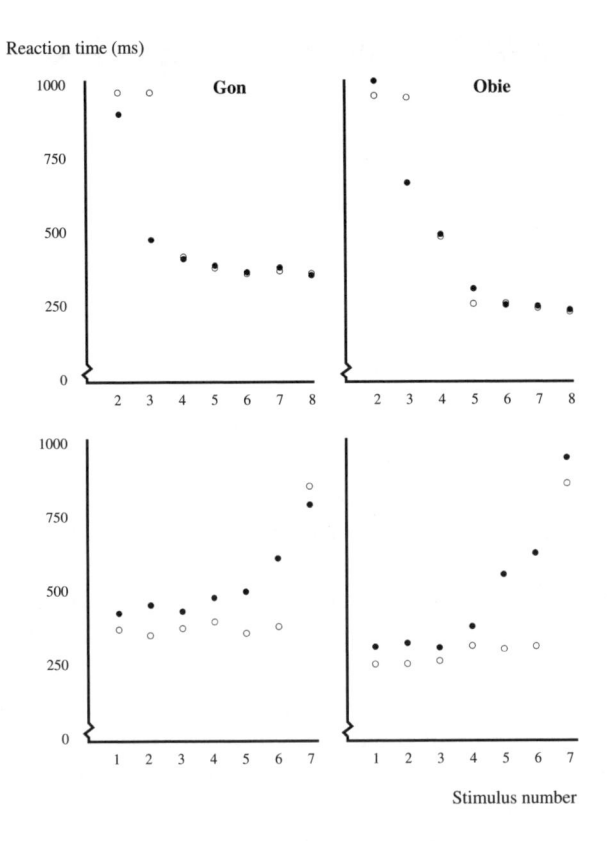

Figure 5-20
Reaction times for discrimination of vowels in the synthetic [o]–[a] continuum by the Japanese macaques (GON and OBIE). The upper panel in each figure indicates the results of trials in which the background vowel was a typical [o] (Stimulus No.1), and the lower panel indicates those of trials in which the background vowel was a typical [a] (Stimulus No.8). Open circles correspond to female voices and filled circles to male voices.

Chapter 6: Perception of species-specific vocal sounds

Production and perception of grunts

Thus far, there have been no precise experimental analyses concerning the perception of species-specific vocal sounds by the chimpanzee in the laboratory. In the first part of this chapter, the production and the perception of grunts will be described. Chimpanzees often vocalize vowel-like sounds. According to Marler and Tenaza (1977), these vocal sounds are rough and soft grunts which are related to feeding, general arousal and social excitement. Thus, they are not expressions of aversive emotional states. Usually, grunts have a harmonic structure and formants. Before analyzing the perception of grunts, the production of grunts was studied, and acoustical analyses of grunts were conducted. Basic vowels in common with human language are [i], [u] and [a]. Lieberman et al. (1972) reported chimpanzee supralaryngeal vocal tract area functions modeled on a computer and indicated the best approximations to the human vowels [i], [a], and [u]. It is of interest to know the repertoire of vowel-like vocal sounds of the chimpanzee.

Recently, I reported that the chimpanzee required long reaction times for discrimination of synthetic [i] from [u] and [e] from [o]; that is, chimpanzees need long latencies for discrimination between vowels based

Table 6-1 Number (N), mean duration and frequencies of the fundamental and the first three formants of chimpanzee grunts.

	[u]*	[u–o]*	[o]*	[a]*
N	24	18	20	20
Duration (ms)	244	232	129	133
Fundamental (Hz)	269	276	311	-
First formant (Hz)	353	546	730	1074
Second formant (Hz)	1997	2118	1972	2089
Third formant (Hz)	4176	4070	4091	4409

Perception of species-specific vocal sounds

on differences in the frequency of the second formant (Kojima & Kiritani, 1989, and Chapter 5). In this study, the generality of the mode of vowel perception in chimpanzees was examined using grunts and synthetic vowel-like sounds (grunts).

Production of Grunts

The subject was a female infant chimpanzee (Pan). The vocal behavior of the infant was observed for about 10 hours a day, 7 days a week, from her first day of life to one year. Vocal sounds and situations in which the chimpanzee vocalized were described in notebooks, and were taped. Vocalizations recorded on the tape recorder were analyzed by sound spectrographs (see Chapter 3).

The author perceived these grunts as [u]*, [o]* or [a]* (asterisks indicate the perception and identification of chimpanzee grunts by the author). Grunts which were perceived as intermediate grunts between [u]* and [o]* ([u-o]*) were also uttered. The chimpanzee did not vocalize typical [i]* and [e]*. Table 6-1 shows the mean duration, fundamental frequency, and frequency of the first three formants. Figure 6-1 shows these grunts on the

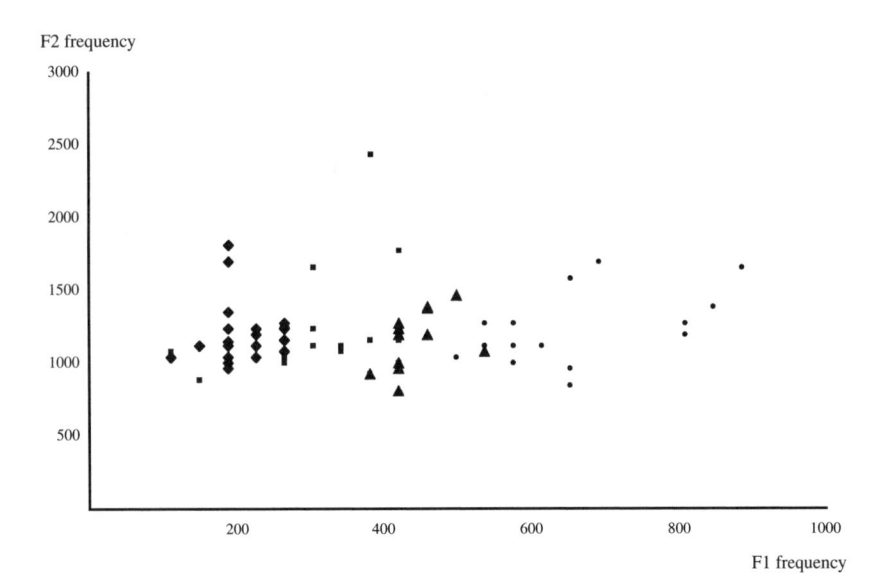

Figure 6-1
Grunts vocalized by an infant chimpanzee in the F1-F2 plane. Diamonds indicate grunts heard as [u]*, squares indicate grunts [o–u]*, triangles indicate grunts [o]* and circles indicate grunts [a]*. Each formant frequency value was divided by 1.7, which enables direct comparison between these results and those of Lieberman et al. (1972).

first (F1)-second (F2) formant plane. Each formant frequency value was divided by 1.7, which enables direct comparison between these results and those of Lieberman et al. (1972). As shown in Figure 6-1 and Table 6-1, the frequency of the second formant is similar between grunts. A statistical analysis was conducted on the first and second formants. No significant differences were obtained in the case of the second formant. In the first formant, there were significant differences between all pairs except those of [u]*-[u-o]* and [u-o]*-[o]*. Thus, the first formant differentiates the grunts. There were differences also in fundamental frequency (F0 (or H1)) and duration between vowel-like sounds (grunts). Grunts [u]* and [u-o]* had lower F0 and longer durations than grunts [o]* and [a]*, although it was difficult to measure F0 for grunts [a]*.

The infant chimpanzee vocalized vowel-like sounds (grunts) which were heard as [u]*, [o]* or [a]* by the author. She did not vocalize the vowel-like sounds [i]* or [e]*. A large pharynx is necessary to pronounce the vowels [i] and [e] (see Chapter 5). The position of the larynx is high and the pharynx is small in the chimpanzee (e.g., Lieberman et al., 1972; Lieberman, 1975). The differences in the shape of the vocal tract may explain differences in the repertoire of vowels (grunts) between chimpanzees and humans. These grunts in the chimpanzee had similar second formant frequencies. The frequencies of the first formant differed between grunts, as shown in Figure 6-1 and Table 6-1. The F2 frequencies are related to the position of the tongue in the antero-posterior dimension. With a short vocal tract due to a high larynx and small pharynx, it may not be easy to produce a variety of F2 frequencies.

There are discrepancies between formant frequencies and the author's perception of these grunts. In particular, the frequencies of the second formant of the grunts are too high. Effects of the normalization of the size of the vocal tract may be related to these discrepancies (see Chapter 2). Because an infant chimpanzee pronounced these grunts, the fundamental and formant frequencies were usually high. These factors may have influenced the author's perception and identification of these grunts. The prototype or magnet effect (see Chapters 2 and 4) may also affect the perception of grunts by the author. There are only five vowels, [i], [e], [a], [o] and [u], in Japanese. The typical frequencies of the first and the second formants of the five Japanese vowels are presented in Table 2-1. The Japanese [u] is a high back unrounded vowel [ɯ] with high second formant frequency. Thus, Japanese vowels [a], [o] and [u] have a similar second formant frequency. The repertoire of Japanese vowels may affect the identification of grunts by the author.

Using computer-implemented modeling, Lieberman et al. (1972) reported chimpanzee supralaryngeal vocal tract area functions and the best approximation to the human vowels [i], [a], and [u]. The present study confirmed their general prediction that it is difficult for the chimpanzee to pronounce a variety of vowels. They reported a vowel triangle, which is different from that of humans, as the best approximation. In the present study, a vowel line rather than a triangle was observed.

Laryngeal activity is relatively independent of activity of the supraralyngeal vocal tract in humans. For chimpanzees, however, the fundamental frequency correlated with the repertoire of grunts. These two activities may not be independent and may interact with each other in the chimpanzee. This limitation may negatively affect the emergence of speech in the chimpanzee.

It is not clear whether chimpanzees vocalize these grunts in different ways depending on social context in the field. Chimpanzees vocalize [u]* or [ou]* when they hear strange sounds, and [o]* before a mild attack. However, these grunts are also vocalized in a different context. I will report that Pan uttered grunts [o]* for milk and grunts [a]* for a banana reward in a vocal operant differentiation experiment (Chapter 8). These results suggest that they have an ability to differentiate grunts for requesting different foods.

Perception of Grunts

The subjects used were two female chimpanzees (Popo, 7 years old and Pan, 5 years old when this experiment was conducted). A human subject was used in the experiment on the perception of grunts.

Grunts which were heard as [u]*, [o]* or [a]* were selected from the vocal library for the first perception test. In the first test, a digital filter removed a harmonic sound or combinations of harmonic sounds (formant) of a grunt, and the subjects were required to discriminate filtered vocal sounds from the original grunt. Figure 6-2 shows an example of the sonograms (left panel) and the power spectra of an original grunt and two filtered grunts. The original grunt, <ORG> (labels used in figures are enclosed in parentheses < >), was heard as [o]*. For one of the filtered sounds, all the components except for harmonics that constitute the main part of the first formant were deleted. That is, only the main part of the first formant remained (in this study, this stimulus was called <F1>. A similar notation was applied to <F2>). When the main parts of both the first and second formants remained, the stimulus was called <F1,2>. For the other filtered grunt shown in Figure 6-2, only the second harmonic sound was deleted

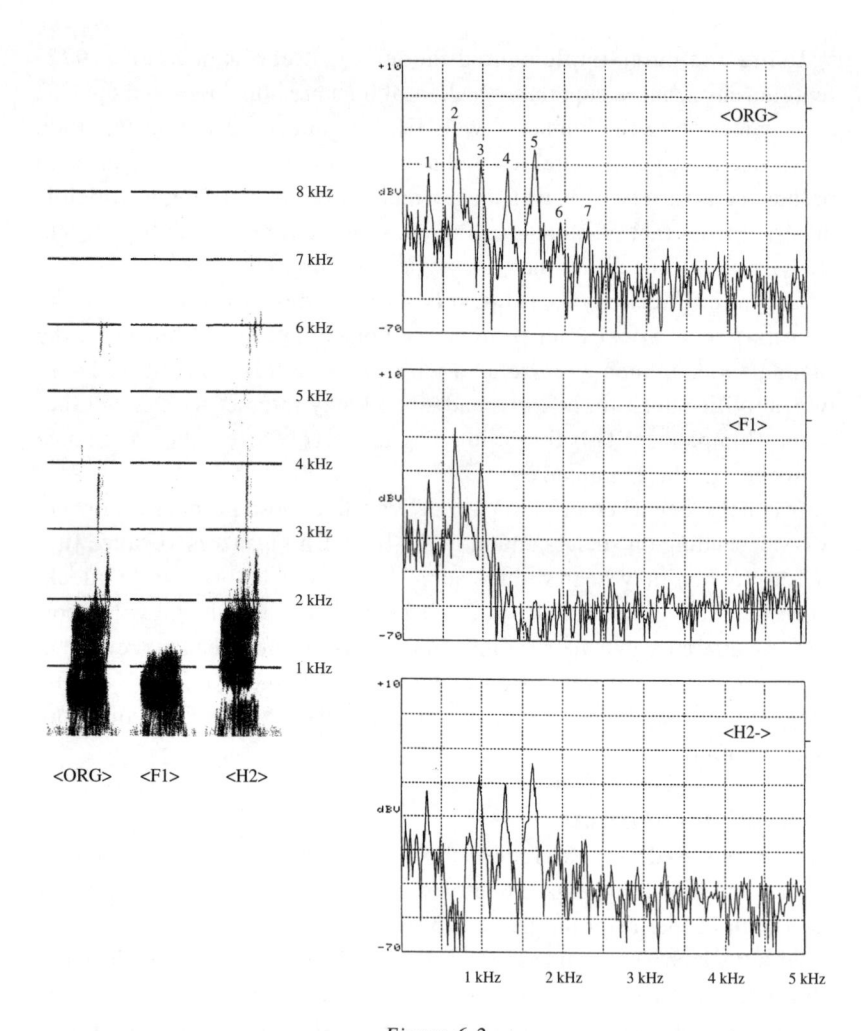

Figure 6-2
An example of the chimpanzee vowel-like vocal sounds (grunts) used in the first test. The sonograms (left panel) and power spectra (right panel) of the original grunt <ORG> and filtered grunts <F1> and <H2-> are also shown. <F1>: All components except for main part of F1 were deleted from the original voice. <H2->: Only the second harmonic sound was deleted from the original voice. The duration of the original voice was about 72 ms. In this and subsequent sonograms, the bandwidth of the analysis filter was 300 Hz. Numbers in the <ORG> panel indicate harmonic sounds.

(<H2->). A similar notation was applied to <H3-> and others. When only the second harmonic sound remained, it was called <H2>. A similar notation was applied to <H3> and others. When both the first and the second harmonic sounds were deleted, the stimulus was called <H1,2->. When both the first and the second harmonic sounds were presented, the stimulus was called <H1,2>. These notations were applied to other vocal stimuli (see Table 6-2).

The upper panels of Figures 6-3, -4 and -5 indicate sonograms of grunts used in the first test. The original grunt in Figure 6-3 was heard as [o]*. Nine filtered grunts were presented (see the x-axis of these figures). The original grunt in Figure 6-4 was heard as [u]*. Seven filtered grunts were presented. The original grunt in Figure 6-5 was heard as [a]*. Five filtered grunts were presented. In the perception task, the intensity of the filtered stimulus matched that of the original grunt, which was about 80 dB SPL (rms; dB re 20 µPa; SPL, sound pressure level).

The left panel of Figure 6-6 shows two sets (low- and high-frequency sets) of synthetic grunts in the F1 (first formant) - F2 (second formant)

Table 6-2 Notations of vocal stimuli used in this chapter.

Abbreviation	Explanation
ORG	original vocal sound
F1	only the first formant of the original vocal sound was presented, and other components were deleted
F1-	only the first formant of the original vocal sound was deleted
F2	only the second formant of the original vocal sound was presented
F2-	only the second formant of the original vocal sound was deleted
F1,2	both the first and second formants were presented
H1	only the fundamental (or the first harmonic sound) of the original vocal sound was presented
H1-	only the fundamental was deleted
H2	only the second harmonic sound was presented
H2-	only the second harmonic sound was deleted
H3	only the third harmonic sound was presented
H3-	only the third harmonic sound was deleted
H4	only the fourth harmonic sound was presented
H4-	only the fourth harmonic sound was deleted
H5	only the fifth harmonic sound was presented
H5-	only the fifth harmonic sound was deleted
H1,2	both the first and second harmonic sounds were presented
H1,2-	both the first and second harmonic sounds were deleted
H1,3	both the first and third harmonic sounds were presented
H1,3-	both the first and third harmonic sounds were deleted
H2,3	both the second and third harmonic sounds were presented
H2,3-	both the second and third harmonic sounds were deleted
H1,2,3	the first three harmonic sounds were presented

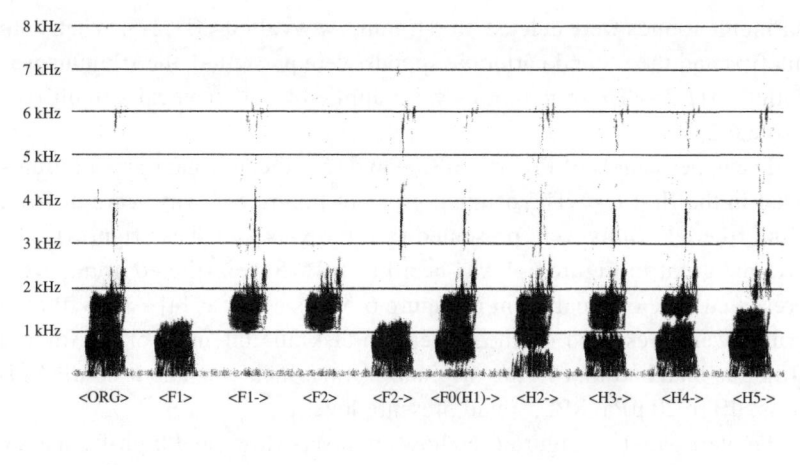

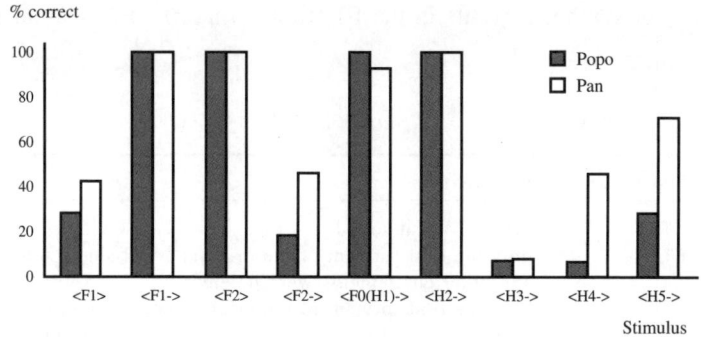

Figure 6-3
Upper: The original grunt [o]* and filtered grunts used in the first test. This is the same voice presented in Figure 6-2 <F1> and <F2>: All components except for main part of F1 and F2 were deleted from the original voice. <F1-> and <F2->: Only main part of F1 and F2 were deleted from the original voice. <F0 (H1)->, <H2->, <H3->, <H4-> and <H5->: Only F0 (H1), H2, H3, H4 and H5 were deleted from the original voice. Lower: The results of the first test for the two chimpanzees.

plane used in the second test. Each set of grunts had a central grunt and four peripheral grunts. The frequencies of F1 of the central grunts (C) in each set were 0.6 and 1.0 kHz and those of F2 were 1.8 and 2.5 kHz for the low- and the high-frequency sets, respectively. The F1 frequencies of the peripheral grunts 1(I) and 2(II) were 200 Hz lower and 200 Hz higher, respectively, than those of the central grunts. The F2 frequencies of the peripheral grunts 3(III) and 4(IV) were 200 Hz lower and 200 Hz higher, respectively, than those of the central grunts. Thus, only the frequency

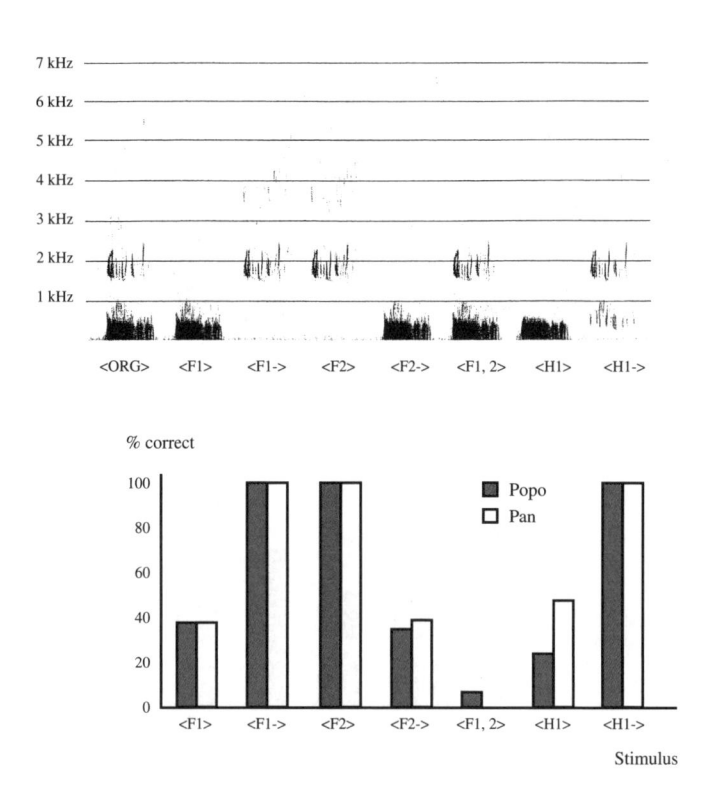

Figure 6-4
Upper: The original grunt [u]* and filtered grunts used in the first test. <F1,2>: Both main parts of F1 and F2 remain in the filtered voice. The duration of the original voice is about 128 ms. Lower: The results of the first test for the two chimpanzees.

of F1 was changed in peripheral grunts 1(I) and 2(II), and only the F2 frequency was changed in peripheral grunts 3(III) and 4(IV). The fundamental frequency was 100 Hz. The duration of these synthetic grunts was 245 ms with 15 ms rise and fall times, and the intensity was about 80 dB SPL. The frequency of the third formant was 3500 Hz and 4000 Hz for the low- and the high-frequency sets, respectively. The bandwidth of each formant was 100 Hz. The task used was RT II.

Figures 6-3, -4 and -5 show the results of the first test. The lower panel in each figure shows the percentage of correct responses for the two chimpanzees in the first test. As for the combination of harmonics ('formants': apostrophes indicate that the combination of harmonics is not the precise description of formants), when lower harmonics that constitute

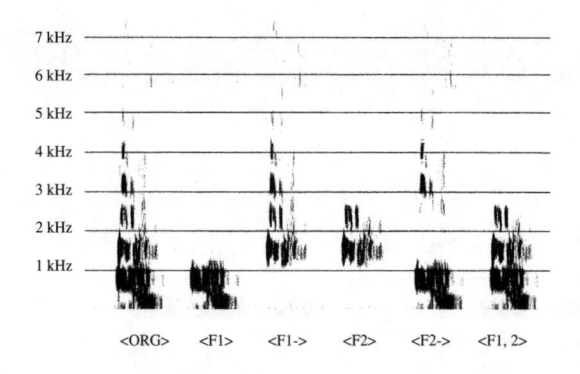

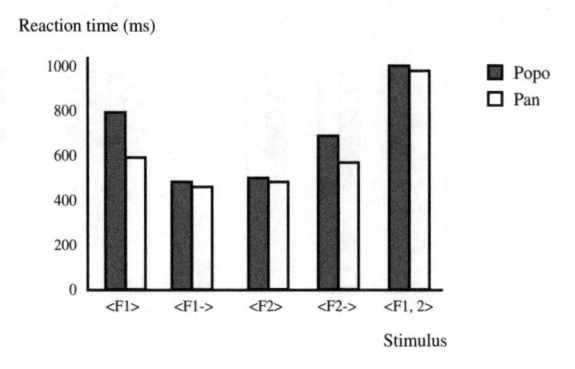

Figure 6-5
Upper: The original grunt [a]* and filtered grunts used in the first test. The duration of the original voice is about 100 ms. Lower: The results of the first test for the two chimpanzees. Reaction time data are presented.

F1 remained in the filtered grunt, as in the case of <F1> and <F2->, the percentage of correct responses was low. Consistent with the findings of the previous experiment (Kojima & Kiritani, 1989 and Chapter 5), F1 is more important than F2 not only for the perception of human vowels, but also for the perception of chimpanzee grunts. In regard to harmonic sounds, the percentage of correct responses was good when the fundamental or the second harmonic sound (<F0 (H1)-> or <H2->, respectively), which is related to F1, was deleted, than when the fourth or the fifth harmonic sound, which is related to F2, was deleted from the original grunt (<H4-> or <H5->, respectively). The human subject showed perfect discrimination of all the stimuli except for stimuli without the third or the fourth harmonic sound (<H3-> or <H4->). The human subject showed 80% correct responses to these stimuli. In the perception of 'formants' and harmonic sounds, the

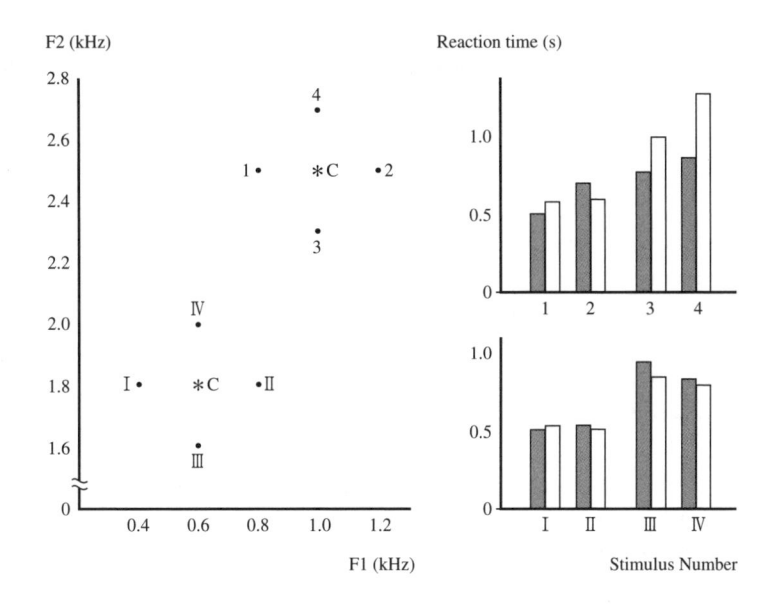

Figure 6-6
Left: Two sets of synthetic grunts in the F1-F2 plane used in the second test. Right: The results of the second test for the two chimpanzees (grey and white columns).

chimpanzee subjects showed almost perfect performance for <F1->, <F2>, <F0 (H1)-> and <H2->. The human subject showed longer mean reaction times to stimuli <F0 (H1)-> (286 ms) and <H2-> (300 ms) than to stimulus <F1-> (233 ms). Thus, compared with the chimpanzee subjects, the human subject was relatively less sensitive to individual harmonic sounds.

Similar results were obtained when the chimpanzee grunt heard as [u]* was used. As shown in Figure 6-4, when lower harmonics remained in filtered grunts, as in the case of <F1> or <F2->, performance was poor. F1 is more important than F2 in the perception of the grunt. When the main harmonic sounds remained in the filtered grunt (<F1,2>), performance deteriorated. The human subject showed perfect discrimination except for <F1,2>. The percentage of correct responses for <F1,2> was 70 %. There was a similar tendency between chimpanzee and human performance, although reaction times by the latter were shorter than the former.

Figure 6-5 shows the perception of the grunt heard as [a]*. There were few miss trials in the discrimination of this grunt except for <F1,2>. Thus, reaction time data is presented. When lower harmonics remained in filtered grunts, as in the case of <F1> and <F2->, longer reaction times were necessary for discrimination than under <F1-> and <F2> filtering conditions. The human subject showed perfect performance for all these stimuli including <F1,2>. The human subject showed a similar tendency in his reaction times, although they were shorter than those of the chimpanzees.

The right panel of Figure 6-6 shows the results of the second test. Consistent with the previous study and the first test, both subjects required longer reaction times for discrimination of the central grunt from peripheral grunts 3(III) and 4(IV) than for that from the peripheral grunts 1(I) and 2(II). These results also suggest that F1 (or lower-frequency components) is more important than F2 or higher-midfrequency components for the perception of these synthetic grunts in the chimpanzee.

The results of these tests and those of the previous experiments indicate that F1 or lower-frequency components are more important than F2 or higher- midfrequency components in the perception of vowels and grunts by the chimpanzee. One interpretation is related to the W-shaped auditory sensitivity functions of the chimpanzee (see Chapters 4 and 5). Difference thresholds for frequencies ($\triangle F$) may not influence the results, because the values of $\triangle F$ were about the same, between 0.5 kHz and 2 kHz (Kojima, 1990 and Chapter 4).

The perception of grunts and the synthetic grunts may be explained by the repertoire of vowel-like vocal sounds (grunts) of the chimpanzee. As described above, the frequency of F1 differs between grunts. Chimpanzees may be sensitive to differences in F1 and insensitive to differences in F2, which could account for the results of the test on perception of vowels and grunts.

Another interpretation is related to the masking phenomenon (Moore, 1989). Grunts are a kind of quasi-resonant nuclei (Oller, 1980). The fundamental frequency is usually low and main frequency components are concentrated in the lower frequency range. Human vowels also have rich low-frequency components. Thus, it is possible that the lower frequency components or F1 mask the higher (midfrequency) components or F2. This masking effect makes it difficult for the chimpanzee subjects to perceive the higher components. The W-shaped auditory sensitivity may augment this tendency. The low fundamental frequency may also influence the perception of each harmonic sound and the results for two harmonic sounds may fall in a single critical band or an auditory filter. The psychophysical tuning curves measured by Serafin et al. (1982) and the critical bandwidth measured by Gourevitch (1970) showed only slight differences between macaque monkeys and humans. However, there are no data on the critical bandwidth or the auditory filter in the chimpanzee. Further experiments on basic auditory functions such as frequency selectivity in chimpanzees are necessary. These interpretations of vowel and grunt perception, in terms of auditory sensitivity, vowel repertoire and masking are not mutually exclusive.

The human subject showed better performance in the perception of grunts. Humans are sensitive to both first and second formants, although they may be slightly more sensitive to the second formant than the first (see Chapter 5). In the perception of 'formants' and harmonics, compared with the chimpanzee subjects, the human subject is relatively less sensitive to individual harmonic sounds.

It is necessary to consider the spectral pattern and the fundamental frequency of chimpanzee grunts and human vowels. It is not clear whether the chimpanzees show the same mode of perception to vocal sounds with high fundamental frequency and strong higher frequency components. This is the main subject of the next experiment.

Perception of whimpers and squeaks

In this section, the perception of whimpers and squeaks will be examined. These vocal sounds are related to aversive emotions and are of short duration and vocalized in series (Marler and Tenaza, 1977). Sometimes whimpers grade into squeaks and then to screams with increasingly aversive emotions. Although the fundamental frequency of whimpers is low, that of squeaks is high. In addition, squeaks often have strong high-frequency components. Thus, in this experiment the generality of the mode of the perception of species-specific vocal sounds was examined in the chimpanzee. Are lower frequencies important even for aversive vocal sounds with high fundamental frequency and rich higher mid-frequency components? First, a series of six vocalizations changing from whimpers to squeaks was recorded and analyzed acoustically. Then, discrimination of each vocal sound was examined by pairing with other members in the series. Finally, I attempted to identify the harmonic sounds that were most important for the perception of these vocal sounds by removing the fundamental, a harmonic sound or a combination of harmonics, as in the previous section.

The same two female chimpanzees and a human subjects were employed. Vocal sounds used in this experiment were recorded from Pan when she was 0–6 months old. Acoustic analyses were conducted using the same apparatus as in the first section of this chapter. The upper panel of Figure

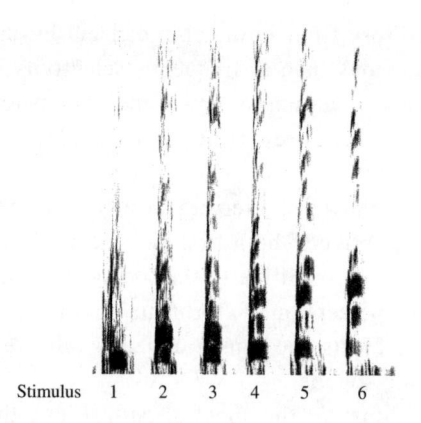

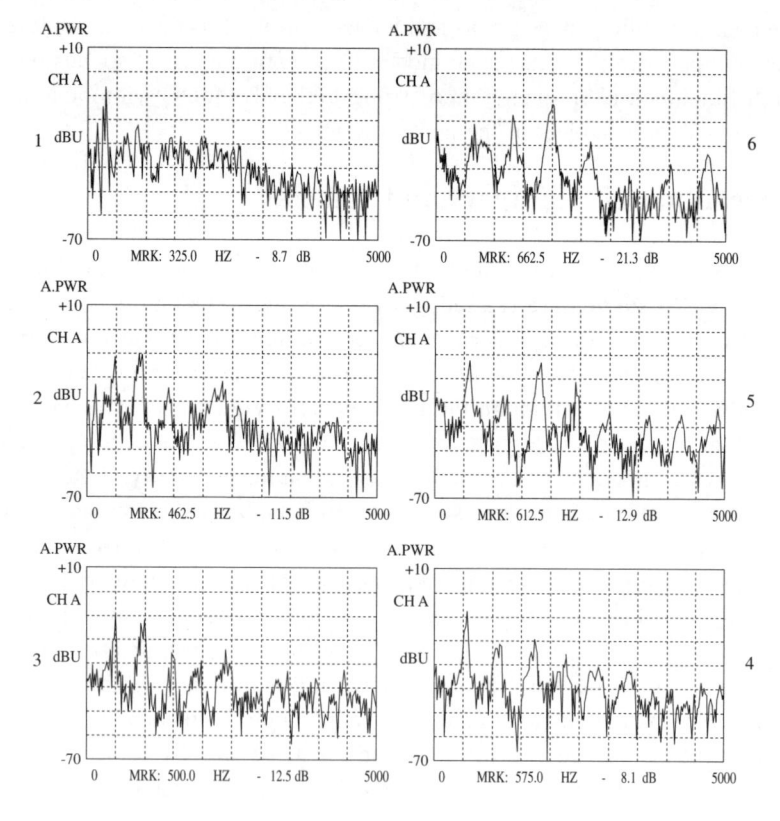

Figure 6-7
Upper: A whimper-squeak continuum (series) from Stimulus 1 (whimper) to Stimulus 6 (squeak). Lower: Power spectrum of each vocal sound in the continuum. Mean duration of these voices is about 48 ms. The Y-axis is the same as in Fig. 2.

6-7 shows the whimper-squeak continuum from Stimuli 1 to 6. The upper panels of Figures 6-8, -9 and -10 indicate the original vocal sounds taken from the series (Stimuli 1, 4 and 6) and the filtered vocal sounds. The fundamental tone and/or its harmonics were removed from the original vocal sounds by the digital filter program. For Stimulus 1 (see Figure 6-8), which had a similar spectral pattern to grunts, the importance of the fundamental and the second harmonic sound was examined (see the x-axis of each figure and Table 6-1 for stimuli used). For Stimulus 4 (see Figure 6-9), which had the strongest fundamental and was relatively rich in higher frequency components, the importance of the fundamental, the second and

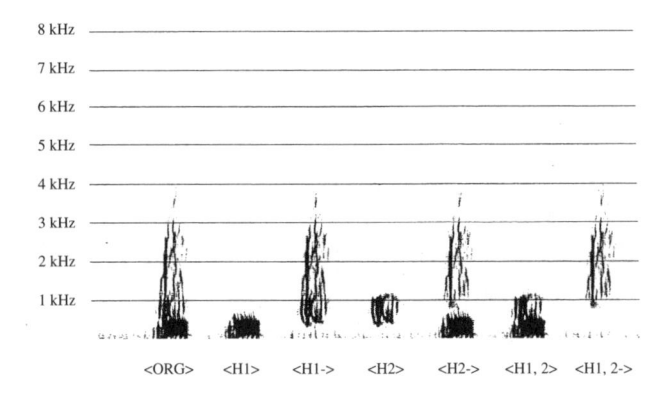

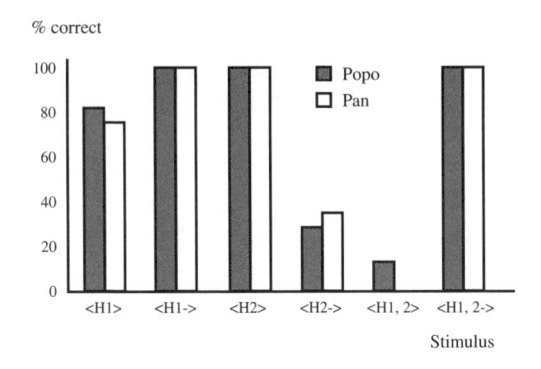

Figure 6-8
Upper: Sonograms of the original and filtered whimpers (Stimulus 1). <H1,2>: Both H1 and H2 remain in the filtered voice. <H1,2->: All components other than H1 and H2 remain in the filtered voice. The same notation of filtering operations is employed in the following two figures. Lower: Performance for the discrimination of filtered whimpers from the original.

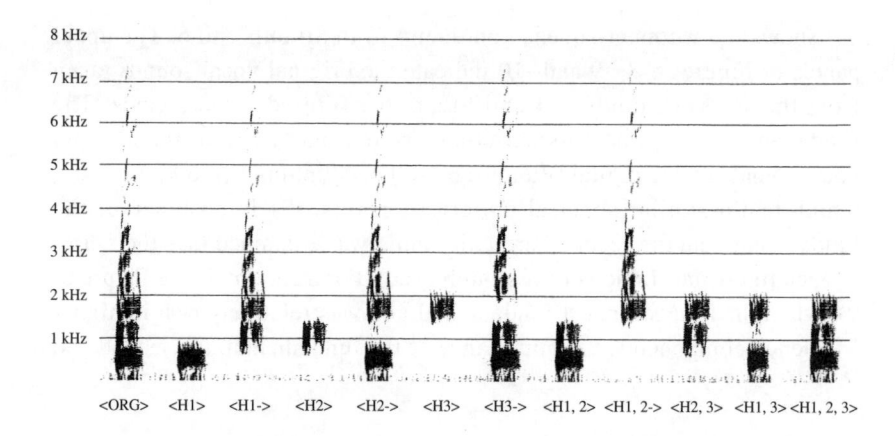

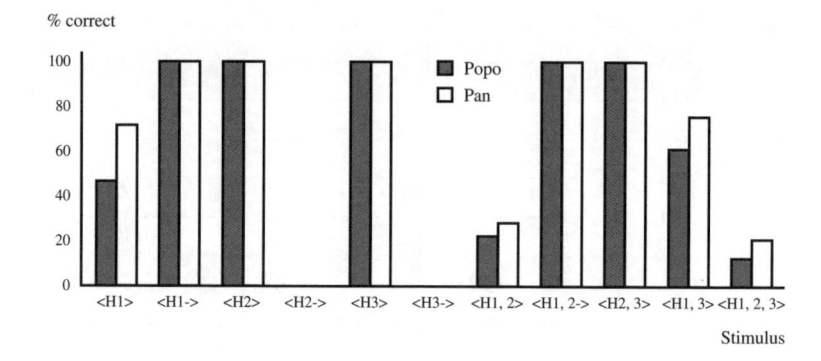

Figure 6-9
Upper: Sonograms of the original and filtered vocal sounds between whimper and squeak (Stimulus 4). Lower: Performance for the discrimination of filtered vocal sounds from the original.

the third harmonics was examined. The original and 11 filtered sounds were used. For Stimulus 6 (see Figure 6-10), which had the strongest third harmonic and a weak fundamental, the fundamental, the second, third and fourth harmonic sounds were used. In the perception task, the intensity of vocal stimuli was about 80 dB SPL. All vocal stimuli were digitized at a rate of 50 kHz and presented binaurally through the earphones, as in the grunt experiment.

The same apparatus and task (RT II) were employed. For discrimination of the whimper-squeak continuum, a member was paired with other members in the continuum, and the chimpanzee subjects were required

Perception of species-specific vocal sounds

Figure 6-10

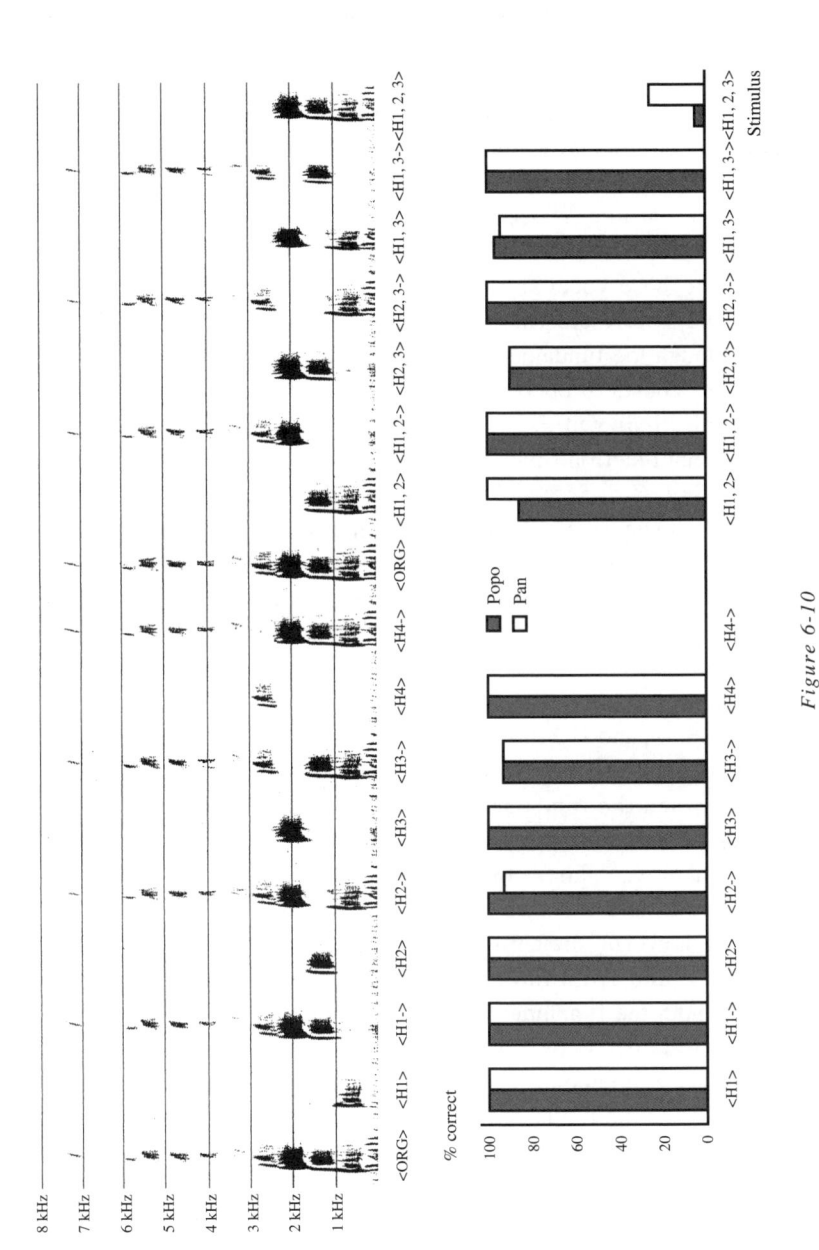

Upper: Sonograms of the original and filtered squeaks (Stimulus 6). Lower: Performance for the discrimination of filtered squeaks from the original.

to discriminate between these two sounds. For the discrimination of filtered vocal sounds, the background voice was always one of the original calls and the target stimulus was one of the filtered vocal sounds.

The lower panel of Figure 6-7 presents the acoustic analysis of the whimper-squeak continuum. The fundamental frequency of these vocal sounds increased gradually from Stimulus 1 through to Stimulus 6 (325, 463, 500, 575, 613 and 663 Hz, respectively). The difference in the fundamental frequency between adjacent voice pairs increased in the order of Stimulus pairs 2-3, 4-5, 5-6, 3-4 and 1-2. A visual inspection of sonograms of these vocal sounds suggests that the spectral patterns of Stimuli 2 and 3 were closest and those of Stimuli 4, 5 and 6 were also similar, although the fundamental frequency of Stimulus 6 was relatively weak. These acoustic properties may be reflected in the way these vocal sounds are discriminated.

Popo's mean reaction times for the discrimination of adjacent voices were 1311, 889, 675, 545 and 536 ms, for Stimulus pairs 2-3, 4-5, 5-6, 3-4 and 1-2, respectively. This is the same order as that of the differences in fundamental frequency. Pan showed similar mean reaction times except that her shortest reaction time was for the discrimination of Stimulus pair 5-6. Mean reaction times for Pan were 1002, 708, 693, 519 and 480 ms, for Stimulus pairs 2-3, 4-5, 3-4, 1-2 and 5-6, respectively.

Figures 6-8, -9, and -10 show the discrimination of voices filtered from original vocal sounds. For Stimulus 1, as shown in the lower panel of Figure 6-8, when the fundamental sound was paired with the original vocal sound, errors occurred in 17–23% of the trials. When the second harmonic sound was paired, their performance was perfect. When both the fundamental and the second harmonic sound were paired with the original call, however, the chimpanzees found it difficult to discriminate the filtered sound from the original. These results suggest that the presence of both the fundamental and the second harmonic sounds were important for the perception of this call, but the fundamental was more important than the second harmonic sound. This is supported by the finding that when the fundamental was removed from the original voice, the chimpanzees easily discriminated the filtered voice from the original voice. In contrast, when the second harmonic sound was deleted from the original, the chimpanzees scored only 29–36% correct responses. The human subject showed perfect discrimination of these stimuli. The longest mean reaction time was observed for stimulus <H2-> (368 ms), not for <H1,2> (264 ms).

As shown in the lower panel of Figure 6-9, when the fundamental, the second or the third harmonic sound of Stimulus 4 was paired with the original sounds separately, the chimpanzees could discriminate perfectly the second or the third harmonic sound from the original. The performance for the fundamental, however, was much lower, that is, 46–71%. These results indicate that the fundamental is more important for the perception of the original call than the second or the third harmonic sound. This is supported by the finding that, although deletion of the second or the third harmonic sound resulted in 0% correct responses, the chimpanzees showed perfect performance when the fundamental sound was removed. Moreover, the role of the second harmonic sound was more important than that of the third harmonic sound. Comparison of results for <H1,2> and <H1,3> revealed that the performance for <H1,2> was worse than that for <H1,3>. The human subject showed perfect discrimination of these stimuli. The human subject showed almost the same mean reaction times for stimuli <H1,3> (301 ms) and <H1,2,3> (305 ms).

For Stimulus 6, as shown in the lower panel of Figure 6-10, when one of the first four components was paired with the original, the chimpanzees discriminated perfectly. Thus, each harmonic sound was perceptually different from the original sound. Only when all of the first three harmonics were combined was it difficult for the chimpanzees to discriminate the filtered voice from the original voice. When one of the first three components was removed, the chimpanzees could discriminate easily (higher than 90% correct responses). However, when the fourth harmonic sound was deleted from the original voice, their performance severely deteriorated. Thus, the fundamental and the second and third harmonics were almost equally important for the perception of voice. With regard to the fundamental, second and third harmonics, however, <H1,2> was the most important for Popo. For Pan, <H2,3> and <H1,3> were more important than <H1,2>. This individual difference is consistent with that in the grunt discrimination experiment. The human subject showed perfect performance except for <H4->. Performance for <H4-> was 60% correct responses. The mean reaction time for <H1,2,3> was 331 ms. This reaction time was shorter than that for <H4->, which was 681.3 ms.

Results for discrimination of Stimuli 1 and 4 replicated the results of the grunt experiment. When a higher component was strong and the fundamental was weak, as in the case of Stimulus 6, however, the higher component became important for the perception of the vocal stimulus (squeak). This tendency was more evident for Pan than for Popo. Although the fundamental and the second harmonic were weaker than the third harmonic in Stimulus 6, they were still important for the perception of the squeak. These results suggest that both strong components and lower components (the fundamental and the second harmonic sounds) may be important for the discrimination of aversive whimpers and squeaks.

These results suggest that the interpretation by masking may be adequate. When higher components are strong and lower components are weak, higher components are not masked by the lower components. In addition, the high fundamental frequency of Stimulus 6 may promote the perception of each harmonic sound and may contribute to the high level of performance for Stimulus 6. It is possible that the strong higher-frequency component masks the weak lower-frequency components. However, the lower components remained important. These results are consistent with those of the perception of grunts in the first section of this chapter and of the perception of human vowels in chimpanzees (Kojima & Kiritani, 1989 and Chapter 5).

Why is the chimpanzee sensitive to the fundamental and the first few harmonics? One possibility is that the fundamental tone contains information on the arousal level or emotional state of the vocalizer, which is the most important aspect of chimpanzee social interactions. The importance of higher harmonics (May et al., 1988), of resonance frequency (Hauser et al., 1993) or of the relative harmonic level (Le Prell & Moody, 1997) has been reported in analyses of macaque vocal sounds. In this experiment, it was shown that the strong third harmonic sound of Stimulus 6 was as important as the fundamental for the perception of the squeak. Further experiments are necessary to understand not only the perceptual, but also the functional importance of higher harmonics.

The human subject showed better perception of species-specific vocal sounds of the chimpanzee (grunts and whimper and squeak) in this study. Humans are sensitive to both first and second formants, although they may be slightly more sensitive to the second formant than the first (Kojima & Kiritani, 1989 and Chapter 5). In the perception of harmonics of whimpers and squeaks, the human subject was relatively less sensitive to individual harmonics than the chimpanzees.

Appendix: Perception of coo sounds in the Japanese macaque

In the appendix, the perception of coo sounds will be examined. Japanese macaques vocalize coo calls in many social situations in which one individual

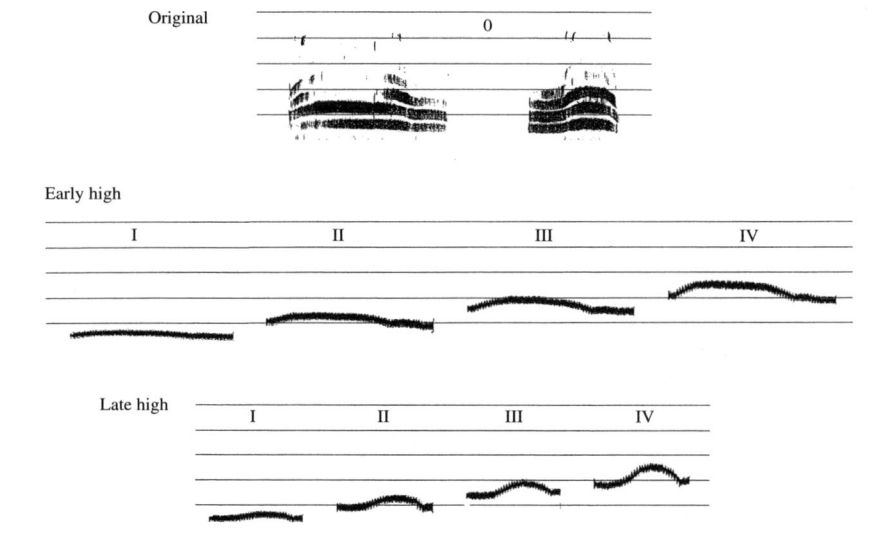

Perception of species-specific vocal sounds 91

Figure 6-11
Coo calls of the Japanese monkey used in the experiment. Original (O): natural early high (left) and late high coo calls. Synthetic early high and late high coo calls. The fundamental (I) and the first three harmonic sounds (II, III and IV) are synthesized separately.

seeks contact with others. Coo calls are tonal sounds with harmonics; they are often frequency-modulated. These calls are classified into seven types on the basis of their fundamental frequency, the degree of frequency modulation, and the position of the peak of frequency modulation (Green, 1975). Japanese macaques vocalize each type of coo in a distinct social context. Thus, each type of coo call probably has a specific communicative function (Green, 1975). Interestingly, Japanese macaques show a right ear (left hemisphere) advantage for the discrimination of early high coos from late high coos (Petersen, et al., 1978; Heffner & Heffner, 1984).

The discrimination of early and late high coo calls was investigated in the Japanese macaque, using an auditory delayed matching to sample task. As coo calls have a harmonic structure, it is important to identify the most important harmonic sound for the discrimination of early and late high coos. Is it the fundamental or some higher harmonic sound? The experiment reported here was designed to answer this question.

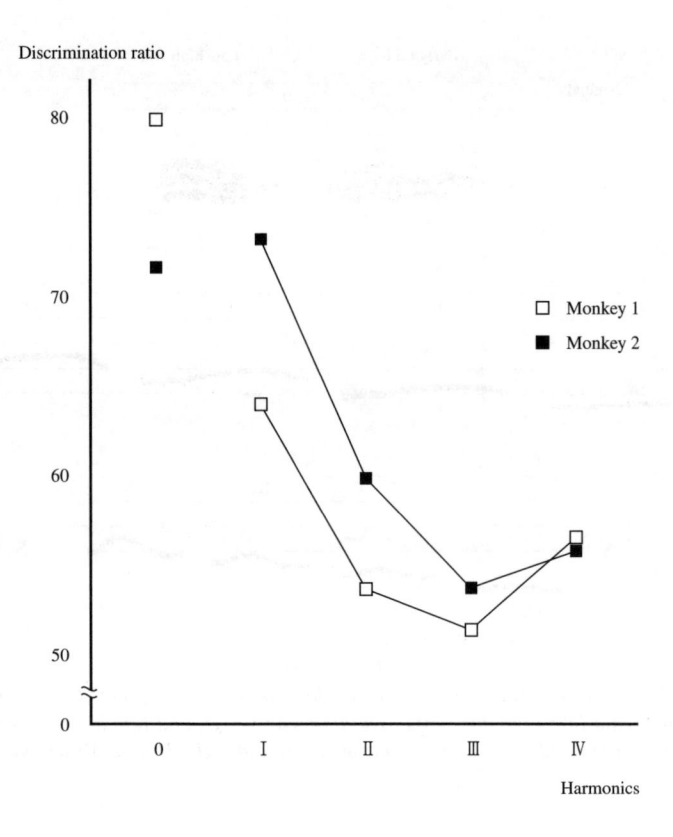

Figure 6-12
Results of the original learning and transfer test. As shown, the largest transfer was observed in the discrimination of the fundamental pair (I).

Subjects were two male Japanese macaques. They had experience on the auditory matching to sample task employed in the present study.

The monkeys were trained and tested in a chamber located in the soundproof room. One wall contained a panel with a key. The following natural and synthetic coo calls were used (see Figure 6-11): (a) Two natural coo calls (O), i.e., an early high (EH) and a late high coo (LH); (b) Synthetic sounds replicating the fundamental (I) or one of the second, third and forth harmonics (II–IV) of each natural coo call. These sounds were digitized at a rate of 33.3 kHz and presented through a loudspeaker. The intensity of the sounds was about 65 dB SPL at the monkey's ear level. A pellet dispenser delivered a piece of apple or sweet potato as reward. The chamber was interfaced to a personal computer, which controlled the experiment.

The subjects had been trained on a GO/NO GO auditory delayed matching to sample task (Kojima, 1985, and Chapter 3 in this book). First, the monkeys were trained to discriminate the natural (original) EH and LH coo calls. After the monkeys had mastered the discrimination of natural coo calls, transfer tests were administered. The transfer tests used paired synthetic features of the EH and LH calls (fundamental or harmonics). For example, the monkeys had to discriminate between the synthetic second harmonic of the EH coo and that of the LH coo.

Figure 6-12 shows the results of the original learning and transfer tests. As shown, the largest transfer from the original coo sounds (O) discrimination was observed in the discrimination of the fundamental pair (I). The discrimination ratio was lower in higher harmonics, and it was almost at a chance level for the discrimination of the third harmonic pair (III). The discrimination of the fourth harmonic pair (IV) improved slightly for both monkeys.

The present results suggest that the fundamental is the greatest contributor to the discrimination of coo calls. Although the task employed was different, the chimpanzee showed a similar perception of grunts, whimpers and squeaks. Thus, attention to low frequencies may be common to nonhuman primates. It was reported that the second and third harmonics were more important than the fundamental tone in early and late high coos (May et al., 1988). However, there are differences in the stimuli and testing procedure employed between May et al.'s study and the present one: while each harmonic pair was presented separately in the present study, they presented pairs of the second and the third harmonics at the same time. Moreover, while a matching to sample task was used in the present study, a successive discrimination task was employed in their study. These differences may be responsible for the differences in results obtained for these two studies.

Chapter 7: Auditory cognition

Acquisition of audio-visual intermodal matching to sample

The integration of information from different modalities is an important cognitive ability in animals (Ettlinger, 1977). In this chapter, integration of auditory and visual information in chimpanzees will be discussed (see Hashiya & Kojima, 1997, 2001a, b). Humans communicate through an auditory-vocal channel, that is, by spoken language. Spoken language is supported by the ability to perform audio-visual intermodal integration. There are many factors that may account for the lack of spoken language in nonhuman primates. The ability to perform audio-visual intermodal integration may be one of them. Are monkeys and apes endowed with the ability? Only a few investigations have reported audio-visual intermodal matching to sample in monkeys (Dewson & Burlingame, 1975; Dewson & Cowey, 1969; Gaffan & Harrison, 1991; Murray & Gaffan, 1994). This indicates it may not be easy for monkeys to integrate auditory and visual information. In other words, they may lack one of the important bases for spoken language. Is the same true for apes? Audio-visual intermodal integration has been studied in two species of apes, chimpanzees and bonobos. Although bonobos showed excellent performance, chimpanzees did not (Savage-Rumbaugh, 1987). Does this mean the performance of chimpanzees was not different from that of monkeys? In other words, are bonobos exceptional in audio-visual integration among nonhuman primates? Several factors other than species difference may affect these results. For example, rearing history may be one of the factors. But other factors were not elucidated in prior research. To determine whether chimpanzees can perform intermodal integration, it may be important to find better procedures for training audio-visual matching to sample in nonhuman primates. Recently, Gaffan and his coworkers reported the training procedure of an audio-visual matching to sample task (Gaffan & Harrison, 1991; Murray & Gaffan, 1994) for monkeys. There may be other procedures which promote acquisition of audio-visual matching to sample. In the present study, a chimpanzee was trained on an audio-visual intermodal matching to sample task and acquisition processes and characteristics of matching behavior were compared with visual intramodal matching.

The subject was a female chimpanzee, Pan, 8 years old when the experiment was conducted. Apparatuses and basic procedures were reported in Chapter 3. In the present study, 15 sound-producing objects that the subject was familiar with were used. Table 7-1 and Figure 7-1 show these sound-producing objects. In the acquisition sessions, 5 pairs of 6 objects were used. The remaining 9 objects were used in the test sessions.

Acquisition

A total of 76 sessions was necessary for the subject to acquire the audio-visual intermodal matching to sample task. It was not easy for the subject to master the task. Several procedures were attempted in the first 48 acquisition sessions, but no improvement in performance was observed. After the 49th session, a trial with an audio-visual sample and a trial with an auditory sample were alternated. This procedure was employed thereafter. In the first 57 sessions, the Objects 1-2 pair was used. Another 4 pairs, that is, Objects 3-4, 2-3, 2-4 and 5-6, were introduced in this order after the 58th session. A single pair was used in each session. In the audio-visual sample procedure, the experimenter made sounds using the objects

Table 7-1 A list of sound-producing objects used in the present study

Stimulus number	Object
1	Bell 1
2	Toy motor horn
3	Rattle 1
4	Rattle 2
5	Rattle 3
6	Toy clarinet
7	Bunch of keys
8	Cup and spoon
9	Squeaking toy
10	Bell 2
11	Castanets
12	Toy tambourine
13	Pebbles in a tube
14	Bell 3
15	Whistling toy

Figure 7-1
Sound-producing objects used in the experiment.

in front of the subject. The subject could observe and hear the object. In the auditory sample procedure, the subject heard but could not see the object. The test stimulus consisted of a pair of pictures, one of which matched the sample stimulus.

Figure 7-2 shows the acquisition of the audio-visual intermodal matching to sample task. These results are those for the auditory sample procedure. Results for audio-visual trials are not presented in this figure. Performance on the audio-visual trials was almost perfect after 10 sessions. Although the results are not presented, 29 sessions with several training procedures were interposed during the first 19 sessions shown in this figure. Thus the 19th session in this figure is actually the 48th training session. The audio-visual and auditory sample procedures were alternated at the 20th (49th) session. Although performance was not stable, it suddenly improved. At the 29th (58th) session, the object pair was changed from Objects 1-2 to Objects 3-4. The performance improved and remained at a high level. One component of the pairs was changed at the 40th–41st and 42nd–43th sessions, that is, Objects 2-3 and 2-4 pairs. The performance level was at about 90% correct. The subject showed a high performance

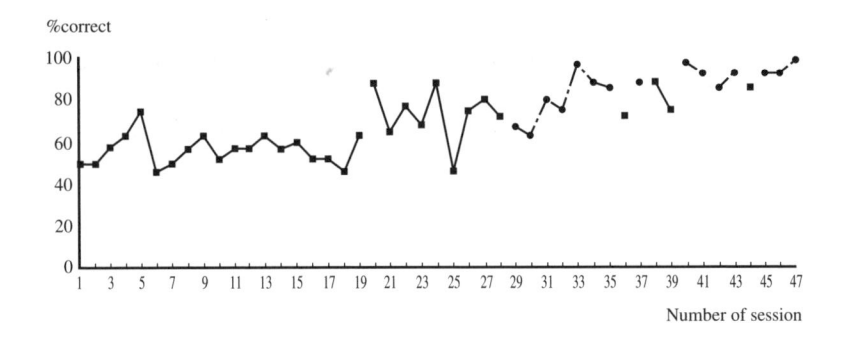

Figure 7-2
Percent correct responses in the acquisition of audio-visual intermodal matching-to- sample performance. Only the results in the auditory sample condition are shown (see text).

level with the introduction of a new pair consisting of new objects (Objects 5-6) at the 45–47th (74–76th) sessions.

In contrast with a large body of data on visual matching to sample, only a few studies have reported the acquisition of the audio-visual intermodal matching to sample task by monkeys (Dewson & Burlingame, 1975; Dewson & Cowey, 1969; Gaffan & Harrison, 1991; Murray & Gaffan, 1994). Except for Gaffan and his co-workers' studies, acquisition procedures and processes have not been described in these studies. In the present study, the chimpanzee subject showed similar difficulties in mastering the audio-visual matching to sample task to those found in previous studies. Sound-producing objects that were familiar to the subject were used as sample stimuli and audio-visual and auditory sample trials were alternated. These two procedures were effective in allowing the chimpanzee subject to acquire the audio-visual matching to sample task. The extent to which these procedures can be generalized should be examined in other chimpanzees and in other nonhuman primate species.

The performance of auditory discrimination depends on the tasks employed. For example, discrimination of sounds is usually easy when a reaction time task (a kind of Go/ No Go procedure) is used as in Chapter 4. On the other hand, when a sound-color matching task (a kind of Yes/ No procedure) is employed, it is difficult for nonhuman primates to acquire the task, as in this chapter. The task dependency in auditory experiments shows a contrast with visual experiments that are not at all or less task dependent. In general, we are inclined to ignore negative data. To study the task dependency may promote our understanding of the nature of auditory stimuli.

Unlike chimpanzees, bonobos have shown excellent audio-visual matching performance (Savage-Rumbaugh, 1987). There may be several factors other than species difference that should be considered in explaining the apparent difference between chimpanzees and bonobos. One of the factors may be the auditory experience of subjects. Further studies are necessary to answer this question.

Tests

After the subject acquired the task, the effects of audio-visual, auditory and visual sample procedures were examined. In visual sample trials, objects were presented without being used to produce sounds. Six pairs of objects, that is, Objects 2-4, 1-3, 2-6, 1-5, 4-6 and 3-5, were used in this test. Then, the effects of massed and alternated sample presentation were examined. In this test, 5 pairs of objects, that is, Objects 5-6, 3-4, 3-5, 4-5 and 4-6 pairs, were used. Under the massed sample presentation condition, audio-visual samples were presented in the first 50 trials, then auditory samples were presented in the second 50 trials. Under the alternation condition, audio-visual and auditory samples were alternated in 100 trials. Next, a transfer test was conducted. In this test, all the 15 sound-producing objects were used. Audio-visual samples were presented in the first 10 trials and auditory samples were presented in the following 50 trials in this test. Transfer of performance to thirty-eight pairs, including 4 new object pairs, was examined.

Figure 7-3 shows percent correct (upper panel) and reaction time in s (lower panel) for audio-visual, auditory and visual samples for each object pair. In both audio-visual and visual sample conditions, the subject showed a high level of performance and short reaction times. In the auditory sample condition, performance dropped to 80% correct and reaction times increased. Statistical analyses showed that there were significant differences in performance level and reaction times between the audio-visual and auditory samples and between the visual and auditory sample conditions.

Figure 7-4 shows percent correct for massed and alternated sample presentations for each object pair. The subject showed higher performance in the alternated than in the massed sample presentation condition. Results of mean percent correct for massed and alternated sample presentations were 70.0% and 83.6%, respectively.

Figure 7-5 shows transfer of audio-visual intermodal matching to sample performance to new object pairs. Both members of pairs with an asterisk represent new objects for the subject. Although performance often dropped to 60% correct in the first 5 pairs, performance was maintained at a high level in subsequent pairs. Even when pairs of new objects were introduced, the subject showed relatively high performance. A statistical analysis was performed for the first 20 sessions in which new pairs were introduced that indicated there was no difference between sessions with new (82% correct) and old (89.75% correct) pairs.

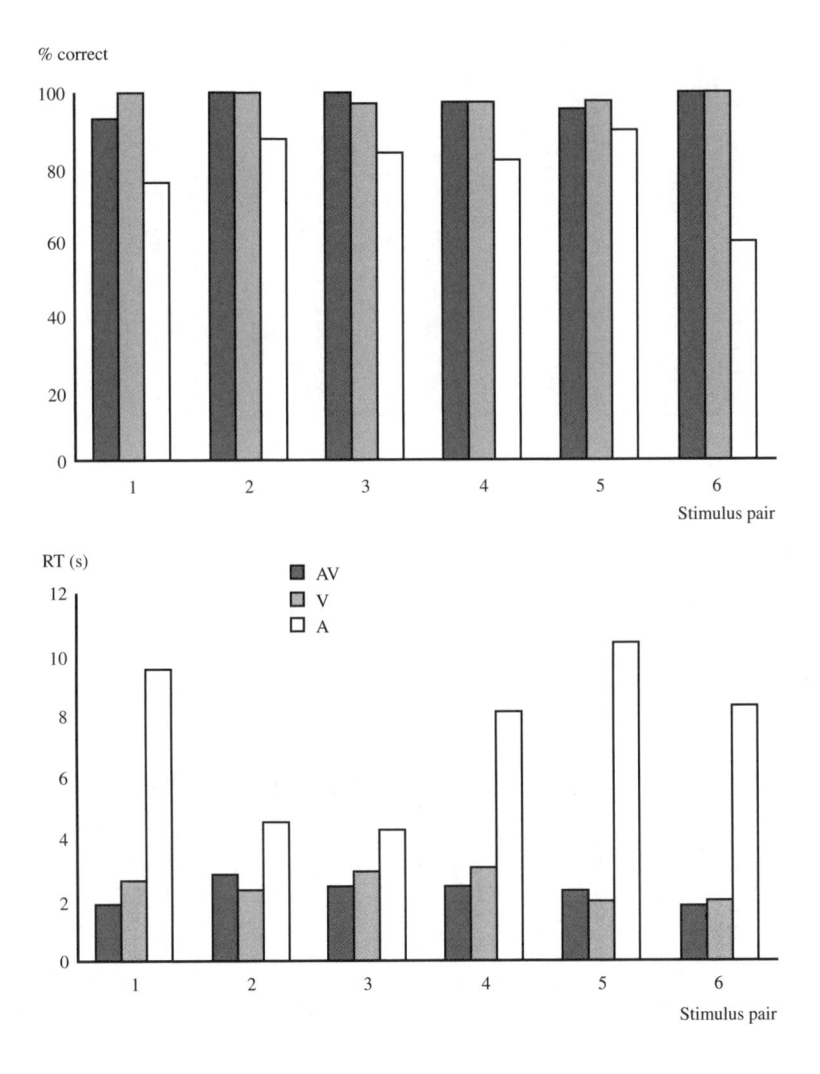

Figure 7-3
Effects of sample modalities on matching performance. Percent correct responses (the upper panel) and reaction time in seconds (the lower panel) in the audio-visual sample (AV), visual sample (V), and auditory sample (A) conditions for each object pair.

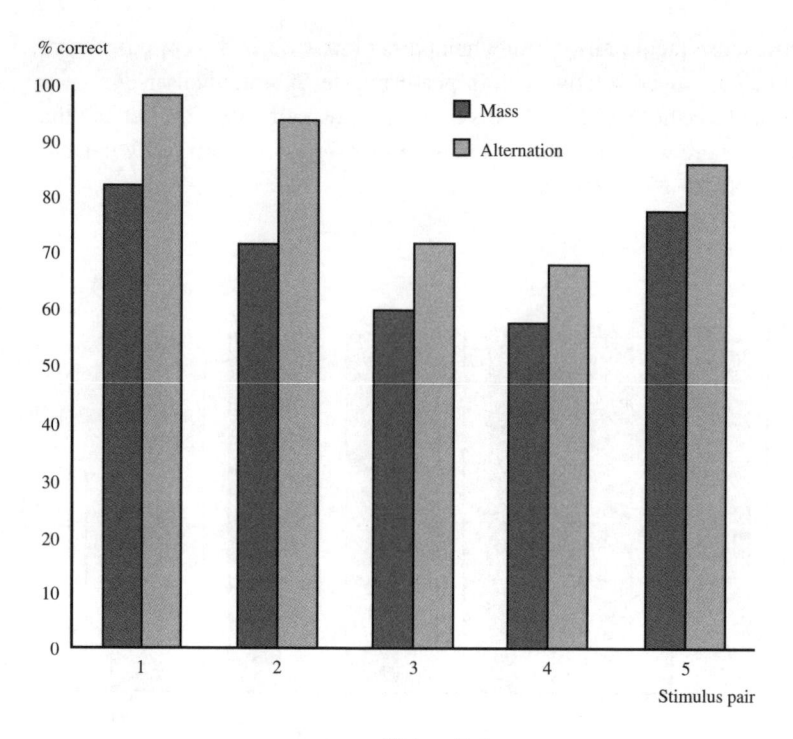

Figure 7-4
Effects of massed and alternation conditions on matching performance for each object pair.

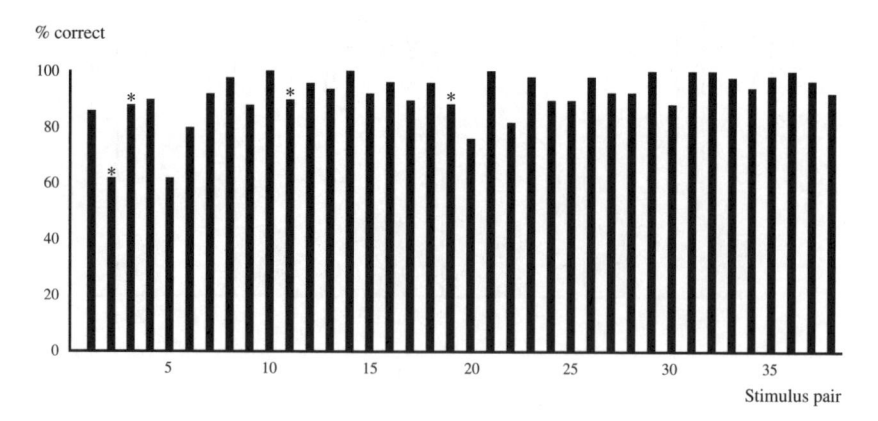

Figure 7-5
Transfer of performance in the auditory sample condition to 38 novel object pairs. The bars with asterisks indicate that both members of the pair were novel for the subject.

Performance for audio-visual and visual sample trials was almost equivalent, revealing that auditory stimuli did not effectively produce correct responses in audio-visual sample trials. Even if performance reached to 90% correct responses in auditory sample trials, reaction times were about 10 s, and thus were about 5 times longer than those for audio-visual and visual sample trials. This indicates that compared with visual samples, auditory samples may not be as effective as discriminative stimuli. This is consistent with difficulties in acquisition of the audio-visual intermodal matching to sample task and with deteriorated performance in auditory working memory in the chimpanzee (Hashiya & Kojima, 2001b.).

Performance of the chimpanzee subject changed abruptly from chance to 90% correct in the course of the acquisition sessions. The massed/alternated factor was examined for data acquired just after the subject made the sudden improvement in the task. For all object pairs used in this test, the subject showed higher performance to alternated than to massed sample presentation. Higher performance in audio-visual sample trials kept reinforcement rates high, which might have helped to maintain the subject's motivation and attention to the task. Alternated sample presentation may also promote a successful transfer from audio-visual sample to auditory sample presentation.

Transfer of performance to 38 new object pairs was examined. A performance greater than 80% correct responses was observed for most of the pairs, but not for the first several pairs, in which performance was only 60% correct. The same results were obtained even when both objects which constituted a pair were new to the subjects.

Understanding of environmental sounds

In this section, understanding of objects (artifacts) and animals by sounds was examined (see Hashiya & Kojima, 1997; 2001a). The subject and the task were the same as those described in the previous section. All sounds used were recorded in the computer. Table 7-2 shows a list of objects and animals used in this section. Half of the list was familiar and the other half was unfamiliar to the subject. All stimuli in each set were paired with each other. Acquisition was continued until either the subject showed better than 85% correct responses in a session or reached the maximum of 3 sessions.

Figure 7-6 shows the overall results. In general, the subject showed a high level of recognition by sound when it was familiar (93% correct responses). When unfamiliar sounds were presented, the performance was relatively low (73% correct responses). Figure 7-7 shows error rates for

Table 7-2 A list of objects and animals used.

stimulus sets	categories	familiar		unfamiliar	
1	artifacts			steam locomotive	telephone 1
	animals	Japanese macaques	crow		
2	artifacts	deck brush	door 1		
	animals			duck	cow
3	artifacts			steam locomotive	telephone 1
	animals			duck	cow
4	artifacts	deck brush	door 1		
	animals	Japanese macaques	crow		
5	artifacts	automobile	door 2		
	animals			owl	sheep
6	artifacts			steamship	microwave range
	animals	sparrow	large brown cicada		
7	artifacts			steamship	microwave range
	animals			owl	sheep
8	artifacts	automobile	door 2		
	animals	sparrow	large brown cicada		
9	artifacts			scissors	kettle
	animals			elephant	lion
10	artifacts	kitchen knife	faucet		
	animals	cicada 2	brown-eared bulbul		

within and between categories (objects and animals). As shown, the subject showed more errors within each category than between categories. There was no difference in performance between animals and objects.

Figure 7-8 shows performance in the first session for each pair. Percentages of mean correct response were 92% and 58% for within-category familiar and unfamiliar sound-picture pairs, respectively. For a between-categories pair, when familiar stimuli were presented as the sample, Pan showed a 94% correct response rate. This value does not differ from that for within-category familiar pairs. When unfamiliar stimuli were correct, a 79% correct response rate was obtained. This value is higher than that for within-category unfamiliar pairs (see Figure 7-9).

Pan recognized familiar objects and animals only by sounds. Hashiya and Kojima (2001a) reported that she was able to identify between objects and humans and between humans and animals based on sound. Pan showed higher performance for pairs of stimuli taken from different categories. This suggests that Pan recognizes environmental sounds categorically: objects

Auditory cognition

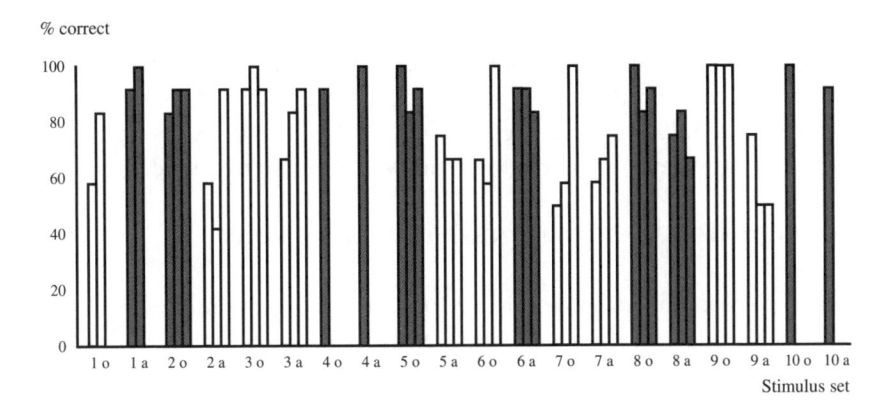

Figure 7-6
Audio-visual matching performance for the ten sets (from 1 to 10) of animals (a) and objects (o). Grey columns are performance for familiar animals and objects. White columns are that for unfamiliar animals and objects. Each column indicates the result of a session.

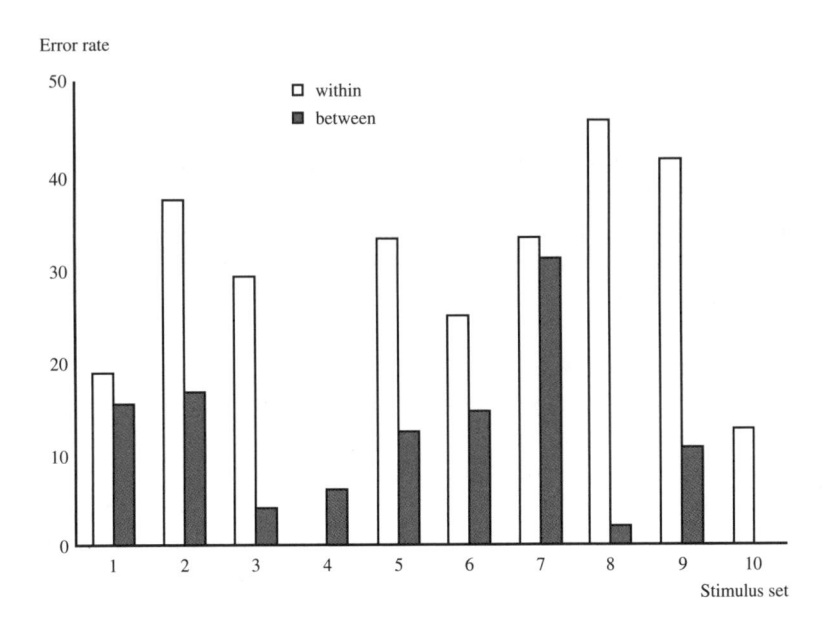

Figure 7-7
Percentage of error response to stimulus pairs from the same (within, white column) and from different (between, black column) categories.

and animals. Another interpretation is that higher performance observed for between-categories pairs may be the result of *exclusion* (Hashiya & Kojima, 2001a), because in between-category pairs with unfamiliar sample the stimulus in the other category was familiar. These results helped to elucidate how the chimpanzee hears the world for the first time.

Recognition of human individuals by voice

For captive chimpanzees, evidence for visual recognition of conspecific and human individuals was reported. Matsuzawa (1990) found very rapid matching of letters with pictures of individual conspecifics and humans by a human-raised chimpanzee. Boysen and Berntson (1986) reported a captive chimpanzee's selective response to the pictures of familiar and unfamiliar human individuals by measuring the subject's heart rate.

Face-voice matching of familiar human or conspecific individuals by chimpanzees has been reported by two laboratory studies. However, transfer tests of the acquired performance using novel stimuli were not conducted by Bauer and Philip (1983) and, thus, the generality of performance was unclear. Though Boysen (1994) conducted a transfer test and demonstrated the generality of performance, it is still unclear whether the performance of matching a particular face and voice was acquired as a result of training or if it reflected the chimpanzees' natural cognition. It is important to eliminate the chance that the particular association to be learned by the subject is derived from already-trained variants.

We tested face-voice recognition of familiar humans. It would be interesting to ask whether a human-raised chimpanzee recognizes familiar human voices without visual information and can match them to visual images.

Familiar individuals
Ten human individuals, 8 males and 2 females, were selected from among the researchers who constantly worked with the subject and staff of the institute who always took care of the subject. They participated in the experiment as a source of auditory and visual stimuli as explained below.

Sample stimuli were voices. Each person who participated in the experiment as a stimulus was requested to read aloud 10 different phrases of a conversation in Japanese obtained from a book. The phrases requested were different for each participant. The duration of each recorded sound was 4 s. The sound intensities of each auditory stimulus ranged from 50 to 70 dB SPL in the experimental booth. Visual stimuli

Auditory cognition

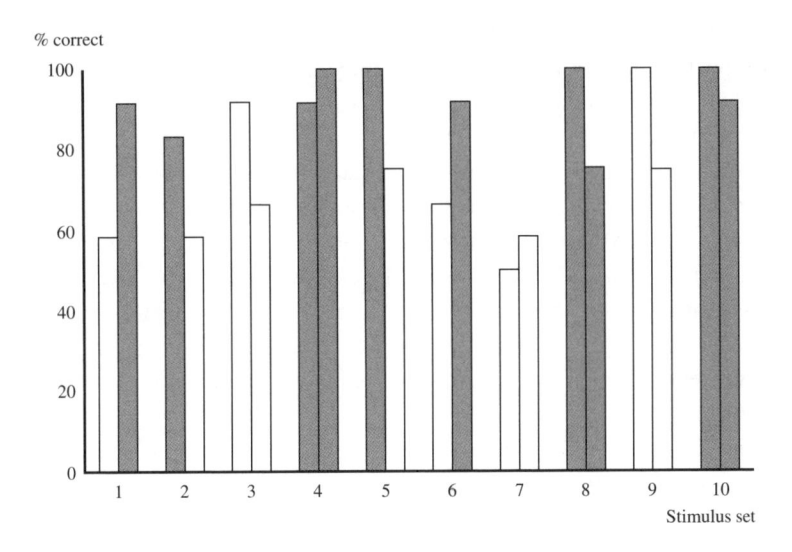

Figure 7-8
Performance in the first session for each pair. The explanation is the same as that for Figure 7-6.

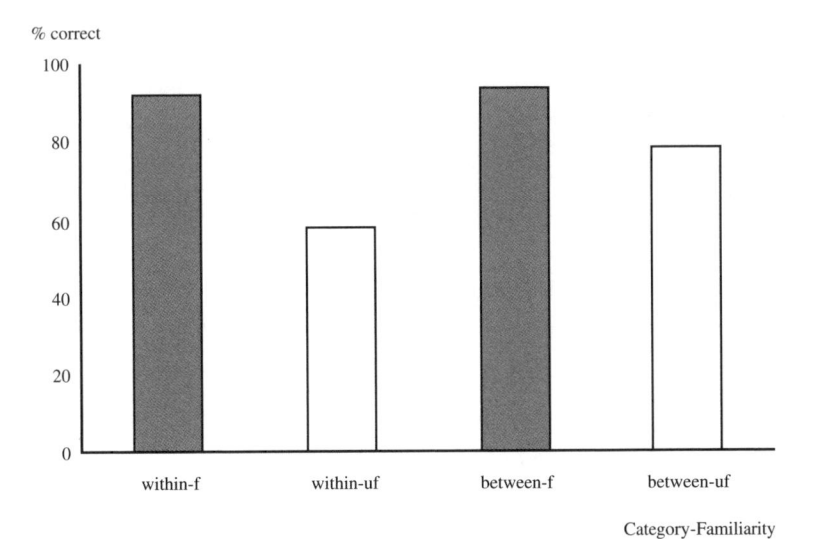

Figure 7-9
Performance in the first session for within-category familiar (within-f) and unfamiliar (within-uf) pairs and between-category pairs with familiar sample (between-f) and those with unfamiliar sample (between-uf).

were color photographs of human faces taken from the front. The eight male participants were randomly separated into 4 pairs, and the two female par-ticipants formed 1 pair. The subject was tested with one of the 5 stimulus pairs in one session. As a control experiment, the matching performance to unfamiliar voices and faces was also tested.

Figure 7-10 shows the results for each session. The subject's performance was significantly better than the chance level in 4 of the 5 stimulus pairs but not in 1 stimulus pair. The total percent correct was 80% and was significantly better than the chance level. For all the tested unfamiliar individual pairs, the subject's performance remained in the range of the chance level. Pan could not match the voices and faces of unfamiliar individuals.

The chimpanzee matched the photographs and recorded voices of familiar humans, despite the subject not having been previously trained to discriminate or categorize such variants. The results suggested auditory-visual intermodal recognition of familiar individuals by chimpanzees.

Speaker identification based on sex difference

This experiment was conducted to determine whether the chimpanzee's ability to perform face-voice matching of human individuals could be generalized to a task that requires the recognition of cues other than individuality, such as sex differences. In humans, Jusczyk et al. (1992) reported that 2-month-old infants can discriminate female voices and male voices.

The sources of the stimuli were unfamiliar males and females who had no previous contact with the subject. Ten people, 5 males and 5 females, participated in the experiment as stimuli. To form choice alternatives, a portrait of a male was always pitted against a portrait of a female.

The performance of the subject was significantly better than the chance level for all the 5 stimulus pairs. The total percent correct was 85%. No increase in percent correct was observed between the first exposure and the second exposure to the same sample stimuli (83% in the first; 87% in the second half of the session).

The results showed that some of the differences that exist between the vocal signals of human females and males are naturally attributed to the different features in their faces, although evidence as to whether the chimpanzee recognizes such differences as sex differences remains inconclusive. The chimpanzee seemed to recognize auditory-visual intermodal relations other than individuality and make use of this ability in speaker identification. At least some of the differences that exist between

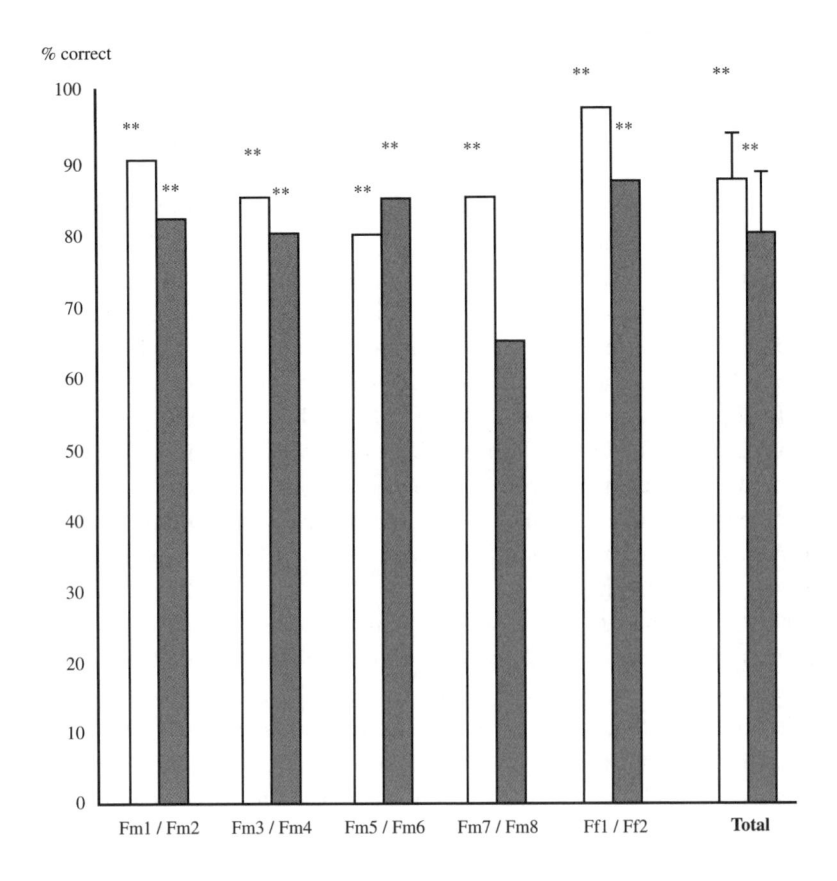

Figure 7-10
Identification of human individuals by voice. F: familiar individual, f: female, and m: male. White columns indicate results for visual intramodal matching-to-sample, and grey columns indicate those for audio-visual intermodal matching-to-sample.

the vocal signals of human females and males can be attributed by the subject to the different features in their faces.

Recognition of chimpanzees by voice

Chimpanzees vocalize various species-specific vocal sounds, e.g., pant hoots and pant grunts, and there have been many discussions on the functions of these vocal sounds (Clark & Wrangham, 1993; Clark, 1993; Clark & Wrangham, 1994; Hauser et al., 1993; Mitani & Nishida, 1993; Mitani & Brandt, 1994; Arcadi, 1996). For example, pant hoots may function to maintain or recruit associates and allies (Clark, 1993; Mitani & Nishida, 1993). Moreover, pant hoots may be directed toward a specific individual (Mitani & Nishida, 1993). Thus, individualities in pant hoots and identification of vocalizers by pant hoots are prerequisites for this hypothesis. Individual differences in these vocal sounds have been identified (Marler & Hobbett, 1975; Mitani et al., 1996). Mitani et al. (1996) noted that pant hoots exhibit a higher degree of individuality than pant grunts. Thus, it is possible that chimpanzees recognize individuals by pant hoots but not by pant grunts (Mitani et al., 1996). However, it has not been examined whether chimpanzees identify vocalizers by pant hoots in practice or whether it is difficult for them to identify vocalizers by pant grunts. It is difficult to test these possibilities in the field because of the difficulties in controlling many variables. Using an audio-visual matching-to-sample task in our laboratory (Hashiya & Kojima, 2001), we examined the identification of vocalizers by pant hoots, pant grunts and screams in a chimpanzee.

The subject was Pan. She was 18 years old when the experiment was conducted. Pan was placed in the experimental booth with her daughter Pal who was born on August 9, 2000. At one of the corners, there was a 21-inch monitor with a touch panel system. In the matching-to-sample task, the sample stimulus was the vocal sound (about 80 dB, SPL) of a chimpanzee, and the test stimulus was a set of 2 pictures of chimpanzees (neutral face) presented side by side on the monitor. One of the pictures showed the chimpanzee that vocalized the sample vocal sound, and the other showed another chimpanzee. The correct response was to touch the picture of the vocalizer. The intertrial interval was 15 s. Three to six responses to the start key on the monitor were required to initiate a trial. Usually, the sample vocal sound was presented 2 s before the presentation of the test pictures and the test pictures were presented for up to 1 min.

Table 7-3 lists the vocalizers, types of vocal sounds, number of vocalizations tested, and number of test trials. About 40% of the pant hoots lacked a climax. These vocal sounds were recorded at the Primate Research Institute, Kyoto University in 1994 and 2001. Of these, about 72% were recorded in 1994. Most sample vocal sounds were session-unique, that is, they were changed from session to session. A daily session consisted of 16 or 24 trials.

Eight pairs of 'duets' of pant hoots were presented, one pair in each session. These duets were a mixture of pant hoots from different individuals or those that occurred naturally. The test pictures were selected from the members of each 'duet' pair. The members of the duet

Table 7-3 Vocalizers, type of vocal sounds, number of vocal sound tested and number of test trials. c: pant hoots with climax, 94: vocal sounds recorded in 1994.

Vocalizer (sex, age)		Pant hoot			Pant grunt			Scream		
		Voc.	(c, 94)	Trs.	Voc.	(94)	Trs.	Voc.	(94)	Trs.
Ai	(♀, 25)	9	(8, 5)	39	4	(2)	30	3	(3)	16
Akira	(♂, 25)	17	(2, 16)	72				3	(3)	14
Gon	(♂, 35)	14	(10, 13)	58				3	(3)	15
Mari	(♀, 25)				6	(0)	48			
Pan	(♀, 18)	7	(2, 2)	58	3	(0)	39			
Pen	(♀, 24)	6	(6, 5)	29	4	(3)	40			
Popo	(♀, 19)	4	(3, 0)	22	1	(0)	30			
Puchi	(♀, 35)	4	(3, 4)	28	5	(5)	30	2	(2)	12
Reiko	(♀, 35)	8	(8, 8)	46	6	(6)	30			
Reo	(♂, 19)	6	(2, 1)	46						

pairs were as follows: 1) Reiko-Ai versus Gon-Akira, 2) Akira-Pen versus Ai-Puchi, 3) Pen-Akira versus Puchi-Ai, 4) Ai-Akira versus Puchi-Pen, 5) Akira-Puchi versus Pen-Ai, 6) Reiko-Ai versus Gon-Akira (using different vocal sounds from those used in 1), 7) Ai-Akira versus Gon-Reiko and 8) Gon-Ai versus Puchi-Pen for a total of 8 test sessions. Sixteen trials were conducted per session.

The subject was an 18-year-old female chimpanzee named Pan who was extensively trained to perform the matching-to-sample task. Figures 7-11, -12 and -13 show the results for identification of vocalizers by pant hoots, pant grunts and screams, respectively. Pan selected the pictures of vocalizers in the initial trial, including one of herself, when pant hoots, pant grunts or even screams were presented. These results clearly show that she identifies her group members using only vocal sounds as cues. Mitani et al. found individuality in the climax part of pant hoots (Mitani et al., 1996), but this part was not necessary for the identification of vocalizers in the present study. Moreover, acoustic individuality was not found in pant grunts in the study by Mitani et al. (1996). Pan, however, easily identified vocalizers by pant grunts. Species and sex differences were found in the screams of chimpanzees and bonobos, but individuality was not (Mitani & Gros-Louis, 1995). Pan selected the vocalizer correctly when the test pictures were of chimpanzees of the same sex, and the results showed she identified vocalizers even by screams.

In the recording of the vocal sounds, a pant hoot by an individual was often followed by pant hoots of other individuals. We examined

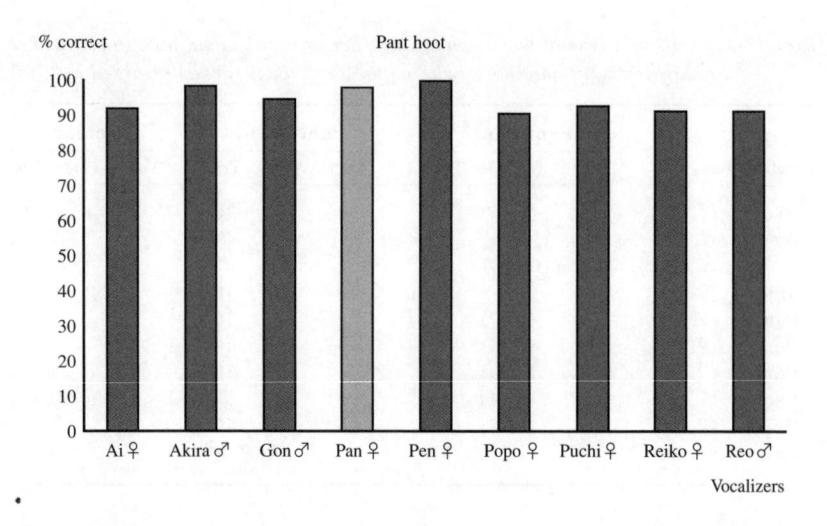

Figure 7-11
Identification of chimpanzees by pant hoots. The light gray column indicates results for Pan (the subject of the experiment).

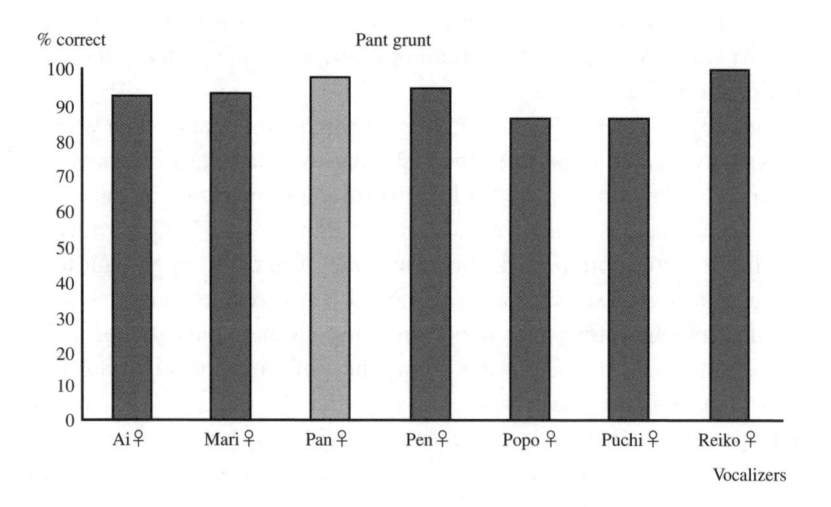

Figure 7-12
Identification of chimpanzees by pant grunts.

whether the subject could recognize vocalizers in 'duets' of pant hoots. Pan identified each vocalizer in 'duets': the percentages of correct

Auditory cognition   111

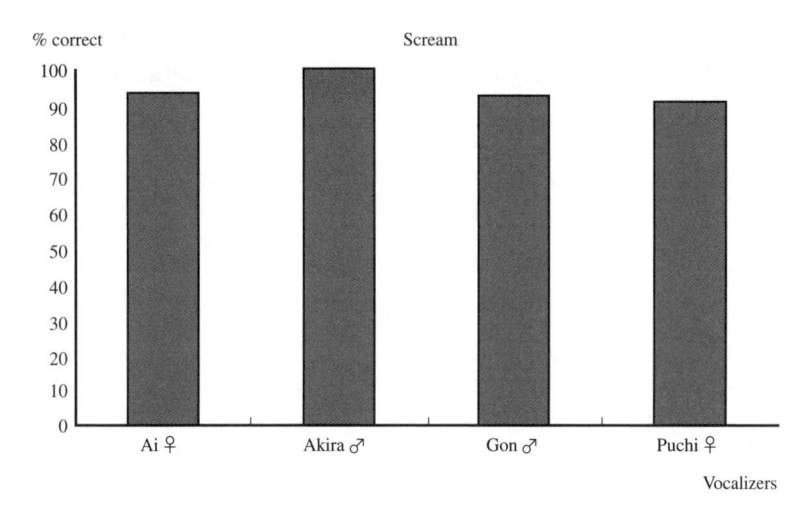

% correct   Scream
100
 90
 80
 70
 60
 50
 40
 30
 20
 10
  0
        Ai ♀   Akira ♂   Gon ♂   Puchi ♀
                                                         Vocalizers

Figure 7-13
Identification of chimpanzees by screams.

identification responses were 87.5%, 93.75%, 87.5%, 81.25%, 81.25%, 93.75%, 100% and 93.75% (the mean was 89.84 %) for the 8 test sessions, respectively. Thus, Pan could identify each member of a duet in pant hoots.

Vocal sounds used in this study were recorded in 1994 and 2001 and there was no difference in the identification of vocalizers between vocal sounds recorded at these two time periods. In 1994, Pan was the youngest female and Reo was the youngest male, and they were 11 and 12 years old, respectively. The present results, especially those for Reo, suggest that the acoustic individualities of the vocal sounds of the chimpanzees are preserved from at least about these ages. Captive chimpanzees are sexually mature at about these ages (Coe et al., 1979).

These results of the present study clearly show that Pan could identify all members of her group only by making use of vocal sounds. Chimpanzees usually pay very close attention to social events and the vocal sounds of other members (de Waal, 1982; Nishida, 1983). It has been reported that the proportion of pant hoots with a let-down phase decreased in more interactive social situations (Clark & Wrangham, 1993). These acoustic differences may help chimpanzees to understand social interactions which are not readily visible. However, identification of vocalizers may also be another very important aspect of understanding these social interactions. If chimpanzees can identify vocalizers not only by pant hoots, but also by pant grunts and screams, they would have a deeper understanding of social interactions which are not visible.

The responses of chimpanzees to their own vocal sounds are of interest. Pan chose her picture when her vocal sounds were presented and there was no difference between her performances for her own pant hoots and pant grunts. These results suggest that she identified her vocal sounds and had vocal self-recognition. There is the possibility, however, that Pan selected her picture in response to her own vocalizations because the vocalization did not match the paired pictures of a known group member, i.e., through use of the exclusion principle (see early part of this chapter and Hashiya & Kojima, 2001). To examine this possibility, Pan's own pant hoots and those of an unknown chimpanzee served as the sample in 4 sessions. In a total of 16 trials, the picture of Pan was paired with that of the unknown chimpanzee. Pan selected her picture in 7 out of 8 trials when her pant hoots were played back, but chose the picture of the unknown chimpanzee only in 2 out of 8 trials when unfamiliar pant hoots were played back. When the picture of the unknown chimpanzee was paired with one of the other members, she correctly selected the unknown picture in 16 out of 16 trials in response

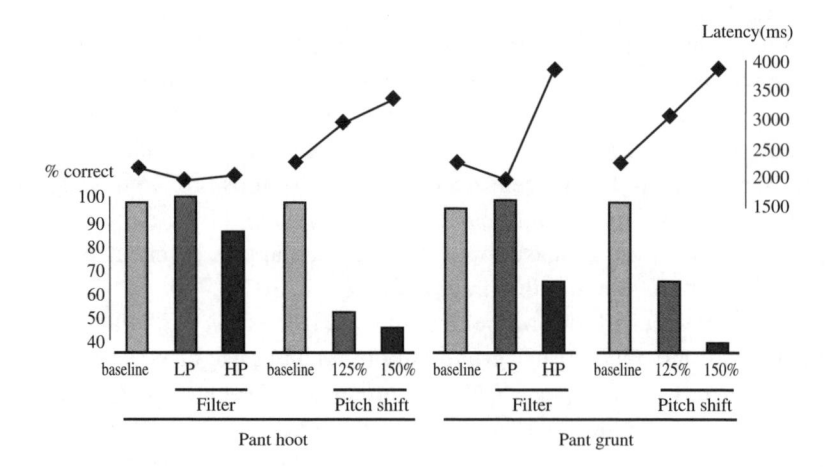

Figure 7-14
Percentages of correct responses (bars) and response latencies (lines) in the acoustical modification test. We examined the effects of filtrations at 1000 Hz (LP: low-pass; HP: high-pass) and pitch shifts (125% and 150%) on the identification of pant hoots and pant grunts. Each value under the modified conditions was compared with that under the baseline conditions

to the playing of the unknown pant hoots. These results indicate that Pan perceived her own pant hoots differently from the pant hoots of other members and suggest that Pan selected her picture based on exclusion when her pant hoots were played back. These results also suggest that Pan may not have vocal self-recognition that corresponds to self-recognition revealed in self-mirror-image experiments in the visual domain (Gallup, 1970).

Effects of acoustical modification

To examine acoustic cues used for vocalizer identification, digital filters and pitch shifts were applied to the original pant hoots and pant grunts. There were four types of sessions: two modification types (filter and pitch shift) x two vocalization types (pant hoots and pant grunts), and these sessions were routinely repeated eight times. Under filtration conditions, the acoustical modifications were low-pass (LP) or high-pass (HP) filtration at 1000 Hz. Under pitch-shifted conditions, the pitches of vocalizations were shifted up 125% or 150% from the original ones. Sixteen vocalizations, 4 for each of 4 chimpanzees (Ai, Akira, Gon and Reiko for pant hoots and Ai, Pen, Puchi and Reiko for pant grunts), were prepared for each vocalization type, and each vocalization appeared once per session; each session consisted of 16 trials. Of the 16 vocalizations, four were acoustically modified in each session. Except for one pant hoot, all other pant hoots lacked a climax.

Figure 7-14 shows the results. The results for the original vocal sounds (baselines) replicated the results described above. A high-pass filter had a mild effect on performance with respect to pant grunts, but not to pant hoots. The application of a low-pass filter had no effect on the identification of vocalizers by pant hoots or by pant grunts.

These results are consistent with the previous results on the discrimination of human speech sounds by Pan (Kojima & Kiritani, 1989 and Chapter 5). Whereas pant hoots are tonal and have rich harmonics, the main component of pant grunts is in the lower frequencies. The results of using the filter may reflect these differences. In nature, vocalizations are filtered in transmission, and the results also suggest that pant hoots are relatively robust against distance and obstacles. On the other hand, pitch shifts of 125% and 150% had a detrimental effect on the identification of vocalizers. Pitch may be an important cue for the identification of vocalizers. In summary, Pan paid more attention to the lower frequencies of the vocalizations and used pitch for individual identification.

Understanding of spoken words

Chimpanzee names

Each chimpanzee in the Primate Research Institute, Kyoto University has a name. When experiments are conducted, we call the name of a chimpanzee subject in the open corral. Pan, the name of the chimpanzee in these experiments, usually responds by pant hoots or other vocal sounds and comes to the experimental room. Other chimpanzees who are not called do not usually come. This indicates that they understand their names.

In this section, the auditory sample stimulus was the name of one of the chimpanzees in the Institute and the visual test stimuli were pictures of them, one of which matched the sample name. The visual sample was also used in different test sessions.

Figure 7-15 shows the results. As shown, Pan did not match the name and the picture, although she showed good matching in visual-visual matching trials. Results were the same when her own name was included in the sample.

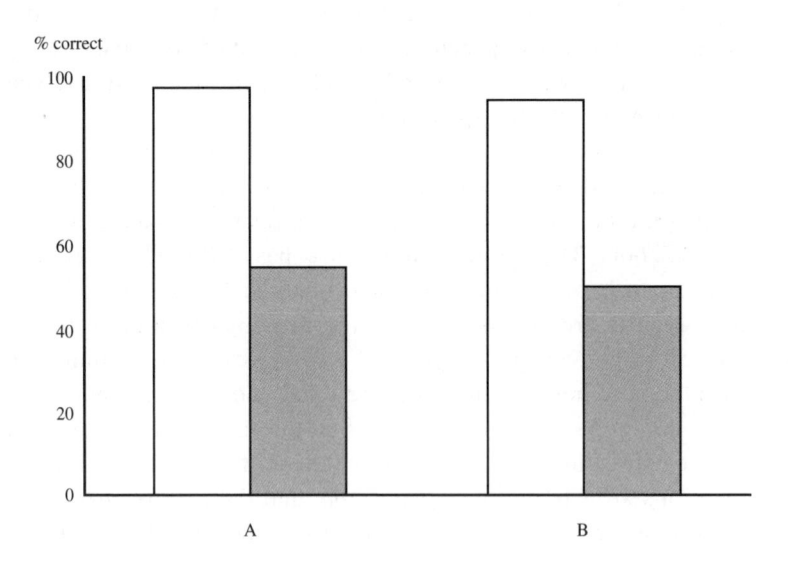

Figure 7-15
Results of the test for the understanding of names. White columns are results for visual face-face matching. Gray columns are those for auditory name-visual face matching. In one condition, the name of the subject (Pan) was included (A). In the other condition, it was not included (B).

These results were surprising. Pan understands her own and her group members' names in the open corral, but she did not understand them in the experimental room.

Onomatopoeia

The results presented in this chapter indicate that Pan understands actual sounds, but she does not understand names (nouns) of animals and objects. Onomatopoeias are words that imitate the actual sound of the object or the action that they signify. In this section, I presented actual sounds, the mixture of actual sounds and their onomatopoeias, and onomatopoeias of ten pairs of object as the sample. See Appendix A for the neural basis of this experiment.

Figure 7-16 shows the results. Pan showed a high performance level for actual sounds. Although it was difficult for Pan to understand spoken words in the laboratory, she showed about a 74% correct response rate for onomatopoeia.

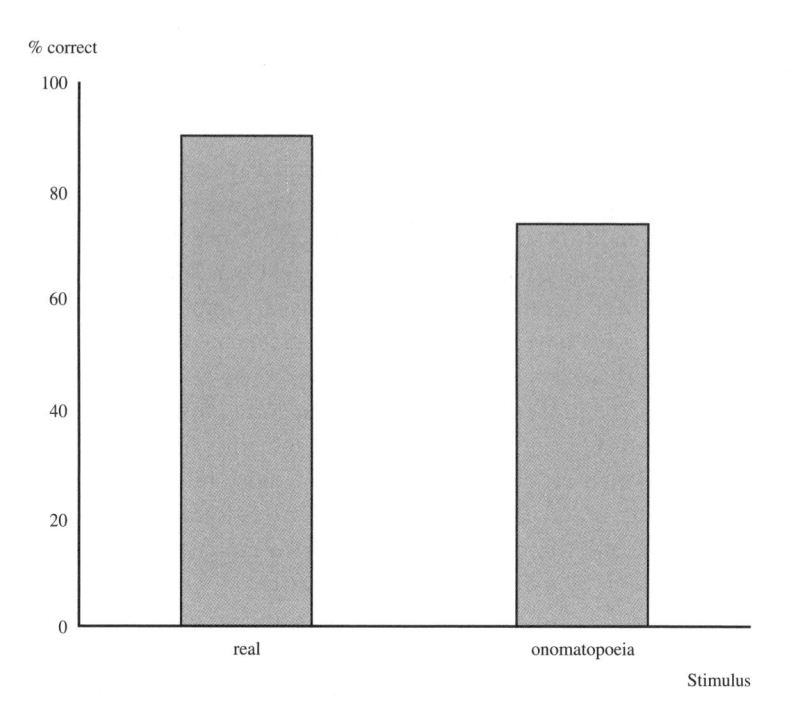

Figure 7-16
Performance for real sound (left) and onomatopoeia (right) of object.

The study of onomatopoeias is of interest, as it pertains to the emergence of language. From the ontogenetic standpoint, Japanese mothers frequently use onomatopoeias when speaking to their infants, and infants first learn the names of objects in the form of onomatopoeia (Fernald & Morikawa 1993; Kobayashi & Ogino 1996). Later, the onomatopoeia is replaced by the canonical name of the object. From the phylogenetic standpoint, many language origin theories propose that onomatopoeias are possible precursors of language (e.g., Rousseau, 1781). These findings are expected to shed some light on the emergence of language.

Auditory working memory

Before testing the generality of the audio-visual matching to sample performance, we examined the effect of sample modalities (visual and auditory) on the subject's matching performance based on working memory. A delay interval was inserted between the termination of the sample presentation and the onset of comparison stimuli, and changes in matching performance as a function of the delay interval were compared between the auditory sample and visual sample conditions. Except for the modalities of sample stimuli, procedures were the same between the conditions.

When the visual stimuli were used as samples, matching performance remained at more than 90% correct. No significant change in matching performance as a function of delay intervals was observed (see Figure 7-17). When the auditory stimuli were used as sample, matching performance deteriorated seriously when the delay interval was lengthened. These results are in clear contrast to those of the visual sample condition.

Previous studies have suggested that performance based on auditory working memory decays easily or is fragile in monkeys (Kojima, 1985 and Appendix B). The present results were comparable to those of previous studies of auditory memory in monkeys. On the other hand, Davenport et al. (1975) reported at least 20 seconds of memory retention in a visual (sample)-haptic (choice) intermodal matching to sample task in chimpanzees. Fujita and Matsuzawa (1990) reported more than 90 seconds of memory retention by a chimpanzee in a constructive matching-to-sample task, which can be regarded as a form of conditional matching to sample task in the visual modality. These findings suggest that the fragility of audio-visual matching to sample performance is not due to the general property of conditional / symbolic matching to sample tasks or of intermodal matching to sample tasks. The sharp decay of the subject's

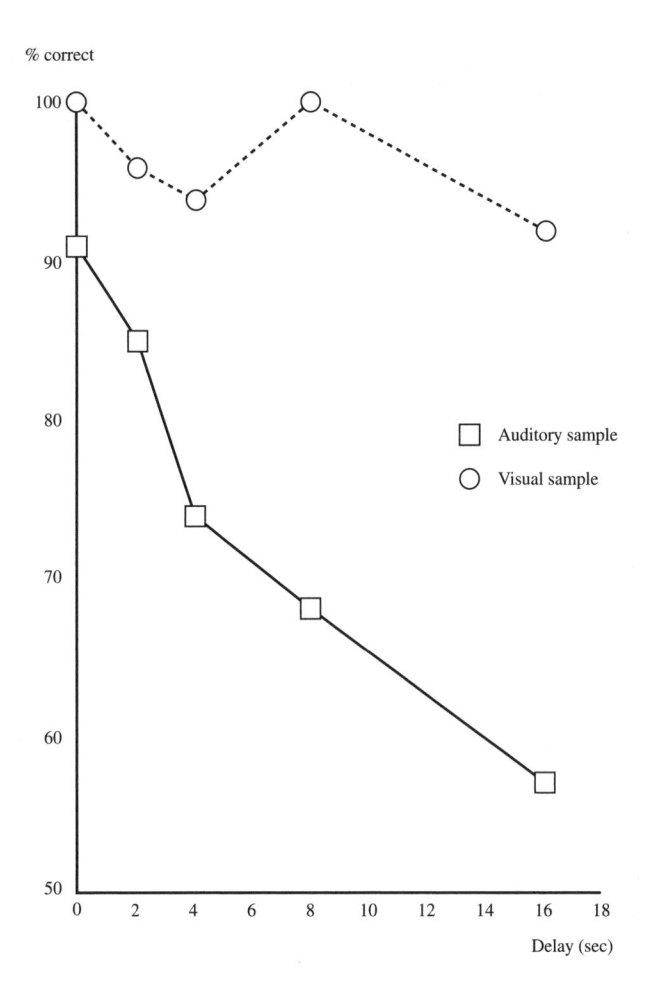

Figure 7-17
Percent correct responses in the conditions as a function of delay interval.

matching performance seemed to reflect the limited ability to process and store auditory information.

Appendix A: PET study of categorization of sound, onomatopoeia and name of object in humans

This is a human positron emission tomography (PET) study that provides a neural basis for the onomatopoeia experiment described above. Recently, a modular architecture of the auditory system has been proposed (Polster & Rose 1998). Neuroimaging studies are expected to further our understanding of auditory modularity. Disorders of auditory cognition suggest that there may be at least two modules: one for spoken language and the other for environmental sounds. In this study, the effects of three types of auditory stimuli on regional cerebral blood flow (rCBF) were examined. Actual sounds, names (common nouns) and onomatopoeias of objects (artifacts) were presented, and human subjects categorized these auditory stimuli while undergoing PET scanning. It is of interest to investigate whether sounds and names have distinct representation in the brain, and if so, to examine whether onomatopoeias activate brain areas related to these two auditory stimuli.

Eight right-handed Japanese male volunteers participated in the present study. Written informed consent was obtained from each subject on forms approved by the Ethics Committee of the National Institute for Longevity Sciences.

In the present study, each subject performed under three experimental conditions and one control condition during the PET scan. Under the experimental conditions, the subjects were required to categorize the sound of various kinds of objects. The subjects were requested to click a computer mouse within 2 s after the presentation of the 300-Hz tone when sounds, onomatopoeias or words related to vehicles were presented. Under the control condition, the subjects were requested to click the mouse in response to the presentation of white noise and to withhold their response to the presentation of a 1000-Hz pure tone.

The rCBF was measured using a SIEMENS PET scanner, after a bolus injection of $H_2^{15}O$ (15 mCi per scan, each lasting 90 s). SPM96 was used to create statistical maps of significant relative rCBF changes (Friston et al. 1995). Comparisons across conditions were made by way of t-statistics, and thereafter transformed into normally distributed Z-statistics. For each comparison, voxels with Z-values > 3.09 ($p<0.001$, without correction for multiple comparisons) were considered to represent regions of significantly changed rCBF.

Table 7-4 and Figure 7-18 show brain activation in response to the three kinds of auditory stimuli compared with that observed under the control condition. All three types of auditory stimuli activated the Heschl's gyrus (HG; the transverse temporal gyrus) in the left temporal cortex. In addition, different loci in the left temporal cortex were activated by the sounds and names of objects: sounds activated the posterior middle temporal gyrus (pMTG) and names activated the

Table 7-4 Regions of increased rCBF in the experimental conditions in contrast to the control condition. Coordinates of the peak activation and the associated z-values are shown.

Left hemisphere			Right hemisphere		
Region	(x, y, z)	z-value	Region	(x, y, z)	z-value
Sound-control					
Transverse temporal gyrus	-56, -14, 10	3.72	Superior temporal sulcus	52, -14, 10	4.11
Middle temporal gyrus	-68, -36, -8	3.64			
Putamen	-30, -4, -8	4.25			
Cerebellum	-34, -54, -44	3.58			
Onomatopoeia-Control					
Transverse temporal gyrus	-58, -14, 8	5.41	Superior temporal sulcus	66, -14, 2	5.29
	-56, -8, 2	5.37		62, -2, -2	4.81
	-52, 8, -8	4.48		54, -18, 0	4.49
Middle temporal gyrus	-68, -38, -6	4.45	Anterior temporal cortex	40, 4, -22	3.35
Inferior temporal gyrus	-42, -6, -40	3.98			
	-42, 4, -38	3.41			
Precentral gyrus	-2, -22, 70	3.95			
Name-control					
Transverse temporal gyrus	-56, -12, 8	3.50	Transverse temporal gyrus	62, -2, 0	5.73
Superior temporal gyrus	-54, 8, -6	4.44		70, -4, 16	3.38
Precentral gyrus	0, -24, 74	3.79			

Coordinates are in mm, relative to the anterior commissure, corresponding to the atlas of Talairach & Tournoux (1988). All of activations are significant at $p<0.001$ ($z>3.09$)

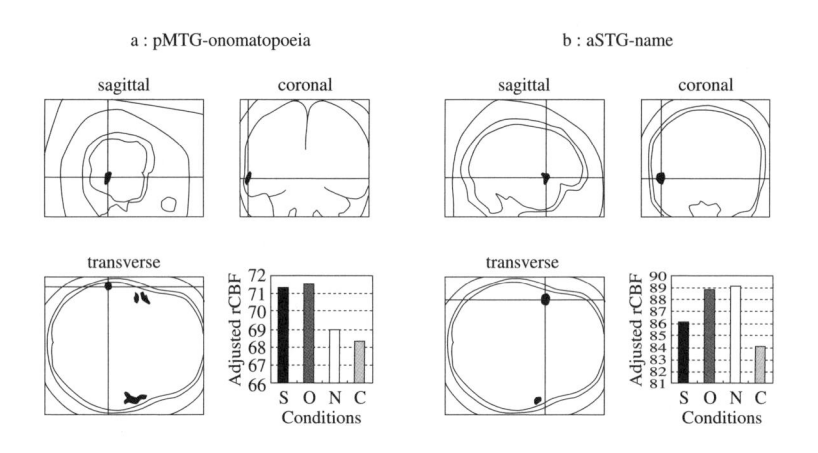

Figure 7-18
Statistically significant activation in the left posterior middle temporal gyrus (pMTG) to onomatopoeia (left). Statistically significant activation in the left anterior superior temporal gyrus (aSTG) to auditory name (right). Adjusted rCBF under each condition for pMTG and aSTG are also shown (S: actual (real) sound, O: onomatopoeia, N: name, and C: control condition).

anterior part of the superior temporal gyrus (aSTG). Onomatopoeias activated a wide area in the superior temporal cortex that covered both the pMTG and the aSTG, which were activated by sounds and names, respectively.

In the right temporal cortex, a similar but slightly different activation pattern was observed: compared with the control condition, only the posterior superior temporal sulcus (pSTS) was activated in response to the sounds of objects, and the HG was activated in response to the names of objects. Sounds did not elicit statistically significant activation in the right HG. Onomatopoeias activated the HG, STG and pSTS, which covered the areas activated by the other two test stimuli. However, the right pMTG was activated neither in response to the sounds of objects nor in response to onomatopoeias.

Recent theories have proposed that the auditory system has a modular architecture, in some respects similar to that of the visual system (Polster & Rose 1998). The present PET results suggest that there may be two modules for the processing of auditory stimuli, both in co-ordination with the HG in the left temporal cortex, at least in relation to categorization. The module in the pMTG may process environmental sounds. The module in the aSTG may be related to the processing of linguistic stimuli. In regard to the categorization of environmental sounds, a PET study by Engelien et al. (1995) showed activation in the left MTG.

Onomatopoeias strongly activated a wide brain area, probably because they are related to both actual sounds and names. They resemble the actual sound of the object, and have comparable canonical names, suggesting that categorization of onomatopoeias may require reference to both the sound and name of objects. The categorization of onomatopoeias may enhance the linguistic demand of the task, for adult subjects usually do not use onomatopoeias. These results suggest that onomatopoeias may bridge the gap between the sound and the name of objects.

It is of interest to examine the relation between onomatopoeias and gestures. Gestures are often regarded as a precursor of language, as the gestural origin theory (Hewes, 1970) and language origin theory based on the mirror system (Rizzolatti & Arbib, 1998) suggest. Kobayashi and Ogino (1996) reported that Japanese infants first learn an action associated with an object. Then, they label the object by a linguistic expression of the action, that is, by an onomatopoeia. Lastly, the onomatopoeia is replaced by a canonical name. There may be a gap between actions and language. Kita (1997) reported that Japanese mimetics (onomatopoeias) often accompany gestures. Thus, onomatopoeias may bridge the gaps not only between actual sound and the name of objects, but also between action and language. These findings were applied to a chimpanzee language study, as described above. A chimpanzee subject was found to have difficulty in understanding auditory names, although she understood the actual sound of objects. Thus, she was trained to understand onomatopoeias in an audio-visual matching to sample task, and she mastered the task.

Appendix B: Auditory working memory in the Japanese macaque

Auditory working memory of the macaque monkey was studied (see Kojima, 1985 for details). Subjects were two male Japanese macaques (No. 282 and No. 287). The task was an auditory Go/No Go matching to sample task described in Chapter 3. The delay interval was between 2 s and 16 s. Figure 7-19 shows the results. As shown in this figure, performance gradually deteriorated as the delay interval lengthened to 16 s. This is similar to the result obtained for the chimpanzee.

When the number of sample tones was increased to three, the monkeys showed the recency effect, but no sign of the primacy effect (see Figure 7-20). These results are not consistent with those of Wright and Rivera (1997), which showed both the primacy and recency effects. This discrepancy may reflect a difference in the variety of sample tones. In my experiment, only 4 tones were used, which increased the forward interference.

Appendix C: Organ playing by a chimpanzee- a comparison between forward and backward fading procedures

A chimpanzee (Pen) was trained to 'play' an 'organ'. There were 8 keys that had different colors and produced different tones on a musical scale from do ($c1$, 259 Hz) to do ($c2$, 517 Hz). Sequences of six key pressings (melodies) were trained by a forward or backward chaining procedure with a fading technique. The effectiveness of the backward chaining procedure is well known. However, we usually learn a sequence from the top, thus I compared effects of the forward and backward chaining procedures with a fading technique. After she mastered the sequences, I tested the effects of key colors and feedback sounds by removing them.

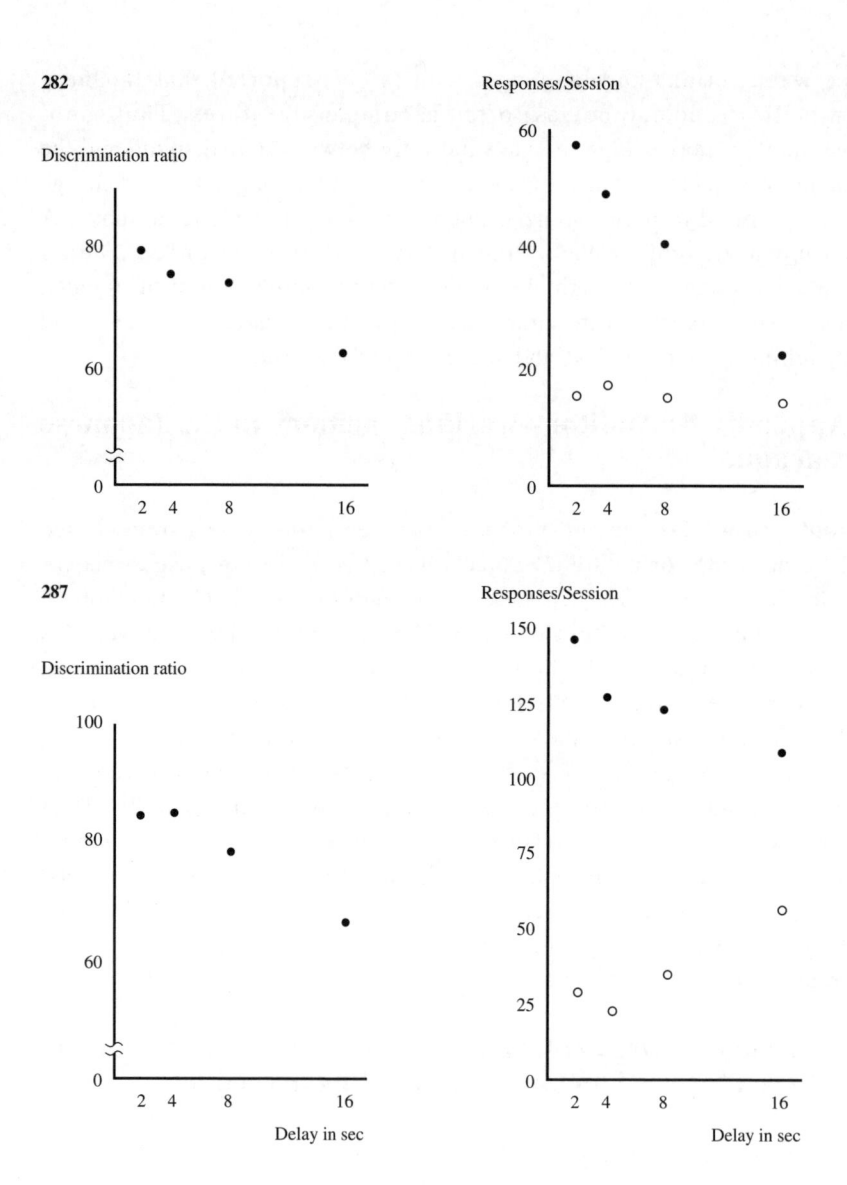

Figure 7-19
Mean discrimination ratio (left panels) and response rate (right panels) as a function of delay interval in each monkey. Filled and open circles in the left panels indicate response rate in GO and NO GO trials, respectively.

Pen learned 3 sequences by each chaining procedure. A typical learning process is presented in Figure 7-21. Although many errors were

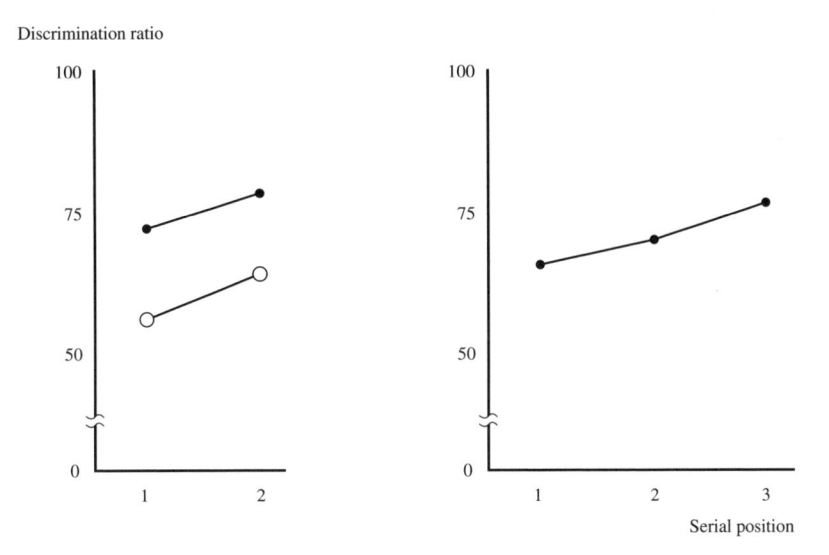

Figure 7-20
Mean discrimination ratio as a function of serial position. Left: two-item sample lists. Right: three-item sample lists. Open circles: Monkey 282. Filled circles: Monkey 287.

observed at the middle of a sequence on the backward fading procedure, there was no difference in the final performance between the forward and backward chaining procedures. Interestingly, there was no change in performance when feedback sounds were removed. The same result was obtained when the color of each key was removed. Thus, sounds and colors of the keys were not important for organ playing by Pen.

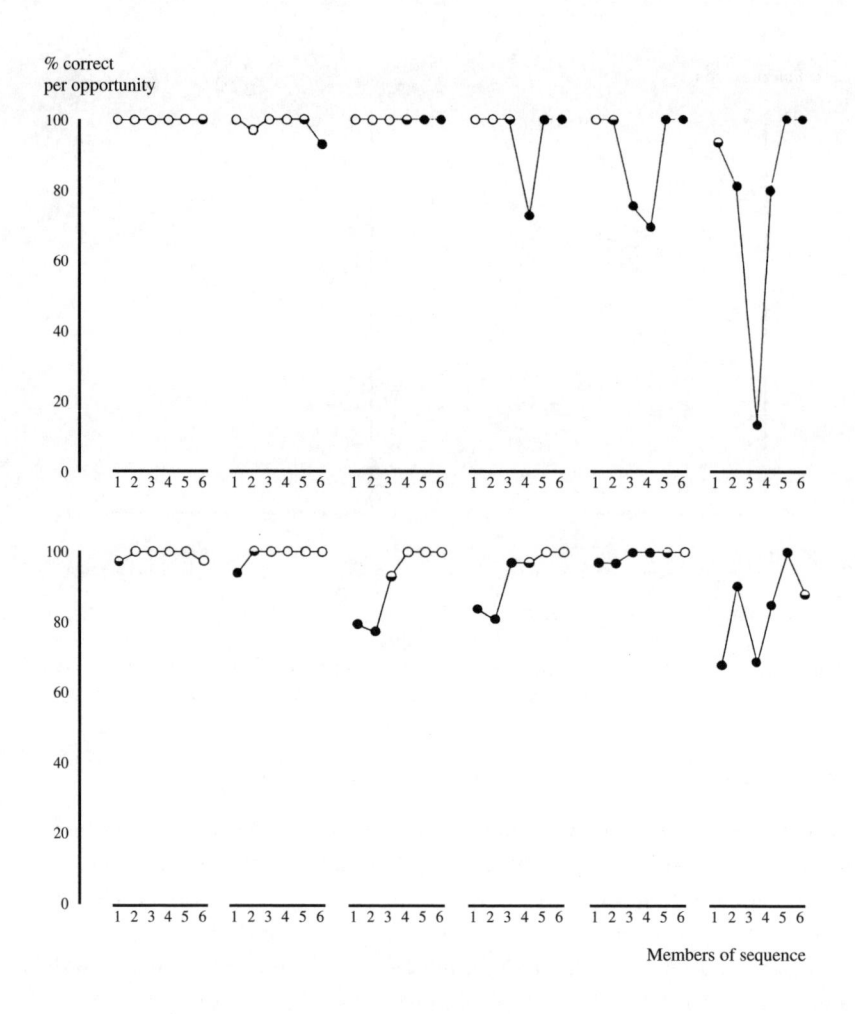

Figure 7-21
Typical performance in the backward (upper) and forward (lower) fading procedures. A sequence consisted of six items (six different key presses). Open circles indicate illuminated keys and black circles indicate dark keys. Half white (black) circles indicate keys receiving fading of light in five steps. In the last stage, Pen has to press six dark keys. Each key has a different color and different tone on a musical scale.

Chapter 8: Vocal operant

Acquisition

There were many attempts to train chimpanzees to speak human speech sounds. However, most of them failed. The research conducted by Hayes (1951) was the last reported attempt. She successfully trained a chimpanzee infant (Viki) to say 'mama', 'papa', 'cup' and 'up'. These are all the words that Viki learned in 6 years! The articulation of these sounds was different from that of humans. For example, there was no vibration of the vocal cords when Viki uttered 'papa'.

I trained Pan to vocalize [o] for milk, and vocalize [a] for a piece of banana. Figure 8-1 shows the result. As shown, Pan vocalized [a] to get banana. It was very difficult and she failed to vocalize [mo] or [ma].

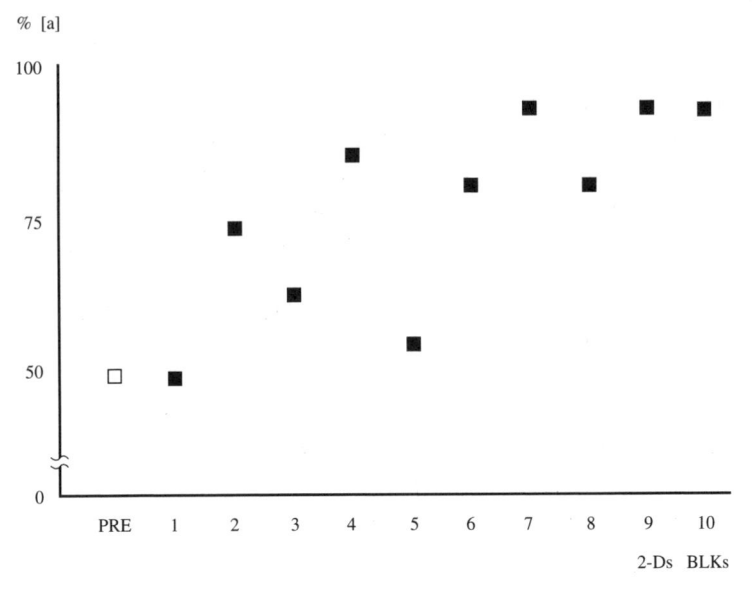

Figure 8-1
Differentiation of vocal response to different foods. Pan gradually learned to vocalize [a] for banana. PRE: before conditioning.

There have been several attempts to condition vocal behaviors in the monkey. Monkeys were conditioned to change vocal response rates (Leander et al., 1972). Monkeys changed the 'topography' of vocal responses (Larson et al., 1973; Sutton et al., 1973). Arbitrarily administered external stimuli controlled the occurrence of vocal behaviors. For example, monkeys were conditioned to vocalize only when a lamp was illuminated (Myers et al., 1965; Wilson, 1975). However, it was very difficult for monkeys to differentiate vocal behaviors according to different external stimuli. For example, monkeys could not vocalize an A call in response to a red lamp and a B call in response to a green lamp. Chimpanzees uttered only a few 'words' even after extensive long-term training. It was difficult to increase their lexicon of 'words'. Thus, difficulties in vocal operant conditioning were common to nonhuman primates, including the chimpanzee.

Chimpanzees may not have the skills necessary to articulate human speech. Humans rapidly change the position of the tongue, and control the air flow in the vocal tract and the vibration of the vocal folds. These movements are accomplished with great skill in humans, and may be related to general motor skill ability. Chimpanzees lack this ability. In 1990, Dr. D. Rumbaugh reported on the speech ability of the bonobo in a symposium of the International Primatological Society in Kyoto, and stated that he will show bonobos who talk at the next meeting. This has not occurred so far.

There are many reasons for the inability of the chimpanzee to speak language. This may not be a simple problem involving only the peripheral auditory and the vocal apparatuses. Auditory and vocal functions of the central nervous system are also important. This is an issue involving the entire system and the system is a result of mutations and natural selection.

Later influences: effects on mother–infant vocal interactions

The effects of vocal training may influence caretaking behaviors. This topic will be presented in the next chapter in detail (Chapter 9). In this section, only individual differences will be discussed. Figure 8-2 shows the occurrence of mother-infant vocal interactions in Pan-Pal, Ai-Ayumu and Kuroe-Kureo pairs (see Table 9-1) in May 2002. As shown, only Pan and Pal showed vocal interactions. Pan vocalized to her daughter by soft grunts, pants or pant grunt-like vocal sounds, and responded to her daughter's screams or squeaks by these vocal sounds. Ai showed vocal interaction between herself and her son, Ayumu, only when he was very young. Ai soon stopped responding by voice to her son's crying vocalizations. Kuroe did not vocalize at all during the observation periods.

These results show that early vocal training in the mother, Pan, influences mother-infant vocal interactions, and thus may influence Pal's vocal behaviors. This is an example of a long-term, cross-generational study.

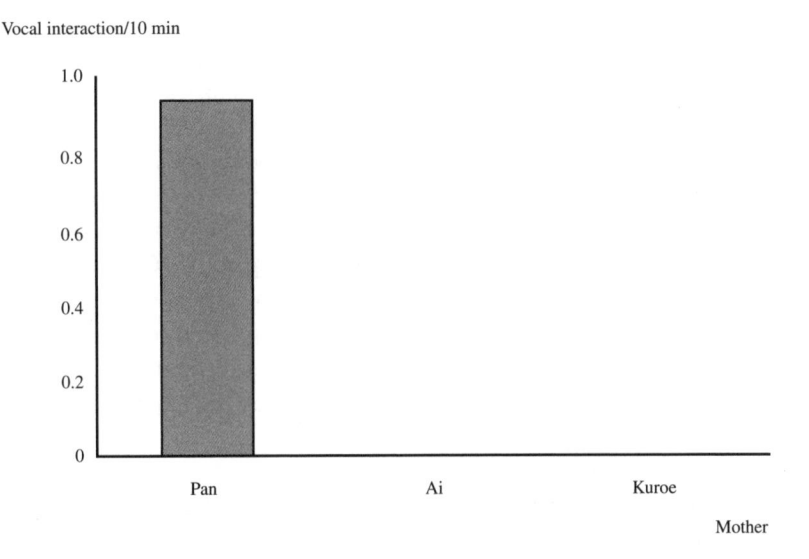

Figure 8-2
Mother-infant vocal interactions in three pairs. Only the Pan-Pal pair showed vocal interactions.

Chapter 9: Early vocal development

Repertoire of non-crying vocal sounds of chimpanzee infants

The following vocalizations were non-crying vocalizations unrelated to aversive emotional states (Figure 9-1). Rather, they were related to excitement or attention. Staccato sounds were short and breathy, and produced in series (see Figure 9-1A). This vocal sound was sometimes accompanied by phonations with frequency modulations (Figure 9-1B). Situations in which staccatos were produced and developmental changes corresponding to them will be described later. Grunts were vowel-like sounds, heard as [u], [o] or [a] by the author (Figures 9-1C, D and E. See Chapter 6). Although the vowel-like sound [ö] was produced several times, the chimpanzee did not produce [i]- and [e]-like sounds. Formant frequencies of grunts have been reported elsewhere (Chapter 6). Laughter sounds were breathy and repetitive, elicited when the chimpanzee infant was tickled.

Early vocal development in chimpanzee infants

Although there have been many studies of vocal development in human infants, few studies have systematically reported on the vocal development of chimpanzee infants (e.g., Hayes, 1951; Marler & Tenaza, 1977; Plooij, 1984). In this chapter, the early development of vocal behaviors in two chimpanzee infants will be described. Humans raised one of the infants and the other was raised by her mother. Many differences between the vocal development of chimpanzee and human infants are expected. Does the chimpanzee infant reach the Goo, the Expansion and the Canonical babbling stages? (See Appendix for the stage theory of early vocal development by Oller [1980].)

A chimpanzee infant raised by humans
One of the subjects was a female chimpanzee (Pan) born in the Primate Research Institute, Kyoto University. A human caretaker and I took care

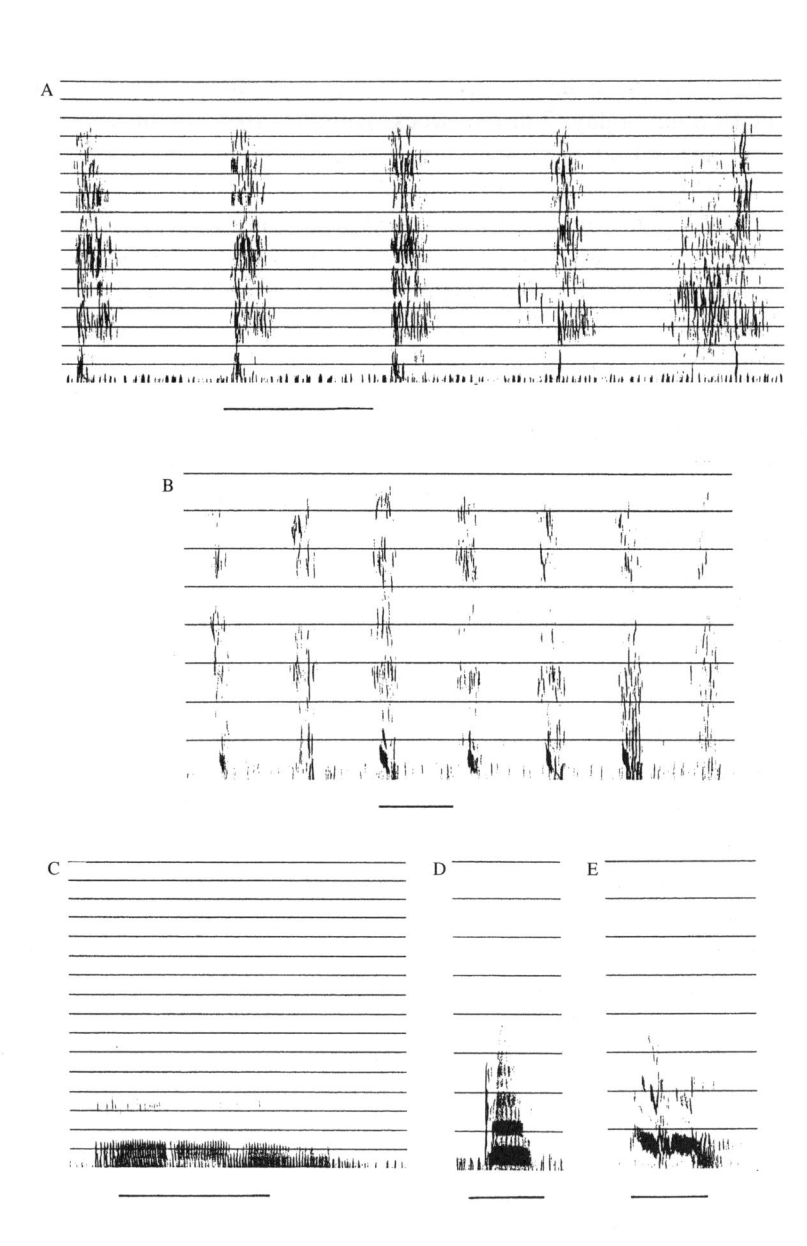

Figure 9-1.
Sound spectrograms of non-crying vocal sounds. A: This staccato was observed within 24 hours after birth. B: A staccato accompanied by phonation with frequency modulation. C: An example of a grunt. D: A coo (CV syllable) uttered by the chimpanzee infant. E: An example of a grunt with frequency modulation. In this and the following sonograms, horizontal lines indicate 1 kHz and time scales indicate 0.2 s.

of her. The vocal behaviors of the chimpanzee infant were observed about 10 hours a day, 7 days a week, from her first day of life. Vocal sounds and situations in which the chimpanzee vocalized were described in notebooks and a total of 2340 minutes of tape recording was conducted. Vocalizations recorded on the tape recorder were analyzed using sound spectrographs (see Chapter 3). In the present study, the vocal behaviors of the chimpanzee infant during the first 18 weeks of life are reported. During the experimental period, vocal behaviors were reinforced by milk.

Development of non-crying vocal behaviors
There were four stages in the early development of non-crying vocalizations in the chimpanzee infant. Three of the four phases were included in the observation period of this paper. These vocal sounds were almost always elicited by environmental stimuli and were occasionally emitted throughout the observation period.

In the first stage (Stage I, 0–3rd weeks [w] after her birth), the chimpanzee infant produced about 14 staccatos or grunts per day in response to various stimuli. One of the non-crying vocalizations (staccatos) was observed within 24 hours of birth (see Figure 9-1A). These vocal sounds were elicited when the caretaker or the author presented low-pitched, loud voices to her. The infant responded with vocalization when she was satiated, alert and gazing at the caretaker or the author. The infant produced more staccatos than grunts in this stage.

In the second stage (Stage II, 4–6 w), non-crying vocalizations of the infant decreased. The author did not hear these vocal sounds on the 41st day. Crying vocalizations also decreased in this stage.

In the third stage (Stage III, 7–18 w), the infant's non-crying vocalizations were readily elicited. These vocal sounds were observed about 85 times a day. Various visual and auditory stimuli elicited staccatos and grunts. For example, when the caretaker approached the infant or when the author spoke to her, she produced grunts. The high level of elicitation was maintained throughout this stage. Her first laughter was observed at 10 weeks after her birth. The infant appeared to imitate environmental sounds (see Figure 9-2).

Although it did not occur during the observation period of this study, the infant decreased vocalizations from the 18th week of life. In this Stage IV (19 w–), the infant seemed to habituate to environmental stimuli. For example, although the infant produced grunts in response to an approaching stranger, she did not respond to the caretaker or the

Early vocal development 131

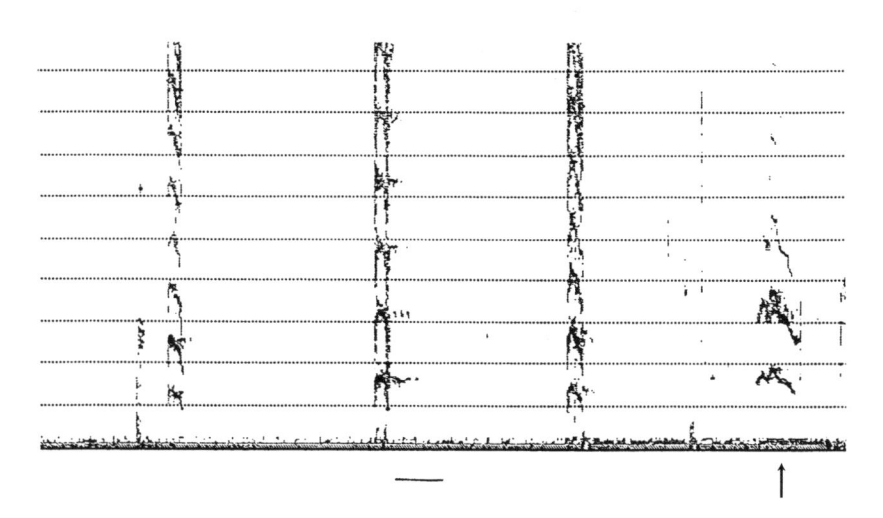

Figure 9-2.
An example of vocal imitation of an external sound by the chimpanzee infant. The chimpanzee infant imitated the same sound just before this episode. The first three sounds were those of a toy presented by the author. The last sound with an arrow is the voice of the chimpanzee infant. The fundamental frequency of this vocal sound was unusually high as a non-crying utterance.

author. Figure 9-3 shows the frequency of staccatos and grunts in the first three stages.

The chimpanzee infant rarely emitted non-crying vocalizations spontaneously. Rather, her vocalizations were almost always elicited by environmental stimuli throughout the observation period. The author could easily elicit vocalizations from the infant in the third stage, but it was difficult in the second and fourth stages. The first two stages of the infant's development correspond approximately to the human Phonation stage. The chimpanzee's third stage has features in common with the human Goo stage. A similar time course for the elicitability of vocalization was observed in human infants by Kaye and Fogel (1980). That is, they observed vocal behaviors of human infants at 6, 13, and 26 weeks, ages that correspond to the Phonation, Goo and Expansion stages, respectively. The elicitation of vocal behaviors increased from 6 to 13 weeks, that is, from the Phonation to the Goo stage. However, it decreased from 13 to 26 weeks, that is, from the Goo to the Expansion stage. Thus, this aspect of vocal behavior in the chimpanzee infant and human infants may have a common basis. However, there were differences between the

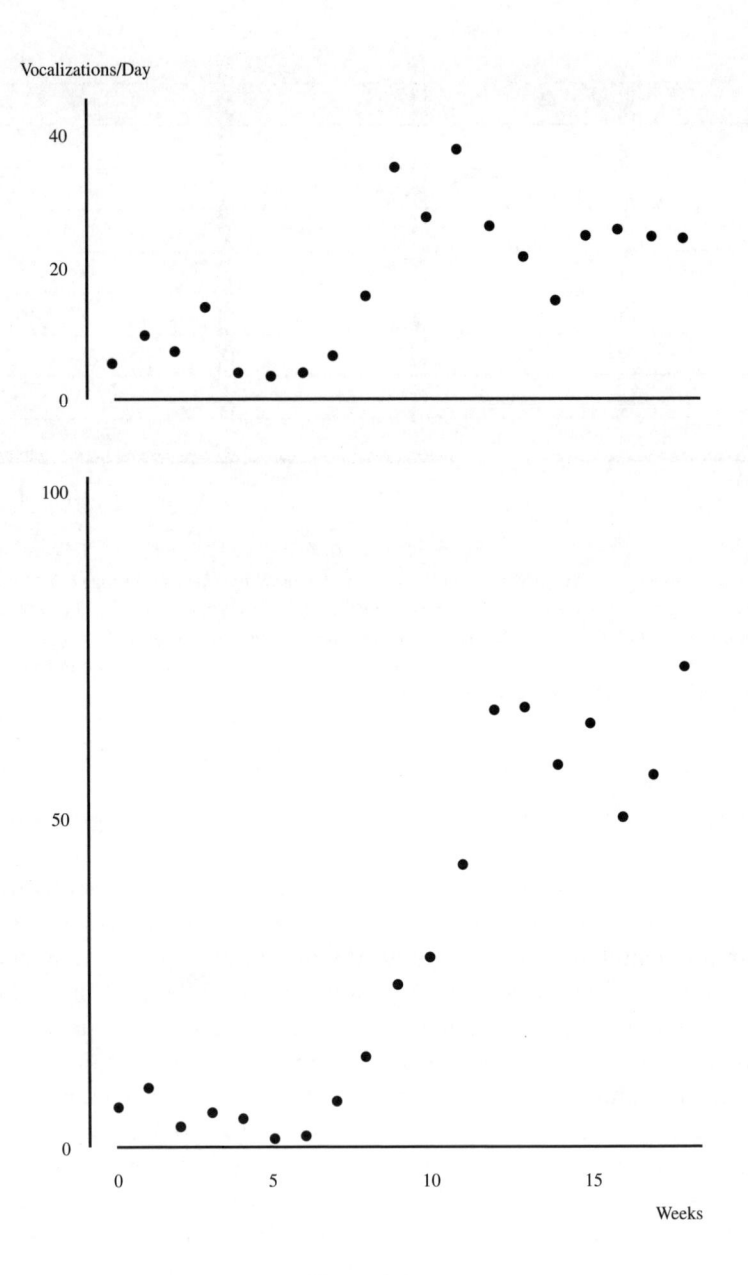

Figure 9-3.
Early developmental changes of staccatos (upper) and grunts (lower) in the chimpanzee infant.

chimpanzee and human infants. Although human infants increased spontaneous vocalizations throughout from the Phonation to the Expansion stage (Kaye & Fogel, 1980), the chimpanzee infant rarely vocalized spontaneously. The spontaneity of vocalization is an important factor for the development of babbling, which is crucial for the development of spoken language. Another difference is the early appearance of non-crying vocalizations in the chimpanzee infant. In fact, in the chimpanzee first stage, which corresponds to the early human Phonation stage, it was easier for the author to elicit non-crying vocalizations from the chimpanzee infant than from human infants. This indicates that some parts of non-crying vocalizations of the chimpanzee infant may be genetically determined.

Throughout these three developmental stages, vocalizations were elicited by the author when the chimpanzee infant was alert and attentive to the author or the caretaker, or to various stimuli presented by us. A similar condition was reported for elicitation of vocalizations in human infants (Kaye & Fogel, 1980; Locke, 1993). This indicates that active interactions between infants and caretakers are important for vocalizations in both species. Usually, chimpanzee mothers do not try to elicit vocalizations from their infants. This absence of interaction may account in part for the limited vocal development of the chimpanzee. The chimpanzee infant was observed to imitate environmental sounds. Acceleration of vocal imitation around the Goo stage was reported in human infants (e.g., Kuhl & Meltzoff, 1982).

Infraphonological analyses of non-crying vocalizations
Preliminary infraphonological analyses (Oller, 1980) of the infant's vocalizations were performed by visual inspection of sonograms because vocal resonance patterns were insufficient. As shown in Figures 9-1C, D and E, no energies at higher frequencies were detected for these grunts. Although grunts were accompanied by normal phonation in the first phase, they often became breathy in the second phase. Frequency modulations of both crying and non-crying vocalizations gradually increased throughout the observation period (see Figure 9-1D). Goos or coos, which were a kind of consonant-vowel (CV) syllable, also increased (see Figure 9-1E).

Analyses of vocalizations suggested that infraphonological features of chimpanzee vocal sounds were similar to those of human infants in the Phonation and the Goo stages. As with quasi-resonant nuclei, the resonance of the vocal tract was concentrated in the low frequencies of the chimpanzee infant's vocalizations. The high larynx may be responsible for this phenomenon. The Goo, a kind of CV syllable generally including very limited formant transitions, increases in both chimpanzee and human infants. Unlike human infants, however, the chimpanzee infant's vocalizations became breathy early in the second stage. This indicates that voluntary control over the vocal cords, which is critical to the development of vocal behavior, is weak in the chimpanzee infant.

In conclusion, the chimpanzee and human infants have similar vocal tendencies, especially when elicited before about 20 weeks, that is, in the Phonation and Goo stages. The larynx of the human infant moves downward in the Expansion stage, permitting greater vocal resonance and expanded vocal repertoires. The larynx of the chimpanzee remains high. Thus, it may be difficult for the chimpanzee to reach the human Expansion stage and therefore to achieve canonical babbling.

A chimpanzee infant raised by her mother

Pan raised the other female chimpanzee infant (Pal). Vocal behaviors of Pal were observed during the audio-visual matching experiment performed by Pan. The duration of the experiment was about 30 min. No conditioning or special elicitation procedures were imposed on vocal behaviors.

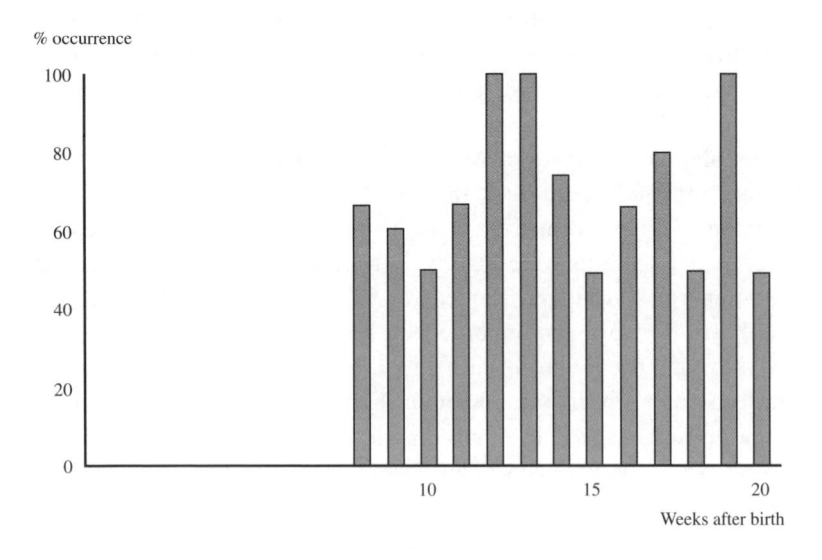

Figure 9-4
Early developmental changes of non-crying vocalization in the mother-raised chimpanzee infant.

Figure 9-4 shows developmental changes in the non-crying vocal behaviors of Pal. The y-axis of the figure indicates percentage of sessions in which vocal behaviors of Pal were observed, irrespective of the number of vocalizations. The chimpanzee infant increased her vocal behavior at about 55 days of age. This persisted for about 150 days and then decreased. From the 30th week of age, Pal often did not vocalize during the 30-minute observation period.

Vocalizations of Pal were almost always elicited, as in the case of Pan. There were external conditions that favored the elicitation Pal's vocal behaviors: vocal sounds of her mother, Pan, human vocal sounds directed to Pan, the existence of other chimpanzees nearby, and the sounds of a door opening. These events often elicited Pal's vocalizations. Pan and Pal were consistent in that they both increased their vocal behaviors at about 55 days of age. Although Pan gradually decreased her vocal behavior in the fourth stage, Pal abruptly decreased her vocalization at about 210 days of age. The different rearing conditions may account for the differences in developmental changes of vocalization between Pan and Pal.

The increase and decrease in Pal's vocal behaviors may be related to changes in her recognition of the external world. Pan accompanied Pal when she performed the audio-visual matching to sample task. We were able to observe Pal's behaviors through a transparent acrylic panel. Before 55 days of age, Pal seemed not to be aware of the existence of the experimenter. When Pal decreased her vocal behaviors, she began to move by herself and habituated to the environmental events. Thus, vocalizations of chimpanzee infants may be related to their recognition of the environment.

Classification and development of crying vocalizations in the chimpanzee infant

So far, development of non-crying vocalizations has been reported. In this section, development of crying vocalizations is reported briefly. Figure 9-5 shows vocalizations related to aversive emotion: scream, squeak, and whimper. Scream (Figure 9-5A) is a long loud call (the mean duration of 107 screams sampled was 488 ms) and is usually accompanied by intense aversive emotions. The mean fundamental frequency of screams decreased gradually from 1664 Hz in the first week to 844 Hz in the 17th week.

Squeak (Figure 9-5B) is also associated with aversive emotional states and was often followed by screams. Squeaks are short vocalizations of

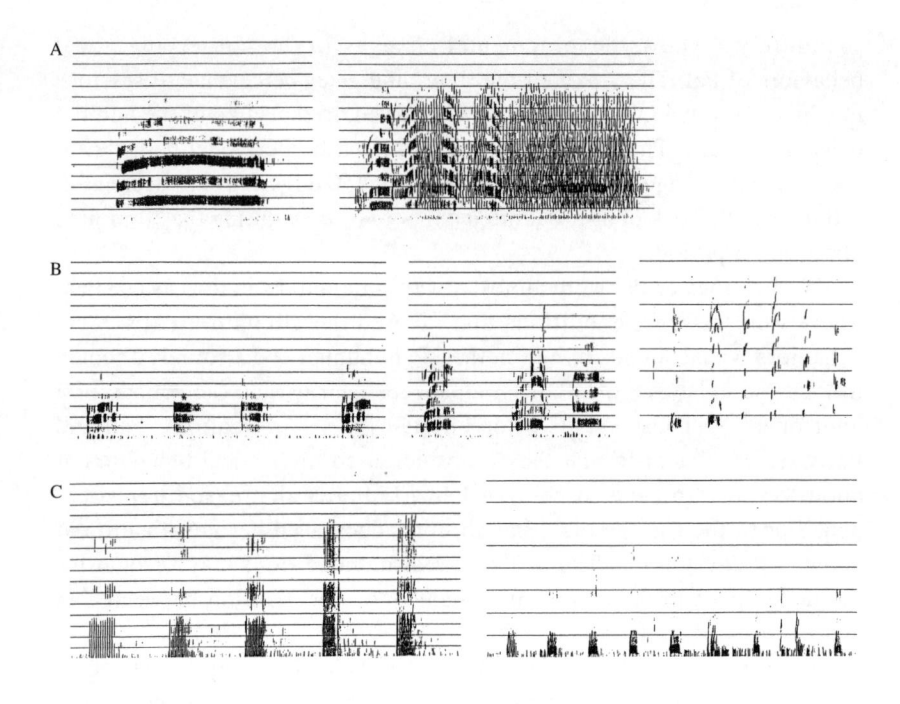

Figure 9-5
Sound spectrograms of aversive (crying) vocal sounds. A: screams, B: squeaks, and C: whimpers.

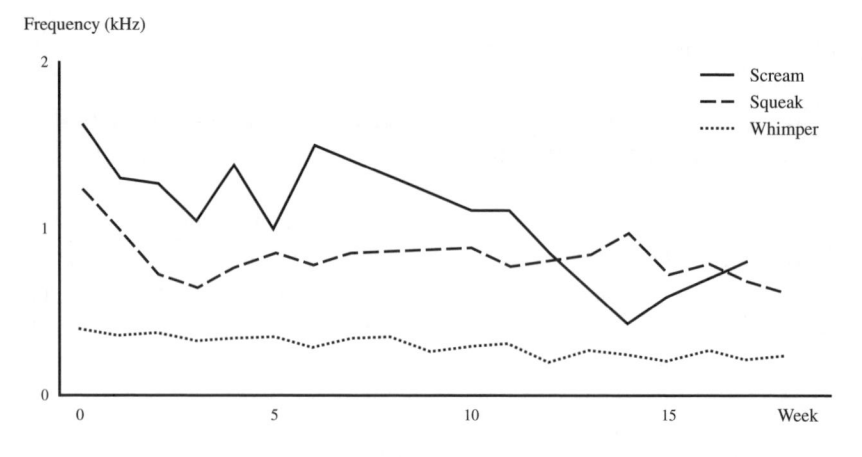

Figure 9-6
Developmental changes in the fundamental frequency of the three aversive vocal sounds.

about 70 ms (the mean of 74 vocal sounds) vocalized in series (the mean number per sequence was 8.3) at about 5.5 voices per second. Squeaks are usually tonal and had a mean fundamental frequency of 1266 Hz in the first week, which decreased gradually to 640 Hz in the 18th week of life.

Whimpers (Figure 9-5C) are associated with relatively mild aversive emotional states. The chimpanzee infant usually vocalized whimpers when she was hungry and wanted milk. Whimpers are short (the mean duration of 168 vocal sounds was 48 ms) and were vocalized in series at about 5.43 voices per second. Whimpers have a clear harmonic structure with a relatively low fundamental frequency. The mean fundamental frequency of whimpers was 404 Hz in the first week, and gradually decreased to 244 Hz in the 18th week of life.

Effort grunt is associated with mild aversive emotion and was produced when the chimpanzee was struggling. This vocalization was sometimes followed by whimpers. Effort grunts are short breathy sounds and were vocalized in series.

Figure 9-6 shows the developmental changes in the fundamental frequency of these crying vocalizations.

Vocal interactions between mother and infant in the chimpanzee

There are frequent and intimate vocal interactions between human mother and infant. Human infants vocalize spontaneously and their mothers respond vocally to infants' vocalizations. Chimpanzees are usually quiet in non-emotional situations. Non-emotional vocalizations of chimpanzees are often elicited in response to external events. The frequency of spontaneous vocalization is low in chimpanzee infants. Do chimpanzee mothers respond vocally to vocalizations of their infants?

The author trained a female chimpanzee (Pan) to vocalize when she was an infant (see Chapter 8). She came to vocalize more frequently than other chimpanzees. She became the mother of a daughter (Pal) on August 9, 2000. The author observed vocal interactions between Pan and Pal for one and a half years just after Pal's birth. To examine the effects of voice training, mother-infant vocal interactions are compared between the Pan-Pal pair and other mother-infant pairs: Ai-Ayumu and Kuroe-Kureo pairs (see Chapter 8).

Vocal interactions of three pairs of chimpanzee mother and infant were observed. The main subject was the Pan-Pal pair (see Table 9-1). The author

Table 9-1 Mother-infant pairs

Mother	Infant		Date of birth
Ai	Ayumu	♂	April 24, 2000
Kuroe	Kureo	♀	June 19, 2000
Pan	Pal	♀	August 9, 2000

Table 9-2 Classification of mother-infant vocal interaction

Abbreviation	Explanation
I/M na/na	Infant vocalized nonaversive vocal sound, then mother vocalized nonaversive vocal sound
I/M a/na	Infant vocalized aversive vocal sound, then mother vocalized nonaversive vocal sound
I-M na	Infant vocalized nonaversive vocal sound to mother, mother did not respond vocally
IO	Other vocal interactions infant initiated
M/I na/na	Mother vocalized nonaversive vocal sound, then infant vocalized nonaversive vocal sound
M-I na	Mother vocalized nonaversive vocal sound to infant, infant did not respond vocally
MO	Other vocal interactions mother initiated

recorded on 8 mm videotapes the vocal sounds and behaviors of Pan and Pal for about 10 min each in the morning before daily experiments and in the evening after a meal. Vocal interactions of other pairs, Ai-Ayumu and Kuroe-Kureo, were also observed. The results of this comparison were presented in Chapter 8.

Behaviors, including vocal behaviors, were observed in a cage room. There are several video cameras and microphones in the room, and behaviors of the mother-infant pair were recorded on 8 mm videotapes (Sony, WV-H1). A total of about 9300 min of recording was made.

Table 9-2 shows the classification of vocalizations and vocal interactions. Aversive vocal sounds were whimpers, squeaks and screams that were uttered mainly by the infant in vocal interactions. Non-aversive vocal sounds of the infant were mainly grunts and staccatos, and those of the mother were pants, soft grunts, pant grunts and others.

Vocal interactions were classified by emotionality of vocal sounds (aversive, a, and non-aversive, na; see Table 9-2), order and direction (mother-initiated and directed to the infant, M, or infant-initiated and directed to the mother, I) and response (with vocal response, /, or without vocal response, -) of vocal interactions. There are seven types of vocal interactions: I/M, na/na; I/M, a/na; I-M, na; IO (other vocal interactions the infant initiated); M/I, na/na; M-I, na; MO (other vocal interactions the mother initiated). See Table 9-2 for further explanation.

Aversive vocalizations of the infant without responses by the mother were not included. Nor were non-emotional vocalizations of the infant not directed to her mother and those not accompanied by mother's vocalizations. Laughter was excluded from the data, because the appearance of laughter was greatly influenced by group members who came into contact with Pal. Thus, I/M, a/na indicates that the infant uttered an aversive emotional voice such as a scream, and then the mother responded with a non-emotional vocal sound like a pant. When the mother vocalized grunts to the infant without responses from the infant, it was described as M-I, na.

Figure 9-7 shows the frequency of each type of vocal interaction in the morning (upper) and in the evening (lower). It is clear that there are more interactions in the evening than in the morning. Because the four types covered about 95% of vocal interactions, Figures 9-8 shows mean interactions of I/M, na/na; I/M, a/na; M/I, na/na; M-I, na.

As can be seen in Figure 9-8, the mother responded by non-aversive vocalizations when the infant uttered aversive vocal sounds such as whimpers, squeaks or screams. The mother responded by pants, soft grunts or vocal sounds similar to pant grunts in this interaction. This interaction decreased gradually, because the infant decreased the frequency of aversive vocalizations. The mother gradually increased vocalizing to the infant with the same vocal sounds without aversive vocal sounds of the infant.

The comparison of vocal interactions between Pan-Pal and other mother-infant pairs was described in Chapter 8.

The chimpanzee is usually very quiet, unless it is emotionally aroused. The spontaneity of non-crying vocalization is usually low. Does a chimpanzee mother-infant pair interact vocally? The answer to this question is yes and no. Vocal interactions were observed between a chimpanzee mother who received vocal training in infancy and her infant. Other mother-infant pairs did not show stable and persistent vocal interactions. Individual differences may account for this finding, but vocal training received in early infancy is more plausible. This is a kind of 'enculturation'. Many aspects of chimpanzee behaviors are not

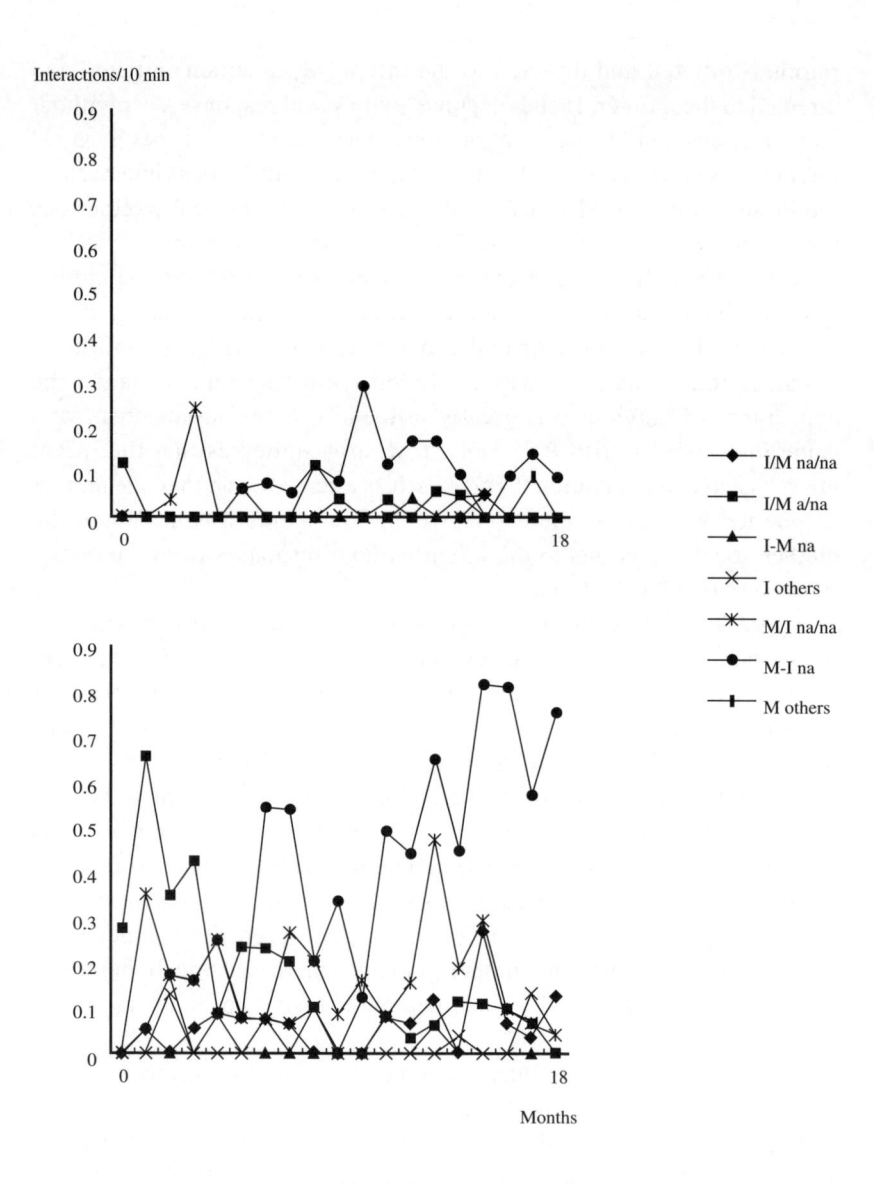

Figure 9-7
Developmental changes in infant-mother vocal interactions. See text and Table 9-2 for details. Upper: vocal interactions in the morning. Lower: vocal interactions in the early evening.

determined by genomes. Chimpanzees, like humans, show plasticity. If humans raise chimpanzees, chimpanzees will show human-like behaviors. Intelligent behaviors by ape 'stars', Washoe, Sarah, Lana and Kanzi, are

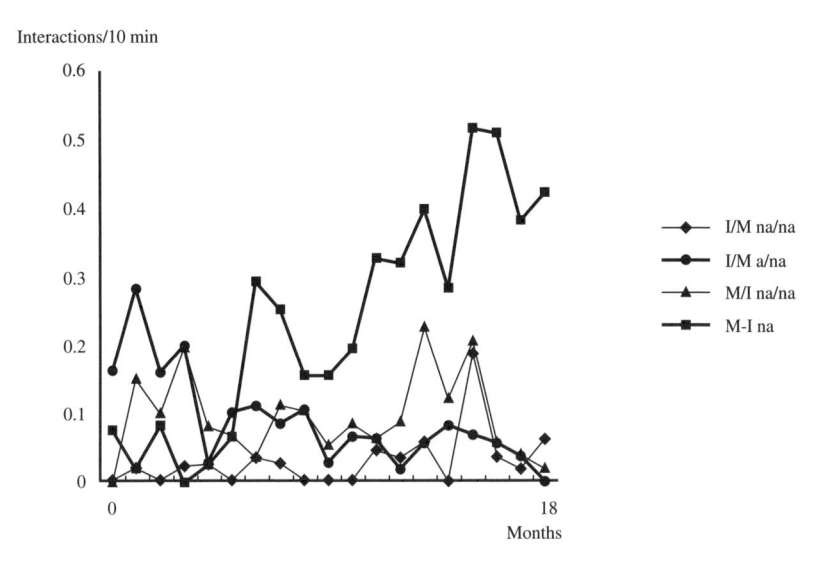

Figure 9-8
Developmental change of infant-mother vocal interaction.

the results of human education or culture. These studies show the great potential abilities of great apes. But, does enculturation have a biological basis? Should we try to find the 'shadow' of human ability or culture in apes? These are old questions concerning the value of such research.

It has been suggested that plasticity in the auditory and vocal functions of the chimpanzee is limited (Hayes, 1951 and Chapter 8). However, the present study showed that the voice training on Pan in early infancy had an influence on her vocal behaviors and vocal interactions with her daughter. It is of interest to examine the effects of infant-mother vocal interaction on the vocal behaviors of Pal.

Why does Pan respond to Pal's crying sounds with pants, soft grunts or pant grunt-like vocal sounds? It has been suggested that pant grunts are submissive vocalizations (e.g., Goodall, 1986). Submissive individuals have often been observed to vocalize pant grunts to dominant individuals. If this is true, is the mother submissive to her infant? Socially the answer is no, but psychologically the answer may be yes. There is a proverb found in both Japanese and English: Nakuko to Jito niha Katenai (You may as well contend against authorities as reason with a crying child). Acoustically, there may be differences between pant grunts directed to a dominant individual and those directed to the infant. For example, pant grunts to a dominant individual are strong and often grade into squeaks or screams. Pant grunt-like vocal sounds to the infant are soft, and are not graded into aversive voices. However, a common mental state may underlie these two vocal behaviors. These vocal sounds may correspond to the same dimension.

Appendix: The stage theory of early vocal development in human infants by Oller

The vocal behaviors of human infants develop in stages. At the age of about 1 year, the typical infant acquires the first words of spoken language (e.g., Oller, 1980, 1986, 1995; Stark,1980). Although human infants usually do not utter words during the first year of life, they do develop a capability to produce the kinds of sounds that are found in words during this period (Oller, 1981). Oller (1980) and Stark (1980) have proposed similar stage theories describing the development of vocal behavior of human infants leading to the first word of spoken language. According to Oller's infraphonological analyses of non-crying utterances, there are five stages of vocal development in human infants. These stages include Phonation (0–1 months of life [mo]), Goo (2–3 mo), Expansion (4–6 mo), Canonical babbling (7–10 mo) and Variegated babbling (11–12 mo). There are characteristic non-reflexive vocalization types for each stage. For example, quasi-resonant nuclei in the Phonation stage, Goo in the Goo stage, fully resonant nucleus, raspberry and others in the Expansion stage, canonical babbling in the Canonical stage and variegated babbling and gibberish in the Variegated Babbling stage.

Chapter 10: Vocal communication

Experimental analyses of vocal interaction of captive chimpanzees during inter-party encounters

There are experimental studies describing social behaviors in which behaviors of a member or members of a group of nonhuman primates are controlled and effects of this manipulation are examined (e.g., Menzel, 1974). In this chapter, we will report on the effects of experimentally produced encounters between parties of a captive chimpanzee group on the production of pant hoots. The pant hoot is a loud and frequent vocalization produced by chimpanzees (e.g. Marler & Tenaza, 1977; Clark, 1993). The acoustic structure of a pant hoot varies greatly, not only between habitats (Mitani et al., 1992; Arcadi, 1996), but also between individuals within the same community (Marler & Hobbett, 1975; Mitani & Brandt, 1994; Mitani et al., 1996) and the vocalization, therefore, conveys the identity of the caller (Bauer & Philip, 1983; Goodall, 1986).

Chimpanzees vocalize pant hoots frequently when they find an abundant food resource (Wrangham, 1977; Ghiglieri, 1984). Therefore, some researchers have suggested that the pant hoot informs other party members of the location of good food resources (Hauser, et al., 1993; Hauser & Wrangham, 1987; Wrangham, 1977; Ghiglieri, 1984). Other researchers suggested that the social context is more important than the ecological context for the production of pant hoots (e.g., Clark & Wrangham, 1994). Many social factors involved in pant hoot production have been considered, such as caller's activity, which can represent spatial dispersion of the party (Mitani & Nishida, 1993), social status (age-sex: Clark, 1993; Marler & Tenaza, 1977; social rank: Mitani & Nishida, 1993; Clark & Wrangham, 1994), alliance and association partner (Clark, 1993; Mitani & Nishida, 1993), estrous females (Clark & Wrangham, 1994), and neighboring communities (Clark & Wrangham, 1994).

Chimpanzees travel in parties which vary greatly in size and age-sex composition. Moreover, fission and fusion of these parties occurs frequently and with great flexibility (Goodall, 1986). When two parties encounter one another visually, chimpanzees show many different social interactions (Goodall, 1986; Nishida, 1970). Pant hoots are also given in this situation (Marler & Tenaza, 1977). Inter-party encounters are different from previously studied contexts of pant hoots. Investigation of pant hoots during encounters may shed new light on proximate factors and functions of the pant hoot.

In this research, we controlled the behaviors of captive chimpanzees in two parties and experimentally produced encounter situations. We observed vocal interactions during inter-party encounters.

Two male and five female chimpanzees were observed for about 6 months at the Primate Research Institute, Kyoto University (Table 3-1). Two parties are often formed spontaneously (Okamoto et al., 2001): Gon-party (Gon, Reiko, Puchi and Kuroe) and Akira-party (Akira, Ai and Pen). They stayed in night rooms from about 17:30 to 08:30, and in an enclosure or corral (about 500 m^2) from 08:30 to 17:30 on weekdays (Figure 10-1,B and C). On weekends, they stayed in their night rooms from Saturday evening (about 17:30) to Monday morning (about 8:30). In addition, one male (Reo) and two females (Popo and Pan) were isolated from the others in rooms nearby (Figure 10-1, D).

Social rank among the subjects could not be precisely determined. From intensive analysis of social behaviors (Okamoto et al., 2001), it was apparent that 2 males (Gon and Akira) were dominant to all females of the other party, and Pen and Kuroe were subordinate to the other females. Dominance rank between the males was uncertain because they seldom showed rank-oriented behaviors. Copulation was not observed during the study period.

To examine the effect of inter-party encounters on pant hoot production, we controlled group composition in the night rooms. There was a shutter between the night rooms (Figure 10-1, c–e). Under Condition 1 (Arrival Condition), the shutter was left open overnight, so all chimpanzees could make contact with one another in the rooms. Under this condition, going outside to the enclosure in the morning simply meant that the same group moved to a different location. Under Condition 2 (Encounter Condition), the night rooms were separated by the shutter and the chimpanzees were divided into the two parties described above. The following morning, the two shutters (Figure 10-1, a and b) out to the enclosure (Figure 10-1, A) were opened simultaneously. Under Condition 2, therefore, going outside involved an inter-party encounter. These two conditions were presented in random order.

We recorded behaviors and vocalizations of chimpanzees for 15 min from when the first individual entered the enclosure. Social interactions

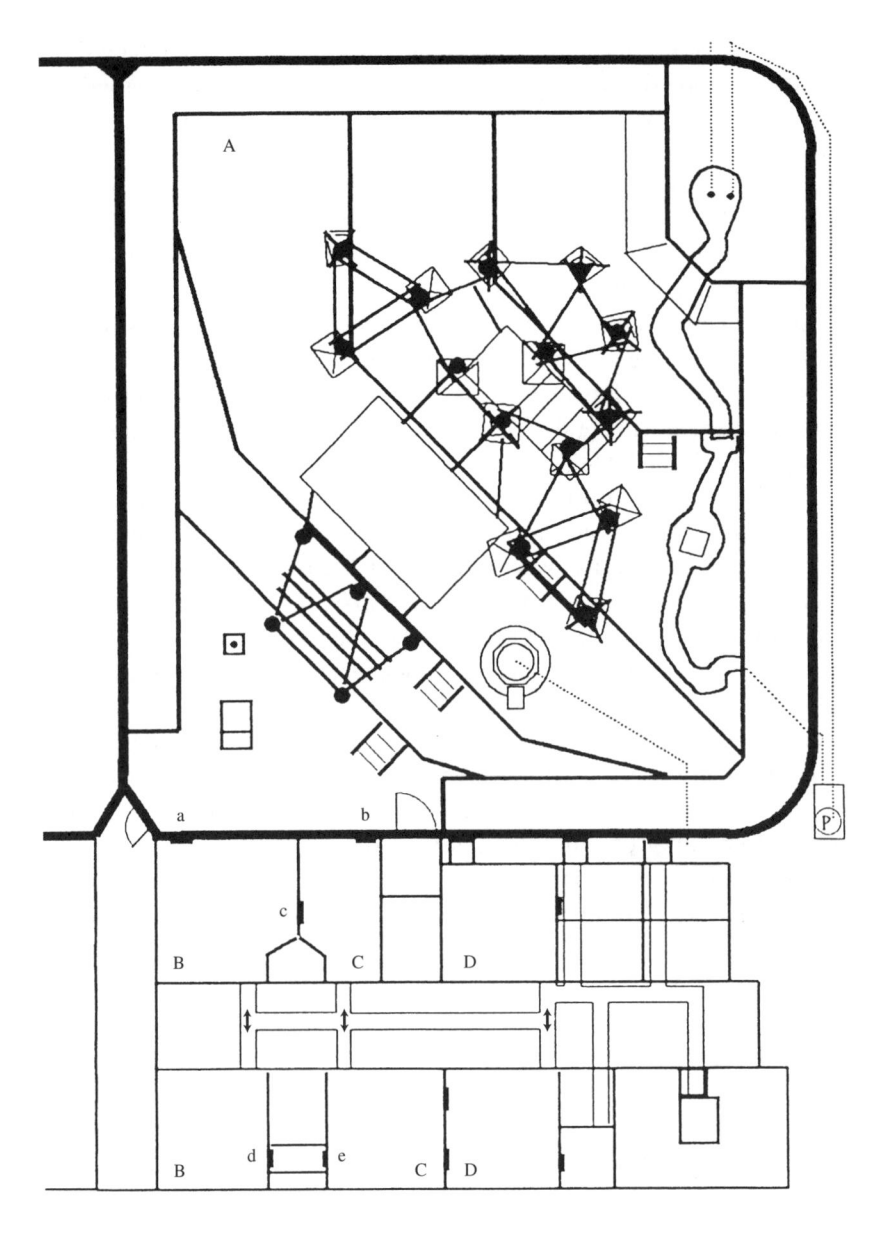

Figure 10-1
Enclosure or corral (A), night rooms (B, C and D), and shutters or doors (a-e).

including attack, charging displays and throwing stones at other individuals were classified as aggressive interactions, and pant grunt, inspect genitals, embrace, kiss, present, peer, groom and touch as affiliative interactions (Okamoto et al., 2001). When chimpanzees vocalized, we recorded the caller's identity, type of vocalization, and the time at the start and end of the vocalization from videotapes. In cases where the same individual vocalized successively and the interval was less than 5 s, it was regarded as one bout of vocalization. Classification of vocalizations followed Clark (1993: Table II). However, we observed only the pant hoot, hoot, bark and cough as non-submissive vocalizations, and squeak, scream and (pant) grunt as submissive vocalizations in this study. Some individuals uttered both non-submissive and submissive vocalizations in the course of one bout of vocalization. We classified this as a mixed type. We omitted data during social excitement among the chimpanzees (Goodall, 1986) from analysis. We analyzed 23 and 22 days for Conditions 1 and 2, respectively.

The frequency of affiliative interaction between Akira-Reiko, Gon-Ai and Akira-Puchi was high under both conditions. The frequency of affiliative interactions was higher under Condition 2 than under Condition 1, although there was no significant difference between conditions for aggressive interactions. The frequency of social excitement (number of days on which social excitement occurred per total observation days) was higher under Condition 2 (14 times / 22 observation days) than under Condition 1 (3 times/ 23 observation days). These results suggest that social tension among chimpanzees was much higher during inter-party encounters (Condition 2) than when no encounter (Condition 1) occurred.

The frequency of non-submissive, mixed and submissive vocalizations (number of vocalizations per 15 min) is shown in Figure 10-2. There were individual differences. At least 93% of the 1008 non-submissive vocalizations recorded under the two conditions were pant hoots, or part of a pant hoot series (introduction, buildup, climax and letdown: Marler & Hobbet, 1975). The two males (Gon and Akira) frequently gave non-submissive vocalizations. The frequency of non-submissive and submissive vocalizations under Condition 2 was higher than that under Condition 1. However, mixed vocalizations showed no significant differences between these conditions.

Chimpanzees frequently gave pant hoots during other chimpanzees' pant hoots. We measured the interval between the ending of the earlier and the beginning of the following vocalization (EB), ignoring submissive vocalizations. In total 466 intervals under Condition 1 and 545 under Condition 2 were measured.

Values of EB have peaks at around 0. Zero and negative values of EB show the duration of overlap of two successive vocalizations. Percentages

Vocal communication

Vocalization bout/15 min

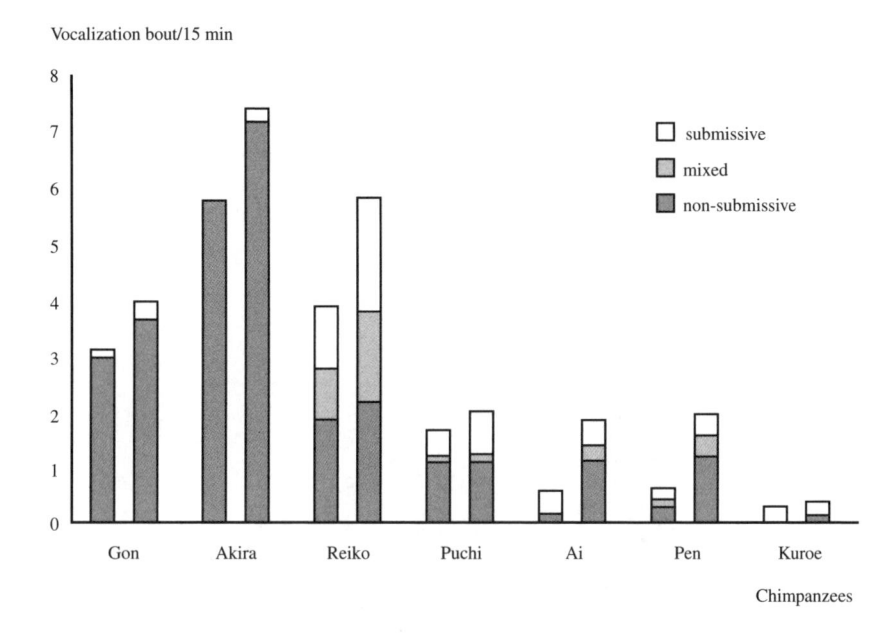

Figure 10-2
The frequency of non-submissive, mixed, and submissive vocalizations uttered by each individual in each condition. . For each chimpanzee, left bar indicates vocalization bouts under Condition 1 (Arrival Condition) and right bar indicates those under Condition 2 (Encounter Condition). The frequency of vocalization is higher under Condition 2 than under Condition 1.

of the number of zero and minus intervals (% of vocalization overlap) were significantly higher under Condition 2 (38.2 %) than under Condition 1 (25.1 %). Moreover, the frequency between males was much higher (Condition 1, 61.5 %; Condition 2, 73.3 %) than the overall cases under both conditions.

These results show that chimpanzees tended to start vocalizing when another individual vocalized, and terminated when the other terminated. As a result, vocalizations were often overlapped. This tendency was most apparent between Gon and Akira, and under Condition 2.

We can describe the cases in which EB showed 0 and negative values as "vocal overlap relations". Table 10-1 and Figure 10-3 show the dyads consisting of earlier and latter vocalizers for each "vocal overlap relation" combining the two conditions. Many vocal overlaps were found even between individuals with few affiliative and aggressive interactions. In

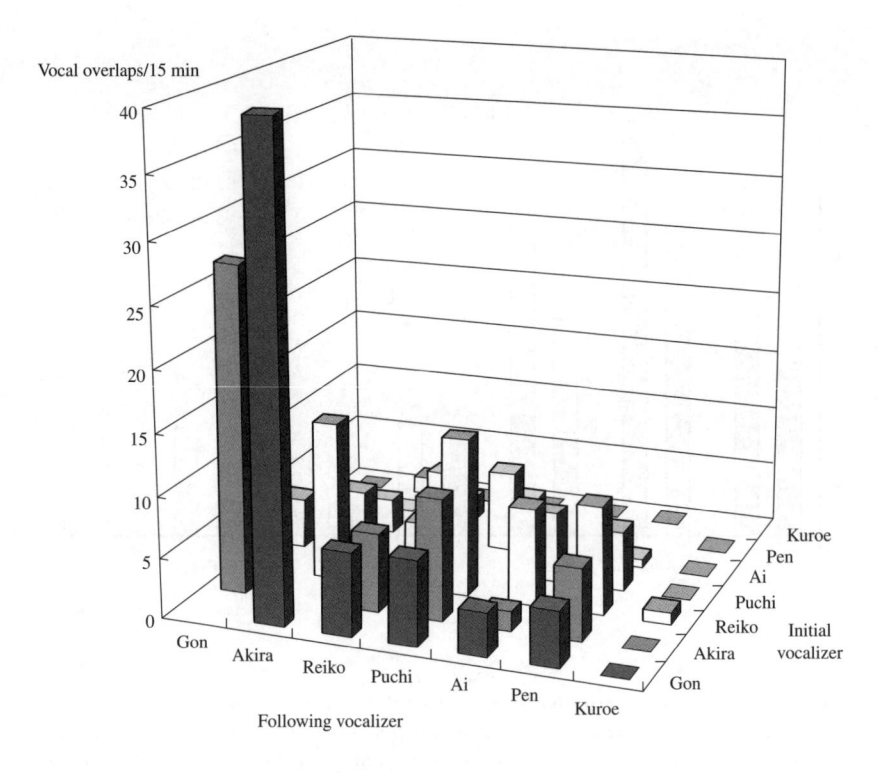

Figure 10-3
Vocal overlap relations between chimpanzees.

particular, vocal interactions between Gon and Akira amounted to 21% of the total. There was a positive correlation between the number of following vocalizations by the two individuals in a given dyad. Thus, there was a tendency for chimpanzees to overlap their vocalizations with those chimpanzees who often overlapped with them.

Chimpanzees changed social behaviors including the production of pant hoots during experimentally produced encounters between parties. This study clearly showed that encounter is a factor that affects pant hoot production.

Pant hoot has been analyzed from various aspects of social context (Reynolds & Reynolds, 1965; Goodall, 1968; Wrangham, 1977; Wrangham & Smuts, 1980; Ghiglieri, 1984; Nishida et al., 1985; Goodall, 1986; Clark, 1993; Mitani & Nishida, 1993). However, such social and ecological factors as dispersion of party, food resources, alliances between males,

Table 10-1 Number of vocal overlaps per 15 min

Initial vocalizer	Following vocalizer								
	Gon	Akira	Reiko	Puchi	Ai	Pen	Kuroe	Room	Unknown
Gon	-	40	7	7.2	3.7	4.5	0	2.5	0
Akira	27	-	6.5	10	1.5	6	0	6.5	1.5
Reiko	13	13	-	13	8	9	1	6	2
Puchi	4.2	5.5	3.5	-	5.7	5	0	0	0
Ai	2.2	3	6	6.7	-	0.5	0	3	0
Pen	0.5	0	2	2.5	2.5	-	0	0	1
Kuroe	0	1	0	0	0	0	-	0	0
Room	6	12	3	0	3	3	0	2	1
Unknown	0	1.5	0	0	0	0	0	0	0

copulation and neighboring communities can be discounted in this study. Therefore, we focus on the influences of social status and inter-party encounter on the production of pant hoots.

Some researchers reported that higher-ranking males vocalize more pant hoots (e.g. Mitani & Nishida, 1993; Clark & Wrangham, 1994) and our results agree. The two dominant males (Gon and Akira) produced most of the non-submissive vocalizations (Figure 10-2). However, Akira produced more vocalizations than Gon. One old female, Reiko, also produced non-submissive vocalizations frequently, while another old female, Puchi, and the other younger females did not often do so (Table 3-1 shows the age of the chimpanzees). Thus, age may weakly influence the production of pant hoots.

Social interactions and "vocal overlap relations" (Table 10-1) show quite different patterns. This means that "vocal overlap" has a different social meaning from the more direct social interactions among chimpanzees.

The frequency of non-submissive vocalizations of each individual increased under the Condition 2, although the composition of vocalization types uttered by each individual was unchanged. Moreover, the interval between vocalizations shortened and the vocalization overlap increased under Condition 2. This tendency was most apparent in vocalizations between males. Thus, inter-party encounters had a proximate influence on the regulation of vocal interactions, especially in the males.

Males tended to overlap their vocalizations with each other. Unless the follower waits until the earlier vocalization has terminated, the earlier vocalization is masked and information cannot be transferred (Masataka & Biben, 1987). Therefore, overlapping of vocalization cannot present cooperative information exchange. Rather, the chimpanzees may be intentionally masking the others' vocalizations by overlapping. The pant hoot may be used as a kind of display. Thus, chimpanzees may try to disturb the pant hoots of rivals and displace them with their own display of overlapping vocalization. Chimpanzees were often observed to accompany pant hoot vocalizations with display behaviors, such as throwing stones, slapping a wall, and stamping on the ground. This hypothesis could be made clearer by considering the form of the social relationship between the males. Rank-oriented behaviors were not observed between them, but the younger Akira was thought to be challenging Gon during the study period. Under such conditions, direct interaction between males may lead to a risk of serious injury for the participants. Therefore, to avoid physical contact, they competed by vocalizing instead of by direct interaction.

Mitani and Nishida (1993) found that the pant hoots of the alpha male tend to receive more vocal responses. Direct confrontation with the alpha male may represent a high risk for other members. Therefore, his rivals may try to confront to him by using vocalizations. Then, after the social rank is established, vocal responses are found to decrease (Clark & Wrangham, 1994). However, pant hoot vocalization may not always prevent direct aggressive interaction. Clark and Wrangham (1994) pointed out that pant hoot invites aggression from higher-ranking individuals. Females and younger individuals utter pant hoots less frequently (Clark, 1993; Clark & Wrangham, 1994; Marler & Tenaza, 1977). This may be because they are less willing to risk aggression from higher-ranking individuals.

Itani (1976) observed that male chimpanzees respond aggressively when they hear the pant hoots of another group. Direct contact with another community can lead to fatal injury (Nishida et al., 1979). These facts suggest that chimpanzees may also use pant hoots as a display to neighboring communities in order to avoid direct interaction.

In conclusion, the primary function of the pant hoot may be as a display to rivals and to other communities in cases where direct contact would lead to a risk of aggressive interaction. Pant hoots made as a display would also convey information about the caller, the location of the caller, and possibly food resources, to other chimpanzees. As a result, chimpanzees may be able to regulate spacing of the party and to attract certain individuals.

Information vocal sounds convey

It has been often reported that acoustic differences in vocal sounds serve to convey many different kinds of information. It is well known that the vervet monkey has different alarm calls for different predators (e.g.,

Struhsaker, 1967). This may be an example of 'semantic' communication (Seyfarth & Cheney, 1982). Could this mode of communication have led to human speech? If so, we may expect that there are many 'semantic' communications among chimpanzees. However, there are few studies that report context-dependent vocal sounds in the chimpanzee. In contrast, we find 'semantic' communication in prosimians (e.g., Oda & Masataka, 1996). Chimpanzee vocal sounds convey rough information about situations and specific information about individuals. In Chapter 7, I described that a chimpanzee can identify the vocalizer by pant hoots, pant grunts and screams, even if I could not identify acoustic parameters that differentiate vocalizers. The identification of vocalizers is another important aspect of vocal communication. Chimpanzees compile extensive memory for social interactions, and may be able to understand situations, especially social situations that they cannot see, by identifying vocalizers.

Chapter 11: Action and language—laterality of the brain

Handedness, actions and language: laterality of the brain

Humans exhibit highly developed actions, such as speech, tool-using behaviors, imitation and gestures. Humans have also developed handedness. Not only language but also actions and handedness are features specific to humans. This does not mean that great apes do not perform actions. Great apes show primitive forms of the behaviors. In this section, I will very briefly review handedness, actions and language behaviors in the non-human primates, mainly chimpanzees, and disorders of action and language. Then, in the next section, I will present data on imitation and body image in the chimpanzee.

Handedness

In humans, the dominant hand tends to be the right hand: about 85–90% of humans are right-handed. Monkeys and apes do not show such biased handedness. Researchers have tried to find evidence of handedness in monkeys and apes. It was reported that macaque monkeys use the left hand for visually guided reaching more frequently than the right hand, while the right hand is used more frequently for object manipulation than the left hand (Beck & Barton, 1972). This research provided an important basis for the postural theory of handedness by MacNeilage et al. (1987). A similar tendency was reported in the chimpanzee (e.g., Hopkins, 1996). These findings suggest that a precursor of human handedness already exists in non-human primates. Another feature of handedness in monkeys and apes is that it is fixed within individuals. Some chimpanzees use mainly the right hand to manipulate objects; others predominantly use the left hand for the same purpose. It is noteworthy that the left hemisphere controls the movements of the right hand and the right hemisphere controls the left hand.

Action and its disorders

Chimpanzees in the wild use a variety of tools. A book by Goodall (1986) provides a list of tools used by chimpanzees. Thus, tool-using behaviors are not specific to humans. However, chimpanzee tools are very primitive. Chimpanzees communicate by gestures. For example, when a chimpanzee begs another individual for food, she/he extends the palm toward the individual (see also Goodall, 1986). However, their gestures are simple, not highly developed, and usually directed to an object or individual. I will report on imitation in chimpanzees in the next section.

The disorders of actions, apraxia, occur when the parietal and/or the frontal cortex is damaged in the left hemisphere. Two types of apraxia are important: ideational apraxia and ideomotor apraxia. The former type is related to sequential behaviors and/or object (tool)-related sequential behaviors. Patients with ideational apraxia were requested to take a match from a matchbox, to strike the match on the matchbox, and then to smoke a cigarette. But they often failed to smoke it. Some patients struck the *cigarette* to the matchbox. The latter type of apraxia is related to relatively simple symbolic gestures, simple object-related behaviors and the imitation of meaningless gestures. Patients with ideomotor apraxia often fail to salute upon request. It is interesting that these behaviors which were found to deteriorate in apraxia are behaviors that are highly developed in humans, that is, object (tool)-using behaviors, imitation and gestures. It is noteworthy that some form of damage to the left hemisphere produces apraxia.

Language and its disorders

Successful attempts to use American Sign Language (Gardner & Gardner, 1969), words in plastic shape (Premack, 1976) or lexigrams (Rumbaugh, 1977) with chimpanzees have been reported, attracting great interest. These 'languages' made use of the visual modality and stood in marked contrast to Hayes' failure in the attempt to use the auditory-vocal channel (Hayes, 1951). There have been many discussions about whether chimpanzees showed language behaviors on the same level as humans. For example, it is not clear whether chimpanzees have grammar. However, these studies clearly showed that chimpanzees have a primitive form of the ability to learn language.

It is well known that the destruction of several parts of the left hemisphere results in disorders of language. Damage to the left inferior frontal gyrus that includes Broca's area produces deficits in the production of language (motor aphasia). On the other hand, damage localized mainly in the left superior temporal gyrus that includes Wernicke's area produces deficits in the perception of language (sensory aphasia). There are many other types of aphasia: transcortical sensory, transcortical motor aphasia and conduction aphasia. Aphasia is often accompanied by alexia and agraphia. Thus, spoken language is considered to be more basic in humans.

It is of significant interest that damage to the left hemisphere produces aphasia, and it should be noted that both language and actions suffer from similar impulsive disorders: echolalia, utilizing behavior and impulsive imitation.

Laterality of the brain

Handedness, actions such as tool-using, imitation, gestures, and language are highly developed in humans, although recent research has shown primitive forms of these behaviors in non-human primates. It is interesting that the left hemisphere mainly controls all these behaviors. In other words, development of the laterality of the brain is deeply related to hominization. This will be discussed in the next section and in the last chapter, Chapter 12.

Imitation and body image

Imitation

Imitation is an ability that is profoundly developed in humans. Through imitation, humans acquire, spread and successfully transmit across generations many cultural behaviors. Without imitation, humans could not have developed modern technologies.

To ask whether the chimpanzee can imitate is not a good question. The answer to this question is clearly 'yes'. A more appropriate question to ask is what kind of behaviors can be imitated by the chimpanzee. Usually, it is not easy for the chimpanzee to imitate arbitrary behaviors performed by humans. If the chimpanzee has an interest in a behavior to be imitated, for example, the manipulation of an object, the chimpanzee readily imitates the behavior. However, when the chimpanzee has no interest in the behavior, imitation does not occur.

In this section, I trained a chimpanzee to imitate many behaviors to answer the question above: What kind of behaviors can the chimpanzee imitate?

The subject was Pen. The molding procedure (Fouts, 1972) was introduced. That is, the experimenter 'molded' the behavior to be imitated in the chimpanzee. Then these behaviors were reinforced when the chimpanzee performed the behavior spontaneously. The training continued until the chimpanzee readily emitted the behavior. Table 11-1A shows the behaviors to be imitated. These behaviors are grouped into 6 categories based on symptoms of human apraxic (imitation disorders) patients. Several behaviors were not necessary to mold.

Action and language—laterality of the brain

Table 11-1A Taught actions

Category	Action No.	Description of actions to be imitated
A	1	both hands were placed on the head
	2	the left hand pointed to the left ear
	3	the left hand pointed to the left eye
	4	the left hand pointed to the nose
	5	the left hand pointed to the mouth
B	6	both hands pointed to the chest
	7	both hands pointed to the neck
	8	the left hand pointed to the left shoulder
	9	the left hand pointed to the right shoulder
C	10	both hands were crossed
	11	the left hand grabbed the righ arm
	12	the left hand was placed on the right hand
	13	the left hand pointed to the righ palm
	14	the left index finger pointed to the tip of the right index finger
D	15	the left foot was lifted and the left hand grabbed it
	16	the left foot was lifted
	17	the bottom was protruded to the experimenter
E	18	the left hand was lifted
	19	both hands were extended sideways
	20	both hands were protruded
	21	the left index finger pointed to the floor
	22	both hands pointed to the floor
F	23	the left hand picked up a pencil

Table 11-1B Novel actions

Category	Action No.	Description of actions
A	24	the left hand pointed to the left cheek
	25	the left hand pointed to the chin
C	26	the left index finger pointed to the right thumb
	27	the left index finger pointed to the right little finger
	28	the left index finger pointed to the back of the right hand
	29	the left hand pointed to the righ arm
	30	the left hand pointed to the left foot
	31	the left hand pointed to the left knee
	32	the left hand pointed to the left shin
D	33	the left hand pointed to the bottom
E	34	both hands were lifted
	35	the left hand was extended sideways
	36	the left hand was protruded
F	37	the left hand picked up a brick

After the training, the chimpanzee subject was tested. In the test, the experimenter performed a behavior to be imitated three times. Behaviors of the subject were recorded. The test consisted of at least 52 trials. Then, fourteen novel actions were introduced (Table 11-1B). The procedure of testing was the same as before. Pen was tested for at least fifteen trials.

The upper panel of Figure 11-1 shows the results for taught actions. As shown in this figure, there are differences in performance among the categories. To imitate simple object-related behaviors was very easy (Category F). For example, imitation of picking up a pencil was perfect. Imitation of behaviors directed to the external personal space was easy, too (Category E). Imitation of behaviors that accompany large postural change was not difficult (Category D). However, it was more difficult to get the chimpanzee to imitate behaviors directed to a non-visible part (for example, face; Categories A and B) than to a visible part (for example, finger; Category C) of the body. The lower panel of Figure 11-1 shows the results for novel actions. A similar tendency was observed for imitation of new actions. In categories A and C, responses were often directed to body parts she had been trained to point to that were proximal to the target.

It was difficult for Pen to precisely imitate a meaningless gesture directed to non-visible parts of the body, for example, the chin or the cheek. The chimpanzee was trained to imitate a pointing action directed to parts of the body, such as the eye, the ear, the nose, the mouth, the chest, the abdomen, and the shoulder. She was then required to point to the chin, for which she had not been trained, by imitation. However, she did not point to the chin and usually pointed instead to the mouth, for which she had been trained. Similarly, when required to point to the cheek, she usually pointed to the eye or the nose. Thus, responses were directed to the facial parts she had been trained to point to that were proximal to the target.

An interesting episode was observed. The behavior to be imitated was pointing to the palm. By molding and operant conditioning, Pen successfully imitated this behavior. In a test trial, I presented only the palm without pointing. However, the subject *pointed* to her palm. These results suggest that, compared with humans, the body image in the chimpanzee may not be as clear or as segmented, and that acquisition of generalized imitation may not be easy for the chimpanzee. Body image in the chimpanzee is the theme of the next section.

Experimental analyses of body image

What kind of body image do chimpanzees have? This is a difficult question to answer, and except for the study by Premack (1975), it has not been

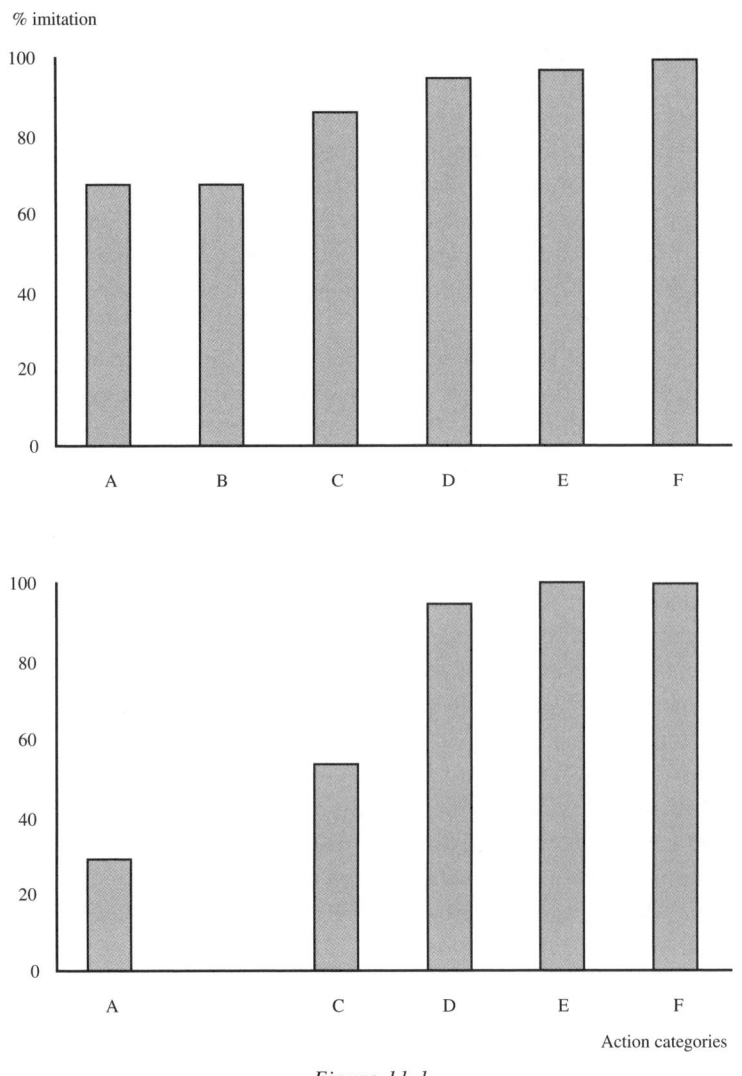

Figure 11-1
Upper: Percent imitation of taught actions in the test sessions for each action category (see Table 11-1A). Lower: Percent imitation of novel actions for each action category (see Table 11-1B).

directly addressed to date. Body image is important because it may be related to action imitation and self-awareness. Action imitation has been studied in chimpanzees (e.g., Hayes & Hayes, 1952; Custance et al., 1995). Custance et al. (1995) reported that two young chimpanzees imitated about

15 (31%) out of 48 novel actions. However, very few responses of their chimpanzee subjects were perfect, and even some of their clearest imitations were flawed in some way. In the previous section, I reported that the degree of difficulty in imitation depended on the actions to be imitated in the chimpanzee. For example, manipulatory actions involving objects can be imitated more easily than meaningless actions. Actions directed to an external space are more easily imitated than self-directed actions. Actions directed to a visible part of the body are easier to imitate than those out of sight. In incorrect imitations, responses were often directed to a body part proximal to the correct target.

The existence of self-awareness or self-recognition in the chimpanzee, which may require body image, was assessed by self-directed actions using a mirror (e.g., Gallup, 1970; Povinelli et al., 1993). These experiments suggest the importance of experimental analyses of body image in the chimpanzee. In the present study, it is assumed that the perception of others' bodies reflects body image. The perception of the body (the human face) was examined in a chimpanzee using a matching-to-sample task with a touch-panel system. The chimpanzee subject was required to touch the part of the face pointed to in the sample phase.

A female chimpanzee was used as the subject (Pan, 7 years old when these experiments were conducted). Throughout the experiments, no food deprivation was imposed.

Experiments were conducted in a large booth (Figure 3-4) using a videodisc player and a 21-inch monitor with a touch-panel system. A personal computer controlled the video disc player to present color pictures of the human face and recorded the position of touch responses on the monitor. Although the monitor had 640×400 pixels, the touch panel system transformed the monitor into a 1024×1024 matrix.

In order to understand the body image in the chimpanzee, discrimination of eight facial parts, that is, the head, forehead, right eye, right ear, right cheek, nose, mouth and chin, was studied (see Figure 11-2). The facial stimuli presented were recorded using the disc player. A series of six experiments were conducted, in which versions of the delayed matching to sample task were employed. The X-Y coordinate of the central point of each facial part was determined. Usually a correct response was a touch response which fell within ±50 of the X-Y coordinate of the central point of each facial part. Responses outside of this rectangular area were incorrect. The area of the rectangle was enlarged to ±60, when the performance of the subject deteriorated.

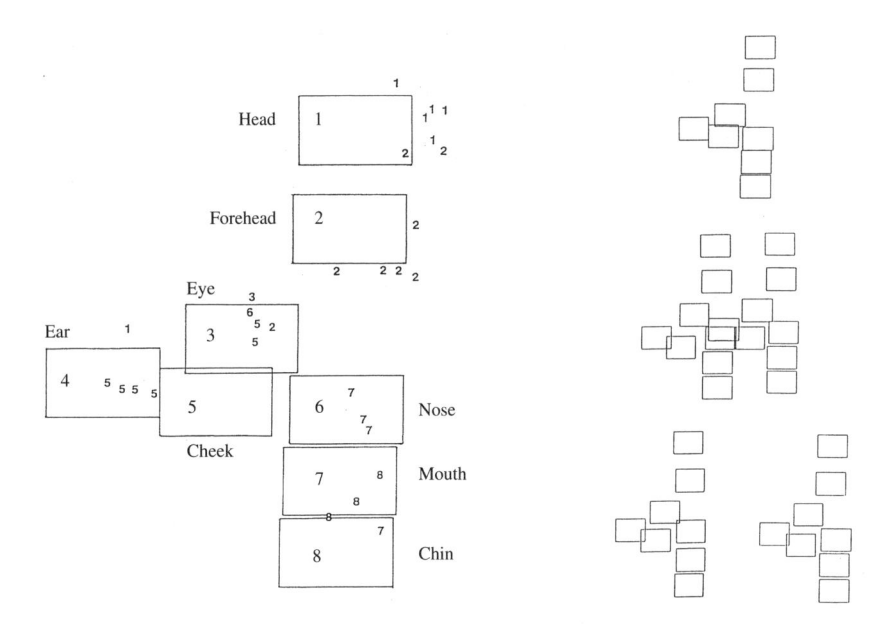

Figure 11-2

Left: Position of each facial part; 1-head, 2-forehead, 3-right eye, 4-right ear, 5-right cheek, 6-nose, 7-mouth and 8-chin. Each rectangle indicates the correct area for each facial part. A response inside each correct area is reinforced. Small numbers in this figure and in Figures 11-5, 11-8 and 11-12 indicate the positions of touch responses in head (1), forehead (2), eye (3), ear (4), cheek, (5), nose (6), mouth (7) and chin (8) trials. All these responses are examples of incorrect responses. Right: Positions of matching face in Experiment 3; upper-center, middle-mid left and right, lower-far left and right positions.

In Experiment 1, a color picture of the experimenter's face was presented on the monitor as the sample, with a picture of an index finger pointing to one of the eight facial parts. A touch response to the tip of the index finger of the sample was required to proceed in the trial from the sample to the delay phase. The sample phase persisted until the subject touched the tip of the index finger. No pictures were presented in the delay phase. After a 2-s delay, the same face with two green dots was presented in the matching (test) phase. The index finger was not presented in the matching face. One dot was located on the sample part, and the other dot was placed on one of the other seven facial parts. Touching the dot on the sample part was a correct response. A response that involved touching any other position on the monitor was incorrect. In this and subsequent experiments, a touch response in the matching phase turned off the photograph on the monitor. When the response was correct, it was followed by a beep sound and reinforced by a piece of fruit. When the response was incorrect, it was followed by a 5-s time-out. The intertrial interval was 3 s.

In Experiment 2, stimuli and response requirements in the sample and delay phases were the same as those of the first experiment. In the matching phase, however, the same face without the dots was presented. A response to the appropriate facial part pointed to by the index finger in the sample phase was a correct response. Touching other areas on the monitor was an incorrect response. In these two experiments, the face in the sample and matching phases (hereafter referred to as sample and matching faces, respectively) was presented in the same location, that is, at the center of the monitor.

The procedures of Experiment 3 were the same as those of Experiment 2 except that the position of the matching face was changed. Four positions were employed in this phase: far left, mid left, mid right and far right on the monitor (see Figure 11-2).

Fifty-six trials were conducted in one session in the three experiments. The criterion of acquisition was to attain a correct-response score higher than 85% in two consecutive sessions.

In Experiment 4, rotation of the facial stimulus was introduced. Three conditions were used. Under the first condition (SFMV; the position of the sample face was fixed and that of the matching face was variable), the sample face was upright and was presented at the center of the monitor. The matching face was rotated and presented in one of eight positions: 0 degrees (upright), 45 degrees, 90 degrees (sidelong), 135 degrees, 180 degrees (upside-down), 225 degrees, 270 degrees (sidelong), and 315 degrees. Under the second condition (SVMF; the position of the sample face was variable and that of the matching face was fixed), the sample face was rotated and presented at the same eight positions as in the first condition. The matching face was presented upright in the center of the monitor. Under the third condition (SVMV; the positions of both sample and matching faces were variable), both the sample and the matching faces were rotated to the same degree, and presented at the eight positions used in the first and second conditions. The conditions of the sample and matching faces were the same as those in Experiment 2. Sixty-four trials were conducted in one session in Experiment 4. The SFMV and SVMF conditions were tested for three sessions and the SVMV condition was tested for two sessions.

In Experiment 5, the matching face was changed to one of two other persons and that of a chimpanzee. The subject knew both the persons and the chimpanzee. The position of the matching face was at the center, or to the left or right of the monitor. The sample face was the same as in Experiment 2. Fifty-six trials were conducted in one session. Each condition was tested for 5 sessions.

In Experiment 6, the sample face was not a photograph, but the experimenter's actual face. Thus, the experimenter pointed to his nose in a face-to-face situation when the sample part was the nose. The same eight facial parts were used. It was not difficult for the experimenter to draw the subject's attention. The matching face was on the monitor, the same facial photograph used in Experiment 2. The task was a simultaneous-matching-to-sample task. Thus, the experimenter continued to point to his nose until the subject made a touch response on the monitor. In this task, a correction procedure was introduced. When the response was incorrect in a trial, the same sample stimulus was presented in the next trial until the subject made a correct response. Fifty-six trials and correction trials were carried out in one daily session. Experiment 6 was continued until the subject's performance exceeded 90% correct responses in a non-correction session.

As shown in Figure 11-3, the subject required 30 sessions to master the task in Experiment 1. Performance improved only gradually. Because there was another non-target dot on the monitor, incorrect responses were often directed to the non-target dot.

Figure 11-4 shows the acquisition of the task in Experiment 2. Eighteen sessions were required to master the task. Although it was difficult to calculate an effective chance level, the performance level decreased to less than 30% correct responses in the first session. Incorrect responses were directed proximal to the target. This tendency was clear when the target had no clear 'landmark' (identifying feature), as in the case of the cheek (see Figure 11-5). Performance varied among the eight facial parts. For target positions without a clear 'landmark', such as the head, forehead and cheek, performance was relatively poor (see Figure 11-6).

Figure 11-7 shows the acquisition of the task in Experiment 3. It took 30 sessions to master the task. The performance level decreased to less than 40% of correct responses in the first three sessions, and was inconsistent before the 20th session. Analyses of error response with respect to position indicated that the responses of the subject were controlled not only by the facial stimulus but also by the positions of the sample face on the monitor. As shown in Figure 11-8, when the face was presented on the far left side in

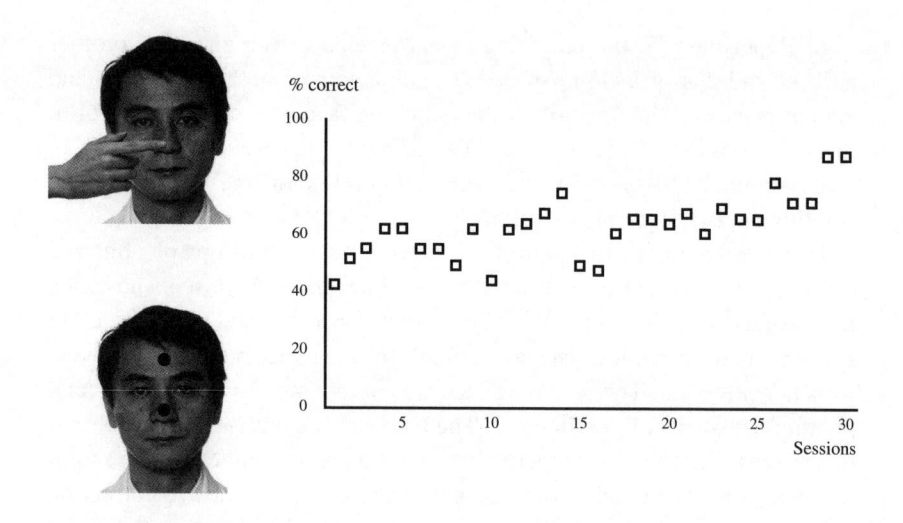

Figure 11-3
Left: Facial stimulus in the sample (upper) and matching (lower) phases in Experiment 1. Right: Acquisition curve of Experiment 1.

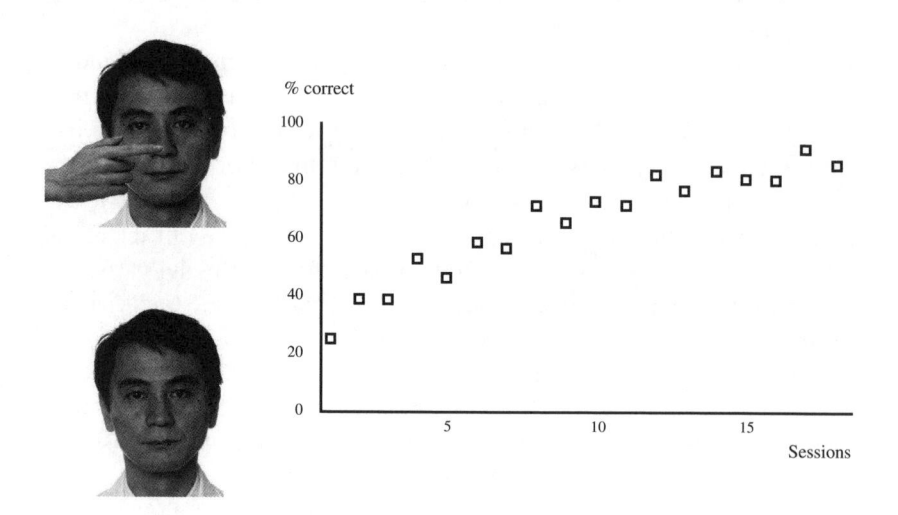

Figure 11-4
Left: Facial stimulus in the sample (upper) and matching (lower) phases in Experiment 2. Right: Acquisition curve of Experiment 2.

Action and language—laterality of the brain

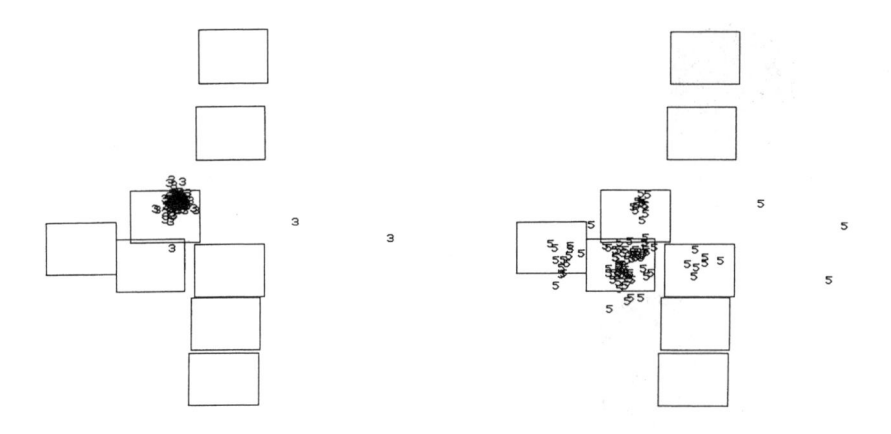

Figure 11-5
Left: Response positions in eye trials (3) from the fifth to 18th acquisition sessions. Most responses are correct. Right: Response positions in cheek trials (5) in the same acquisition sessions. Many responses were directed to adjacent facial parts.

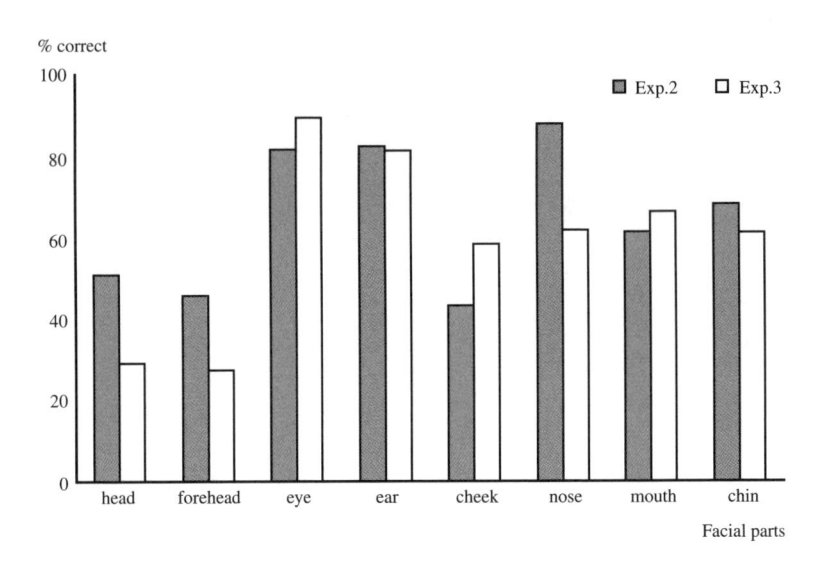

Figure 11-6
Performance for each facial part in the acquisition sessions of Experiments 2 and 3.

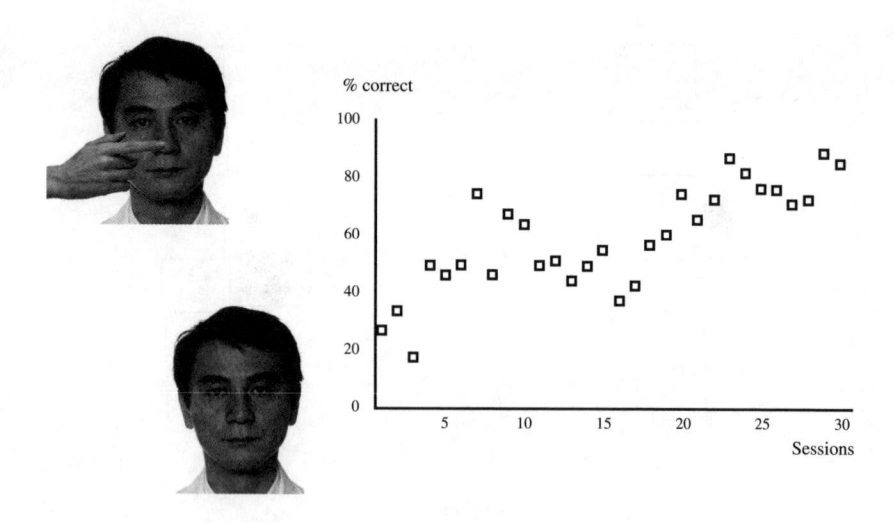

Figure 11-7
Left: Facial stimulus in the sample (upper) and matching (lower) phases in Experiment 3. The position of the face in the matching phase is different from that in the sample phase. Right: Acquisition curve of Experiment 3.

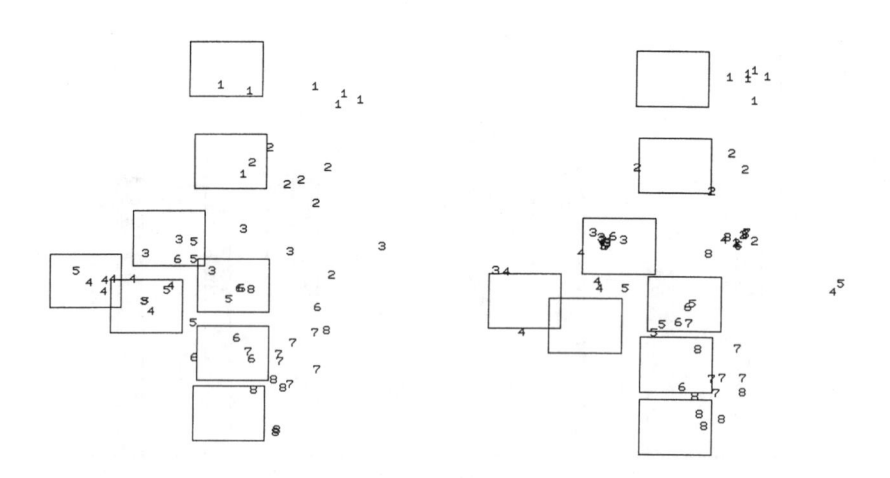

Figure 11-8
Left: Positions of responses in the first acquisition session (far left position). Right: Positions of responses in the third acquisition session (mid left position). Numbers in the figure indicate positions of touch responses. See the explanation of the numbers in the caption of Figure 11-2.

the matching phase, responses were directed to right side of the matching face. Thus, responses fell in between the position of the sample face (the center of the monitor) and that of the matching face. The performance level was particularly low when the target was the head or forehead (see Figure 11-6).

Figure 11-9 indicates performance in Experiment 4 with rotation at each position. Under the SFMV condition, when rotation exceeded ±45 degrees, the performance level decreased abruptly to less than 20% correct responses in the 90-, 135- and 180-degree rotations, and to about 40% correct responses in the 225- and 270-degree rotations. Under the SVMF condition, performance was about 40% for rotations between 90 and 270 degrees. Under the SVMV condition, the decline in performance was small and the subject always scored more than 70% correct responses. Performance differed among the eight facial parts, as shown in Figure 11-10. Under the SFMV condition, the subject made many errors (less than 20% correct responses) when the cheek or forehead was the target position. Under the SVMF condition, the performance level was low in trials in which the cheek, forehead or mouth was the target. In the SVMV condition, the subject made errors when the cheek or head was the target. The subject scored high in the nose trials, because the nose was always located at the center of the rotated face.

Figure 11-11 shows the results of Experiment 5 where the matching face was different from the sample face. The performance level for the substituted human matching faces was high except for the chin and head trials. When the matching face was that of a chimpanzee, performance decreased to a low level, in particular, there were almost no correct responses in the mouth and chin trials. Interestingly, although the position of the ear is different between the human and chimpanzee, a relatively high performance level was maintained in the ear trials (see Figure 11-12). The subject exhibited a very high performance level only in the eye trials.

Figure 11-13 shows the results of Experiment 6. In this task, the sample was not a picture, rather, it was a real face. Because incorrect responses were often observed in the ear (53.1% correct responses), cheek (65.3% correct responses) and chin (61.2% correct responses) trials, a correction procedure was introduced. Performance improved gradually and reached about 90% correct responses at the 19th session. Incorrect responses were directed to facial parts that were proximal to the target in later sessions.

The results of this series of six experiments suggest that responses of the chimpanzee are not completely controlled by facial stimuli. When the difference in position between the sample and matching faces was large,

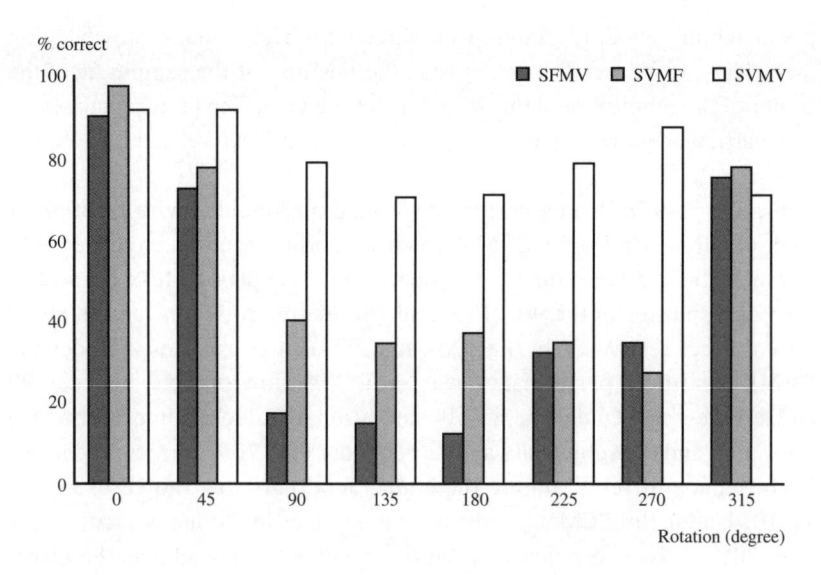

Figure 11-9
Performance for the eight positions for each of the three conditions in Experiment 4.

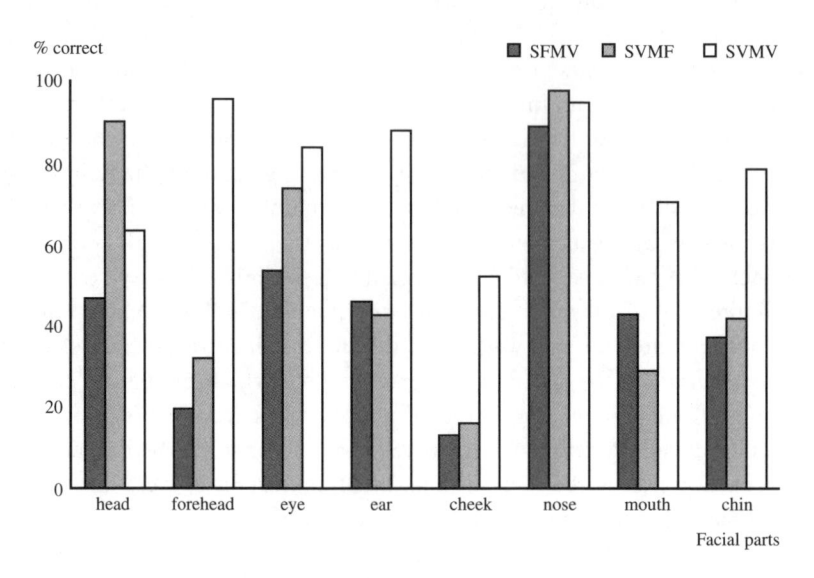

Figure 11-10
Performance for the eight facial parts for each condition in Experiment 4.

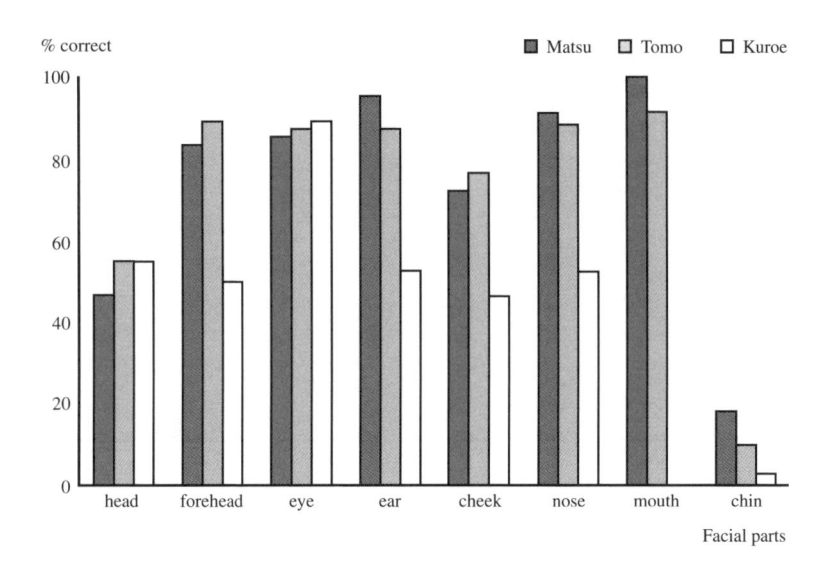

Action and language—laterality of the brain 167

Figure 11-11
Performance for the eight facial parts in Experiment 5. Matsu and Tomo are humans, and Kuroe is a chimpanzee.

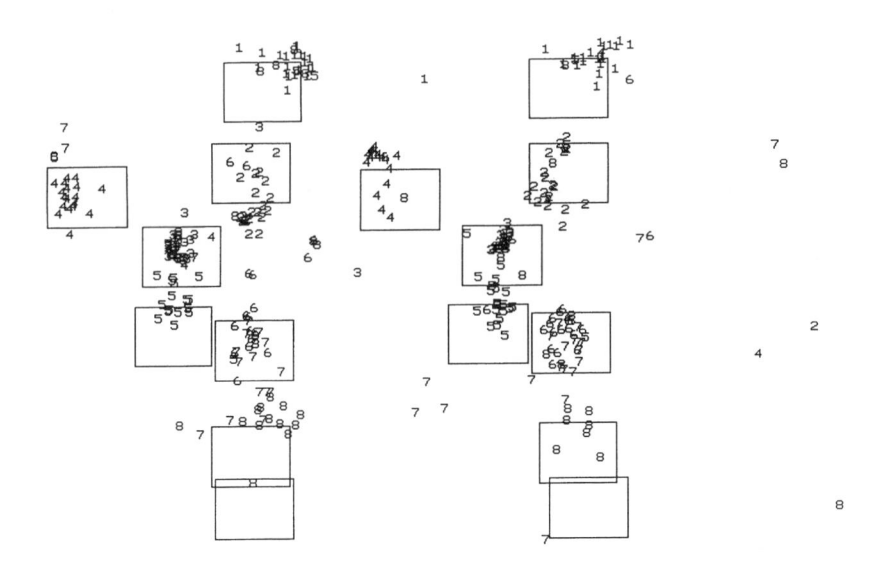

Figure 11-12
Positions of responses to the substitute chimpanzee face (Kuroe) for the left and right positions in Experiment 5. Note that the position of the ear is high. Numbers in the figure indicate positions of touch responses in trials for each facial part. See the explanation of the numbers in the caption of Figure11-2.

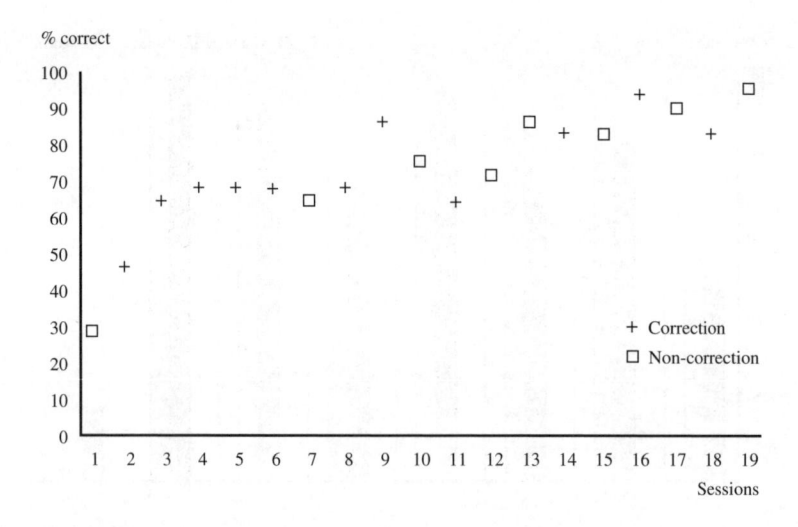

Figure 11-13
Acquisition of the task in Experiment 6. Plus signs indicate performance in correction trials (Correction). Squares indicate non-correction test trials (Non-correction).

performance deteriorated, as shown in Experiments 3 and 4. In these tasks, the position of the sample face was fixed at the center of the monitor, and a response to the sample part was required to proceed in the task from the sample phase to the delay phase. Thus, the position of the sample face controlled the position of responses in the matching phase. When a facial part without a clear 'landmark' was the target, as in the case of the forehead, cheek or chin, performance often deteriorated. When the matching face was replaced by the face of other persons or a chimpanzee, performance often deteriorated. Altogether, these results suggest that the perception of facial parts is not accurate in the chimpanzee and that the body image of the chimpanzee may not be clear or explicit. However, the chimpanzee subject was able to match the human ear to the chimpanzee ear, even though the position of the chimpanzee ear is different from that of the human ear, as shown in Experiment 5. Moreover, performance was transferred from a sample picture to a real face in Experiment 6. Thus, the chimpanzee has a body image but, compared with humans, it may not be as clear or as segmented.

Premack (1975) studied a face construction test using four facial pieces: the eyes, nose and mouth in four chimpanzees and children. Except for Sarah, other chimpanzees failed to construct the face of a chimpanzee. Even

Sarah's construction was not perfect. The results of the present study are consistent with those of the face construction test performed by Premack. Children of about 3 years of age could not properly construct a face in the same task, but most children older than 5 years of age could. There are items in psychological tests for children (e.g., Schopler & Reichler, 1979) that assess the development of body image. It was found using this test that children acquire body image at about 4 years of age.

The body image experiments described in this chapter were derived from my previous study of imitation in chimpanzees (not including the present subject, Pan; see the previous section). Custance et al. (1995) reported that imitation behavior of chimpanzees is not perfect. Fouts (1972) reported that molding, and not imitation, is an effective means to teach sign language to chimpanzees. The present results of body image experiments are consistent with those of the imitation experiments. It will be of interest to examine whether experiences with body image experiments have influences on imitation, and *vice versa*.

As described in the previous section, there are several behaviors that are highly developed in humans, e.g., imitation as well as language, tool-use, handedness. It is of interest that the left hemisphere of the brain mainly controls all these behaviors. Thus, the development of these behaviors may reflect the development of laterality of the brain. Deficits in imitation have been observed in patients with apraxia (disorders of actions without paralysis). Deficits are not equal among the actions of apraxic patients for whom, for example, transitive actions (actions directed to objects) are easier to imitate than intransitive actions. Furthermore, actions directed towards one's own body are more difficult to imitate than those directed towards external space. Concerning actions directed to one's own body, actions directed to visible parts are easier to imitate than those directed to non-visible parts. The chimpanzee showed the same tendency for imitation in this experiment. Apraxia often occurs as a result of damage to the left hemisphere, particularly that of the parietal (and frontal) cortex (Kimura & Archibald, 1974; Kolb & Milner, 1981). What are the functions of the right hemisphere? Deficits in body image occur as a result of damage to the right parietal cortex (Heilman & Valenstein, 1979). A recent functional MRI study by Iacoboni et al. (1999) showed activation in the left inferior frontal and the right parietal cortices during observation and execution (imitation) of finger movement. They interpreted that this activation in the right parietal cortex is related to body schema necessary for imitation. The left and right hemispheres cooperate to produce precise and generalized imitation.

Compared with humans, the lateralization of behavioral and cognitive functions is not clear in the chimpanzee. These may explain the inaccurate imitation and body image in the chimpanzee.

Self-directed actions are a special case. Facial expressions are the most basic mode of communication. They are directed to another individual, rather than to one's self. During the course of hominization, upper limb actions were introduced in communication, as Rizzolatti and Arbib (1998) have suggested. Although the chimpanzee often uses upper limb actions in communication, they are usually directed to another individual or to objects (Goodall, 1968). Self-directed actions rarely occur in the communication of the chimpanzee. On the other hand, humans frequently direct their actions to themselves in communication. Thus, in early hominids the asymmetry of the structures and functions of the brain was enhanced, a tendency that already existed in nonhuman primates (Beck & Barton, 1972; MacNeilage et al., 1987; Hopkins, 1996; Heffner & Heffner, 1984; Hamilton & Vermeire, 1988; Ganon et al., 1998; Yeni-Komshian et al., 1976), fine movements of the hands and fingers and the body image became more elaborate, and they acquired the ability to direct their actions toward their own body in communication.

Recognition of self mirror-image has been interpreted as a sign of self-awareness (Gallup, 1970). Self-directed actions using a mirror are taken as an index of self-recognition. It is reasonable to assume that the body image is related to self-awareness. Some chimpanzees show self-directed actions using a mirror, whereas others do not (Povinelli et al., 1993). It would be of interest to examine the body image in these subgroups of chimpanzees, as the development of body image may be associated with that of self-awareness. The subject of the present study had not been trained to use sign language or artificial languages. Some chimpanzees, however, have learned the name of facial parts. It would also be of interest to examine the body image in these subgroups of chimpanzees.

Appendix: The mirror system

Neuroanatomical and neurophysiological studies

Broca's area (Brodeman's area 44), which is related to the production of speech, is located in the inferior frontal gyrus of the left hemisphere. There is a homologous area in the monkey inferior premotor cortex, area F5, as shown in Figure 11-14 (Rizzolatti et al., 1998). Gallese et al. (1996) found a group of neurons in area F5 that fired with the observation and the execution of the same action, such as picking up food. These neurons fired

Action and language—laterality of the brain

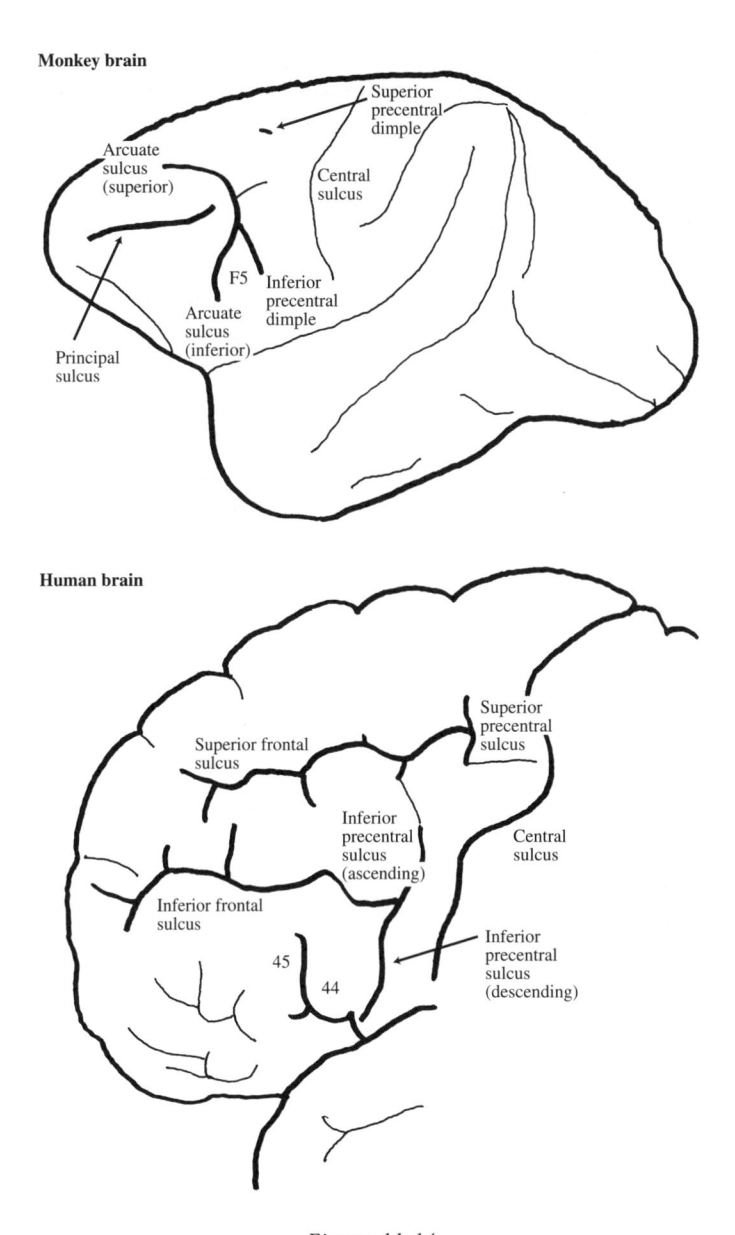

Figure 11-14

The upper panel shows the monkey brain, the lower panel shows the human brain. The superior frontal sulcus and the superior precentral sulcus of the human brain correspond to the superior limb of the monkey arcuate sulcus. The inferior frontal sulcus and the ascending branch of the inferior precentral sulcus of the human brain correspond to the inferior limb of the monkey arcuate sulcus. The descending branch of the inferior precentral sulcus of the human brain corresponds to the inferior precentral dimple. Thus, area F5 is homologous to Broca's area (area 44 [and 45]).

when the monkey observed a human picking up food, and were also fired by his own action of picking up food. Because of this feature, these neurons were called mirror neurons. The mirror neurons are thought to play an important role in the recognition of actions and imitation.

Neuroimaging studies

Human PET studies showed that the Broca's area is related to both the production (execution) and the perception (observation) of speech sounds (Zatorre et al., 1992). Thus, this area in the monkey and human brain share the same feature. In addition, it is reported that Broca's area is activated not only by mouth movement but also by hand movements (Rizzolatti et al., 1996; Grafton et al., 1996; Iacoboni et al., 1999; Nishitani & Hari, 2000). Broca's area was activated when human subjects rehearsed speech sounds, suggesting that this area plays an important role in the 'articulation loop'. In the same way, motor imagery activates Broca'a area. These findings suggest that Broca's area is related to mouth as well as hand actions and to both their production and perception. This is persuasive evidence of a close relationship between the hands and the mouth.

Chapter 12: Conclusion

Vocal functions of the chimpanzee and human speech

There are many differences in the auditory and vocal functions of chimpanzees and humans. Basic auditory functions, such as auditory sensitivity and difference thresholds, differ between these two species (Chapter 4). The perception of speech sounds is also different, and auditory and visual intermodal integration is not easy for the chimpanzee (Chapters 5 and 7). Development of vocal behaviors is profoundly different for chimpanzees and humans (Chapter 9). The vocal tract of the chimpanzee is unlike that of a human. In particular, the position of the larynx is high and the size of the pharynx is small in the chimpanzee (Chapter 6). It is also difficult for the chimpanzee to differentiate vocal responses according to visual cues (Chapter 8). Thus, it is difficult to teach spoken language to a chimpanzee. Compared with human speech, the vocal communication of chimpanzees is not complex (Chapter 10). These results suggest that there may be a great gap between the degree of vocal communication development in these species.

If there are differences in auditory and vocal functions of these two species, we may be able to assume different origins of human speech. Gestural and manual movements are one of the candidates. Early hominids may have a long history of gestural communication. There is much indirect evidence from recent functional brain mapping studies, as described in the previous chapter. For example, Rizzolatti et al. (1996), Iacoboni et al. (1999) and Nishitani and Hari (2000) showed that Broca's area in the left inferior frontal cortex, which is thought to be the motor center of spoken language, is activated by manual movements.

Hand and mouth

There are many similarities between mouth and manual movements. These two types of movements often involve very fine motor skills. They are often used for communication. Deaf people make use of manual sign language instead of spoken language. Kimura (1973; 1993) showed that manual movements are accompanied by human speech. As described in Chapter 11, the left hemisphere of the brain controls both spoken language and manual praxic actions.

Bipedal walking was a very important step toward the evolution of the large human brain. The upright posture made it possible for early hominids to support the large brain. Bipedal walking also freed the upper limbs from the requirements of locomotion. This enabled manual skills, differential movements of the left and right forelimbs, and bimanual coordination. Different movements of the left and the right hands promoted lateralization of the brain. Many researchers reported the superiority of the left hand for visually guided reaching and that of the right hand for praxic movements in the monkey and the ape. This tendency was accelerated by bipedal walking and promoted the development of tool-using behaviors, imitation and gestural communication. Thus, a tendency already existing in the ape (and the monkey) was elaborated.

The development of skilled manual movements provided bases for the development of skilled oral movement. Visual and manual interactions are necessary for the development of skill movements. This promoted auditory and vocal intermodal integrations. Auditory feedback is necessary for the development of canonical babbling, which is vital for the emergence of language. Early hominids acquired the ability to perform intermodal integration gradually. Early hominids are thought to have communicated by gestures for a long time. In those days, oral movements would have played subordinate roles. Gradually, the vocal and auditory channel became dominant, because this channel was more effective.

There are several advantages of the auditory-vocal channel compared with the visual-gestural channel. It is easy to confer a substantial amount of information in a short time using a small amount of energy. Sounds propagate with relatively high speed in air and are robust against obstacles and darkness. It is not necessary for listeners to attend to a sound source. However, because sounds appear one after another, the listener must have a high-speed successive information processing system to interpret sounds.

Hominization and laterality

Praxic manual movements were performed mainly by the right hand. The right hand is controlled by the left hemisphere. The left hemisphere also controlled praxic oral movements, because similar sensory and motor integration was necessary. The F5 area in the monkey inferior premotor cortex is homologous to Broca's area in human brain. As described in

Conclusion

the previous chapter, mirror neurons in F5 fired at the time of the observation and the execution of the same movement. Human PET studies showed that Broca's area is related to both the production (execution) and the perception (observation) of speech sounds. Broca's area is also activated in the production and the perception of manual movements. In addition, Broca's area was activated when human subjects rehearsed speech sounds and imagined actions. These findings suggest that Broca's area is related to mouth as well as hand actions, to both their production and perception, and to their internalization. Sensory and motor integration is the main feature of this brain area. Not only the enlargement, but also the development of the lateralization of the brain accompanied hominization. We might overemphasize the functions of the left hemisphere. The right hemisphere played a complementary role, in domains such as body image and spatial functions. And both hemispheres collaborate to perform skilled manual and speech actions.

Bibliography

Chapter 1

Bickerton, D. *Language and Species*. Chicago: Univ. of Chicago Press, 1990.

Chen, F.-C. & Li, W.-H. Genomic divergence between humans and other hominoids and the effective population size of the common ancestor of humans and chimpanzees. *Am. J. Human Genet.*, 68:444–456, 2001.

Cleveland, J. & Snowdon, C.T. The complex vocal repertoire of the adult cotton-top tamarin, *Saguinus oedipus oedipus*. *Zeitschr. Tierpsychol.*, 58:231–270, 1982.

Elder, J.H. Auditory acuity of the chimpanzee. *J. Comp. Psychol.*, 17:157–183, 1934.

Elder, J.H. The upper limit of hearing in chimpanzee. *Am. J. Physiol.*, 112:109–115, 1935.

Gallese, V., Fadiga, L., Foggasi, L. & Rizzolatti, G. Action recognition in the premotor cortex. *Brain*, 119:593–609, 1996.

Gardner, R.A. & Gardner, B.T. Teaching sign language to a chimpanzee. *Science*, 165:664–672, 1969.

Goodall, J. Tool using and aimed throwing in a community of free-living chimpanzees. *Nature*, 201:1264–1266, 1964.

Green, S. Communication by a graded vocal system in Japanese monkeys. In Rosenblum, L.A. (ed.) *Primate Behavior, Vol. 4: Developments in Field and Laboratory Research*. New York: Academic Press, pp.1–102, 1975.

Hayes, K. *The Ape in Our House*. New York:Harper, 1951.

Hopkins, C.D. Sensory mechanisms in animal communication. In Halliday, T.R. & Slater, P.J.B. (eds.) *Animal Behavior*. Oxford: Blackwell, 2:114–155, 1982.

King, M.C. & Wilson, A.C. Evolution at two levels in humans and chimpanzees. *Science*, 188:107–116, 1975.

Kolb, B. & Whishaw, I.Q. *Fundamentals of Human Neuropsychology*. New York: Freeman, 1980.

Kuhl, P.K. & Padden, D.M. Enhanced discriminability at the phonetic

boundaries for the voicing feature in macaques. *Percept. Psychophysic.*, 32:542–550, 1982.
Kuhl, P.K. & Padden, D.M. Enhanced discriminability at the phonetic boundaries for the place feature in macaques. *J. Acoust. Soc. Am.*, 73:1003–1010, 1983.
Lieberman, P. Primate vocalizations and human linguistic ability. *J. Acoust. Soc. Am.*, 44:1574–1584, 1968.
Lieberman, P. *On the Origins of Language: An Introduction to the Evolution of Human Speech.* New York: Macmillan, 1975.
Lieberman, P. *The Biology and Evolution of Language.* Cambridge: Harvard Univ. Press, 1984.
Marler, P. & Tenaza, R.C. Signalling behaviour of apes with special reference to vocalizations. In Sebeok, T.E. (ed.) *How Animals Communicate.* Bloomington: Indiana Univ. Press, pp.965–1033, 1977.
Oller, D.K. The emergence of sounds of speech in infancy. In Yeni-Komshian, G.H., et al. (eds.) *Child Phonology, Vol.1, Production,* New York: Academic Press, pp.93–112, 1980.
Premack, D. *Intelligence in Ape and Man.* Hillsdale: Lawrence Erlbaum Associates, 1976.
Rumbaugh, D. *Language Learning by a Chimpanzee.* New York: Academic Press, 1977.
Seyfarth, R.M. & Cheney, D.L. The ontogeny of vervet monkeys alarm calling behavior: a preliminary report. *Zeitschr. Tierpsychol.*, 54:37–56, 1980.
Snowdon, C.T. Linguistic and psycholinguistic approaches to primate communication. In Snowdon, C.T., Brown, C.H. & Petersen, M.R. (eds.) *Primate Communication.* Cambridge: Cambridge Univ. Press, pp.212–238, 1982.
Snowdon, C.T., Brown, C.H. & Petersen, M.R. *Primate Communication.* Cambridge: Cambridge Univ. Press, 1982.
Struhsaker, T.T. Auditory communication among vervet monkeys (*Cercopithecus aethiops*). In Altmann, S.A. (ed.) *Social Communication among Primates.* Chicago: Univ. of Chicago Press, pp.281–324, 1967.

Chapter 2

Crothers, J. Typology and universals of vowel systems. In Greenberg, J.H., Ferguson, C.A. & Moravcsik, E.A. (eds.) *Universals of Human*

Language. Vol. 2, Phonology, Stanford: Stanford Univ. Press, pp.93–152, 1978.

Fujisaki, H., and Kawashima, T. The roles of pitch and higher formants in the perception of vowels. *IEEE Transact. Audio Electroacoust., AU-16*: 73–77, 1968.

Kuhl, P.K. Speech perception in early infancy: Perceptual constancy for spectrally dissimilar vowel categories. *J. Acoust. Soc. Am.*, 66:1668–1679, 1979.

Kuhl, P.K. Discrimination of speech by nonhuman animals: Basic auditory sensitivities conducive to the perception of speech-sound categories. *J. Acoust. Soc. Am.*, 70:340–349, 1981.

Kuhl, P.K. Human adults and human infants show a "perceptual magnet effect" for prototypes of speech categories, monkeys do not. *Percept. Psychophysic.*, 50:93–107, 1991.

Kuhl, P.K. & Miller, J.D. Speech perception by the chinchilla: Identification functions for synthetic VOT stimuli. *J. Acoust. Soc. Am.*, 63:905–917, 1978.

Kuhl, P.K. & Padden, D.M. Enhanced discriminability at the phonetic boundaries for the voicing feature in macaques. *Percept. Psychophysic.*, 32:542–550, 1982.

Kuhl, P.K. & Padden, D.M. Enhanced discriminability at the phonetic boundaries for the place feature in macaques. *J. Acoust. Soc. Am.*, 73:1003–1010, 1983.

Liberman, A.M., Cooper, F.S., Shankweiler, D.P. & Studdert-Kennedy, M. Perception of the speech code. *Psychol. Rev.*, 74:431–461, 1967.

Lieberman, P. *The Biology and Evolution of Language.* Cambridge: Harvard Univ. Press, 1984.

Lieberman, P. Some aspects of dimorphism and human speech. *Human Evol.*, 1:67–75, 1986.

Lisker, L. & Abramson, A. A cross language study of voicing in initial stops: acoustical measurements. *Word*, 20:384–422, 1964.

Mattingly, I.G., Liberman, A.M., Syrdal, A.K. & Halwes, T. Discrimination in speech and nonspeech modes. *Cog. Psychol.*, 2:131–157, 1971.

Miller, J.L. & Liberman, A.M. Some effects of later-occurring information on the perception of stop consonant and semi-vowel. *Percept. Psychophysic.*, 25:457–465, 1979.

Morse, P.A. & Snowdon, C.T. An investigation of categorical speech discrimination by rhesus monkeys. *Percept. Psychophysic.*, 17:9–16, 1975.

Repp, B.H. Phonetic trading relations and context effects: New evidence for a speech mode of perception. *Psychol. Bull.*, 92:81–110, 1982.

Waters, R.S. & Wilson Jr., W.A. Speech perception by rhesus monkeys: The voicing distinction in synthesized labial and velar stop consonants. *Percept. Psychophysic.*, 19:285–289, 1976.

Chapter 3

Klatt, D.H.. Software for a cascade/parallel formant synthesizer. *J. Acoust. Soc. Am.*: 971–995, 1980.

Chapter 4

Beecher, M.D. Hearing in the owl monkey (*Aotus trivirgatus*): I. Auditory sensitivity. *J. Comp. Physiol. Psychol.*, 86:898–901, 1974.

Brown, C.H. & Waser, P.M. Hearing and communication in blue monkeys (*Cercopithecus mitis*). *Anim Behav*, 32:66–75, 1984.

Elder, J.H. Auditory acuity of the chimpanzee. *J. Comp. Psychol.*, 17:157–183, 1934.

Elder J.H. The upper limit of hearing in chimpanzee. *Am. J. Physiol.*, 112:109–115, 1935.

Fant, G. Acoustic analysis and synthesis of speech with application to Swedish. *Ericsson Technics*, 1:3–108, 1959.

Farrer, D.N. & Prim, M.M. A preliminary report on auditory frequency threshold comparisons of humans and pre-adolescent chimpanzees. *Technical Report No.65–6, 6571st Aeromedical Research Laboratory, Holloman Air Force Base*, New Mexico, 1965.

Fay, R.R. *Hearing in Vertebrates: A Psychophysical Databook*. Winnetka Illinois: Hill-Fay Associates, 1988.

Fukuda, O. Measurements of auditory structures of vertebrates. I. *J. Otolaryngol. Jpn*, 62:1846–1862, 1959.

Itani, J. Vocal communication of the wild Japanese monkey. *Primates*, 4:11–66, 1963.

Jackson, L.L., Heffner, R.S. & Heffner, H.E. Free-field audiogram of the Japanese macaque. *J. Acoust. Soc. Am.*, 106: 3017–3023, 1999.

Kamada, T., Kameda, K. & Kojima, S. Auditory evoked potentials in the Japanese monkey. *J. Med. Primatol.*, 20: 284–289, 1991.

Kojima, S. Comparison of auditory functions between chimpanzee and human. *Folia Primatol.*, 55: 62–72, 1990.

Masterton, B., Heffner, H. & Ravizza, R. The evolution of human hearing. *J. Acoust. Soc. Am.*, 45:966–985, 1969.
Pickles, J.O. *An Introduction to the Physiology of Hearing*. New York, Academic Press, 1982.
Pfingst, B.E., Hienz, R., Kimm, J., et al. Reaction time procedure for measurement of hearing: I. Suprathreshold function. *J. Acoust. Soc. Am.*, 57:421–430, 1975.
Pfingst, B.E., Hienz, R. & Miller, J. Reaction time procedure for measurement of hearing. II. Threshold functions. *J. Acoust. Soc. Am.*, 57:431–436, 1975.
Shaw, E.A.G. The external ear. In Keidel, W.D. & Neff, W.D. (eds.) *Handbook of Sensory Physiology*. Berlin, Springer, vol.5/1, pp.455–490, 1974.
Sinnott, J.M., Petersen, M.R. & Hopp, S.L. Frequency and intensity discrimination in humans and monkeys. *J. Acoust. Soc. Am.*, 78: 1977–1985, 1985.
Stebbins, W.C. Hearing of Old World monkeys (Cercopithecinae). *Am. J. Phys. Anthropol.*, 38:357–364, 1973.

Chapter 5

Baru, A.V. Discrimination of synthesized vowels [a] and [i] with varying parameters (fundamental frequency, intensity, duration and number of formants) in dogs. In Fant, G. & Tahtam, M.A.A. (eds.), *Auditory Analysis and Perception of Speech*. London: Academic Press, pp. 91–101, 1975.
Burdick, C.K. & Miller, J.D. Speech perception by the chinchilla: discrimination of sustained /a/ and /i/. *J. Acoust. Soc. Am.*, 58: 415–427, 1975.
Chiba, T. & Kajiyama, M. *The vowel: its Nature and Structure*, Tokyo: Tokyo-Kaiseikan, 1941.
Fujisaki, H. & Kawashima, T. The roles of pitch and higher formants in the perception of vowels. *IEEE Transactions on Audio and Electroacoustics*, AU-16: 73–77, 1968.
Fukuda, Y., Sakamoto, Y. & Kuroki, S. Promotive effect of residual hearing upon speech reading. *J. Acoust. Soc. Jpn.*, 32:271–276, 1976.
Kojima, S. Comparison of auditory functions in the chimpanzee and human. *Folia Primatol.*, 55: 62–72, 1990
Kojima, S. Early vocal development in a chimpanzee infant. In Matsuzawa, T. (ed.) *Primate Origins of Human Cognition and Behavior*. Tokyo: Springer-Verlag, pp.190–196, 2001.

Kojima, S. & Kiritani, S. Vocal-auditory functions in the chimpanzee: Vowel perception. *Int. J. Primatol.*, 10: 199–213, 1989.

Kojima, S. Tatsumi, I.F., Kiritani, S. & Hirose, H. Vocal-auditory functions of the chimpanzee: Consonant perception. *Human Evol.*, 4:403–416, 1989.

Kuhl, P. Speech perception in early infancy: perceptual constancy for spectrally dissimilar vowel categories. *J. Acoust. Soc. Am.*, 66: 1668–1679, 1979.

Kuhl, P. Discrimination of speech by nonhuman animals: Basic auditory sensitivities conducive to the perception of speech-sound categories. *J. Acoust. Soc. Am.*, 70: 340–349, 1981.

Kuhl, P. Theoretical contribution of tests on animals to the special-mechanisms debate in speech. *Exp. Biol.*, 45: 233–256, 1986.

Kuhl, P.K. Human adults and human infants show a "perceptual magnet effect" for prototypes of speech categories, monkeys do not. *Percept. Psychophysic.*, 50:93–107, 1991.

Kuhl, P.K. & Miller, J.D. Speech perception by the chinchilla: Identification functions for synthetic VOT stimuli. *J. Acoust. Soc. Am.*, 63:905–917, 1978.

Kuhl, P.K. & Padden, D.M. Enhanced discriminability at the phonetic boundaries for the voicing feature in macaques. *Percept. Psychophysic.*, 32:542–550, 1982.

Kuhl, P.K. & Padden, D.M. Enhanced discriminability at the phonetic boundaries for the place feature in macaques. *J. Acoust. Soc. Am.*, 73:1003–1010, 1983.

Liberman, A., Cooper, F., Shankweiler, D. & Studdert-Kenedy, M. Perception of the speech code. *Psychol. Rev.*, 74: 431–461, 1967.

Lieberman, P. *On the Origins of Language: an Introduction to the Evolution of Human Speech.* New York: Macmillan, 1975.

Lieberman, P. *The Biology and Evolution of Language.* Cambridge: Harvard University Press, 1984.

Lieberman, P. Some aspects of dimorphism and human speech. *Human Evol.* 1: 67–75, 1986.

Lisker, L. & Abramson, A. A cross language study of voicing in initial stops: Acoustical measurements. *Word*, 20: 384–422, 1964.

Mattingly, I.G., Liberman, A.M., Syrdal, A.K. & Hawles, T. Discrimination in speech and nonspeech modes. *Cog. Psychol.*, 2: 131–157, 1971.

Miller, G.A. & Nicely, P.E. An analysis of perceptual confusions among some English consonants. *J. Acoust. Soc. Am.*, 27: 338–352, 1955.

Miller, J.L. & Liberman, A.M. Some effects of later-occurring information on the perception of stop consonant and semi-vowel. *Percept. Psychophysic.*, 25:457–465, 1979.

Moody, D.B., May, B., Cole, D.M. & Stebbins, W.C. The role of frequency modulation of complex stimuli by primates. *Exp. Biol.*, 45:219–232, 1986.

Mohr, B. & Wang, W.S.-Y. Perceptual distance and the specification of phonological features. *Phonetica* 18: 31–45, 1968.

Morse, P.A. & Snowdon, C.T. An investigation of categorical speech discrimination by rhesus monkeys. *Percept. Psychophysic.*, 17: 9–16, 1975.

Peters, R.W. Dimensions of perception for consonants. *J. Acoust. Soc. Am.*, 35: 1985–1989, 1963.

Peterson, G.E. & Barney, H.L. Control methods used in a study of the vowels. *J. Acoust. Soc. Am.*, 24: 175–184, 1952.

Singh, S., Wood, D.R. & Becker, G.M. Perceptual structure of 22 prevocalic English consonants. *J. Acoust. Soc. Am.*, 52: 1698–1713, 1972.

Sinnott, J.M., Owren, M.J. & Petersen, M.R. Auditory duration discrimination in Old World monkeys (*Macaca, Cercopithecus*) and humans. *J. Acoust. Soc. Am.*, 82: 465–470, 1987.

Walden, B.E., Montgomery, A.A., Prosek, R.A. & Schwarts, D.M. Consonant similarity judgments by normal and hearing-impaired listeners. *J. Speech Hearing Res.*, 23: 162–184.

Waters, R.S. & Wilson, Jr. W.A. Speech perception by rhesus monkeys: The voicing distinction in synthesized labial and velar stop consonants. *Percept. Psychophysic.*, 19: 285–289, 1976.

Wilson, K.V. Multidimensional analyses of confusions of English consonants. *Am. J. Psychol.*, 76: 89–05, 1963.

Chapter 6

Gourevitch, G. Detectability of tones in quiet and in noise by rats and monkeys. In Stebbins, W.C. (ed.) *Animal Psychophysics: The Design and Conduct of Sensory Experiments.* New York: Appleton-Century-Crofts, 1970.

Green, S. Variation of vocal pattern with social situation in the Japanese monkey (*Macaca fuscata*): a field study. In Rosenblum, L.A. (ed.) *Primate behavior.* New York: Academic Press, pp.1–102, 1975.

Hauser, M.D., Evance, C.S. & Marler, P. The role of articulation in the production of rhesus monkey, *Macaca mulatta*, vocalizations. *Anim. Behav.*, 45: 423–433, 1993.

Heffner, H.J.E. & Heffner, R.S. Temporal lobe lesions and perception of species-specific vocalizations by macaques. *Science*, 226: 75–76, 1984.
Kojima, S. Auditory short-term memory in the Japanese monkey. *Int. J. Neurosci.*, 25: 255–262, 1985.
Kojima, S. Comparison of auditory functions in the chimpanzee and human. *Folia Primatol.*, 55: 62–72, 1990.
Kojima, S. & Kiritani, S. Vocal-auditory functions in the chimpanzee: Vowel perception. *Int. J. Primatol.*, 10: 199–213, 1989.
Le Prell, C.G. & Moody, D.B. Perceptual salience of acoustic features of Japanese monkey coo calls. *J. Comp. Psychol.*, 111: 261–274, 1997.
Lieberman, P. *On the Origins of Language: An Introduction to the Evolution of Human Speech*. New York:Macmillan, 1975.
Lieberman, P., Crelin, E.S. & Klatt, D.H. Phonetic ability and related anatomy of the newborn and adult human, Neanderthal Man, and the chimpanzee. *Am. Anthropologist*, 74: 287–307, 1972.
Marler, P. & Tenaza, R. Signaling behavior of apes with special reference to vocalization. In Sebeok, T.E. (ed.) *How Animals Communicate*. Bloongton: Indiana Univ. Press, 1977.
May, B., Moody, D.J.& Stebbins, W.C. The significant features of Japanese macaque coo sounds: a psychophysical study. *Anim. Behav.*, 36: 1432–1444, 1988.
Moore, B.C.J. *An Introduction to the Psychology of Hearing*. New York:Academic Press, 1989.
Oller, D.K. The emergence of sounds of speech in infancy. In Yeni-Komshian, G.H., Kavanagh, J.F. & Ferguson, C.A. (eds.) *Child Phonology, Vol.1, Production*. New York: Academic Press, pp. 93–112, 1980.
Petersen, M.R., Beecher, M.D., Zoloth, S.R., Moody, D.B. & Stebbins, W.C. Neural lateralization of species-specific vocalizations by Japanese macaques (*Macaca fuscata*). *Science*, 202: 324–327, 1978.
Serafin, S.V., Moody, D.V. & Stebbins, W.C. Frequency selectivity of the monkey's auditory system: Psychophysical tuning curves. *J. Acoust. Soc. Am.*, 71: 1513–1518, 1982.

Chapter 7

Arcadi, A.C. Phrase structure of wild chimpanzee pant hoots: Patterns of production and interpopulation variability. *Am. J. Primatol.*, 39: 159–178, 1996.

Bauer, H.R. & Philip, M.M. Facial and vocal individual recognition in the common chimpanzee. *Psychol. Rec.*, 33: 161–170, 1983.

Boysen, S.T. Individual differences in the cognitive abilities of chimpanzees. In Wrangham, R.W., McGrew, W.C., de Waal, F.B.M. & Heltne, P.G. (eds.), *Chimpanzee Cultures*. Cambridge: Harvard Univ. Press, pp.335–350, 1994.

Boysen, S.T. & Berntson, G.G. Cardiac correlates of individual recognition in the chimpanzees (*Pan troglodytes*). *J. Comp. Psychol.*, 100: 321–324, 1986.

Clark, A.P. Rank differences in the production of vocalization by wild chimpanzees as a function of social context. *Am. J. Primatol.*, 31: 159–179, 1993.

Clark, A.P. & Wrangham, R.W. Acoustic analysis of wild chimpanzee pant hoots: Do Kibale Forest chimpanzees have an acoustically distinct food arrival pant hoot? *Am. J. Primatol.* 31:99–109, 1993.

Clark, A.P. & Wrangham, R.W. Chimpanzee arrival pant hoots: Do they signify food or status? *Int. J. Primatol.* 15: 185–205, 1994.

Coe, C.L., Connolly, A.C., Kraemer, H.C. & Levine, S. Reproductive development and behavior of captive female chimpanzees. *Primates*, 20: 571–582, 1979.

Davenport, R.K., Rogers, C.M. & Russell, I.S. Cross-modal perception in apes: altered visual cues and delay. *Neuropsychologia.*, 13: 229–235, 1975.

Dewson, J.H.III & Burlingame, A.C. Auditory discrimination and recall in monkeys. *Science*, 187: 267–268, 1975.

Dewson, J.H.III & Cowey, A. Discrimination of auditory sequences by monkeys. *Nature*, 222: 695–697, 1969.

Ettlinger, G. Interactions between sensory modalities in nonhuman primates. In Schrier, A.M. (ed.), *Behavioral Primatology. Advances in Research and Theory*. Hillsdale: Lawrence Erbaum, Vol. 1, pp. 71–104, 1977.

Engelien, A., Silbersweig, D., Stern, E., Huber, W., Doring, W., Frith, C. & Frackowiak, R. S. J. The functional anatomy of recovery from auditory agnosia: a PET study of sound categorization in a neurological patient and normal controls. *Brain,* 118: 1395–1409, 1995.

Fernald, A. & Morikawa, H. Common themes and cultural variations in Japanese and American mothers' speech to infants. *Child Develop.,* 64: 637–656, 1993.

Friston, K.J., Holmes, A.P., Worsley, K.J., Poline, J-P., Frith, C.D. & Frackowiak, R.S. J. Statistical parametric maps in functional imaging: a general linear approach. *Human Brain Mapping,* 2: 189–210, 1995.

Fujita, K. & Matsuzawa, T. Delayed figure construction in a chimpanzee (*Pan troglodytes*). *J. Comp. Psychol.*, 104: 345–351, 1990.

Gaffan, D. & Harrison, S. Auditory-visual associations, hemispheric specialization and temporal-frontal interaction in the rhesus monkey. *Brain*, 114: 2133–2144, 1991.

Gallup, G. Chimpanzees: Self-recognition. *Science* 167, 86–87, 1970.

Hashiya, K. & Kojima, S. Auditory-visual intermodal matching by a chimpanzee (*Pan troglodytes*). *Jpn. Psychol. Res.*, 39: 182–190, 1997.

Hashiya, K. & Kojima, S. Hearing and auditory-visual intermodal recognition in the chimpanzee. In Matsuzawa, T. (ed.) *Primate Origins of Human Cognition and Behavior.* Tokyo: Springer-Verlag, pp.155–189, 2001a.

Hashiya, K. & Kojima, S. Acquisition of auditory-visual intermodal matching-to-sample by a chimpanzee (*Pan troglodytes*): Comparison with visual-visual intermodal matching. *Anim. Cognit.*, 4: 231–239, 2001b.

Hauser, M.D., Teixidor, P., Field, L. & Flaherty, R. Food-elicited calls in chimpanzees: Effects of food quantity and divisibility. *Anim. Behav.* 45: 817–819, 1993.

Hewes, G. W. Primate communication and the gestural origin of language. *Current Anthropol.*, 14: 5–24, 1973.

Jusczyk, P.W., Pisoni, D.B. & Mullenix, J. Some consequences of stimulus variability on speech processing by 2-month-old infants. *Cognition*, 43:253–291, 1992.

Kita, S. Two-dimensional semantic analysis of Japanese mimetics. *Linguistics*, 35: 379–415, 1997.

Kobayashi, H. & Ogino, M. Cultural actions on objects and early language development. In: Kojima, S. (ed.) *The Emergence of Human Cognition and Language*, vol 3, Primate Research Institute, Kyoto University, pp.62–65, 1996.

Kojima, S. Auditory short-term memory in the Japanese monkey. *Int. J. Neurosci.*, 25:255–262, 1985.

Kojima, S. & Kiritani, S. Vocal-auditory functions in the chimpanzee: Vowel perception. *Int. J. Primatol.*, 10: 199–213, 1989.

Marler, P. & Hobbett, L. Individuality in a long-range vocalization of wild chimpanzees. *Zeitschr. Tierpsychol.*, 38: 97–109, 1975.

Matsuzawa, T. Form perception and visual acuity in a chimpanzee. *Folia Primatol.*, 55: 24–32, 1990.

Mitani, J.C. & Brandt, K.L. Social factors influence the acoustic variability in the long-distance calls of male chimpanzees. *Ethology,* 96: 233–252, 1994.

Mitani, J.C. & Gros-Louis, J. Species and sex differences in the screams of chimpanzees and bonobos. *Int. J. Primatol.,* 16: 393–411, 1995.

Mitani, J.C., Gros-Louis, J. & Macedonia, J.M. Selection for acoustic individuality within the vocal repertoire of wild chimpanzees. *Int. J. Primatol.,* 17: 569–583, 1996.

Mitani, J.C. & Nishida, T. Contexts and social correlates of long-distance calling by male chimpanzees. *Anim. Behav.* 45: 735–746, 1993.

Murray, E. & Gaffan, D. Removal of the amygdala plus subjacent cortex disrupt the retention of both intramodal and crossmodal associative memories in monkeys. *Behav. Neurosci.,* 108: 494–500, 1994.

Nishida, T. Alpha status and agonistic alliance in wild chimpanzees (*Pan troglodytes schweinfurthii*). *Primates,* 24: 318–336, 1983.

Polster, M. R. & Rose, S. B. Disorders of auditory processing: evidence for modularity in audition. *Cortex,* 34: 47–65, 1998.

Rizzolatti, G. & Arbib, M. A. Language within our grasp. *Trends in Neuroscience,* 21: 188–194, 1988.

Rousseau, J-J. *Essai sur l'origine des langues, ou il est parle de la melodie et de l'imitation musicale,* 1781. Japanese translation.

Savage-Rumbaugh, S. A new look at ape language: comprehension of vocal speech and syntax. *Nebraska Symposium on Motivation: Comparative Perspectives in Modern Psychology,* 35: 201–255, 1987.

Talairach, J. & Tournoux, P. *Co-planar Stereotaxic Atlas of the Human Brain.* New York: Thieme, 1988.

de Waal, F. *Chimpanzee Politics.* London: Jonathan Cape, 1982.

Wright, A.A. & Rivera, J.J. Memory of auditory lists by rhesus monkeys (*Macaca mulatta*). *J. Exp. Psychol.: Anim. Behav. Proc.,* 23: 441–449, 1997.

Chapter 8

Hayes, K. *The Ape in Our House.* New York: Harper, 1951.

Larson, C.R., Sutton, D., Taylor, E.M. & Lindeman, R. Sound spectral properties of conditioned vocalization in monkeys. *Phonetica,* 27: 100–110, 1973.

Leander, J.D., Milan, M.A., Jasper, K.B. & Heaton, K.L. Schedule control of vocal behavior of cebus monkeys. *J. Exp. Anal. Behav.,* 17: 229–235, 1972.

Myers, S.A., Horel, J.A. & Pennypacker, H.S. Operant control of vocal behavior in the monkey *Cebus albifrons*. *Psychon. Sci.*, 3: 389–390, 1965.

Sutton, D., Larson, C., Taylor, E.M. & Lindeman, R.C. Vocalization in rhesus monkeys: Conditionability. *Brain Res.*, 52: 225–231, 1973.

Wilson, W.A.Jr. Discriminative conditioning of vocalizations in *Lemur catta*. *Anim. Behav.*, 23: 432–436, 1975.

Chapter 9

Goodall, J. *The chimpanzees of Gombe*. Cambridge: Belknap, 1986

Hayes, C. *The Ape In Our House*. New York: Harper, 1951.

Kaye, K. & Fogel, A. The temporal structure of face-to-face communication between mothers and infants. *Develop. Psychol.*, 16: 454–464, 1980.

Kuhl, P. K. & Meltzoff, A.N. The bimodal perception of speech in infancy. *Science*, 218: 1138–1140, 1982.

Locke, J.L. *The Child's Path to Spoken Language*. Cambridge: Cambridge Univ. Press, 1993.

Marler, P. and Tenaza, R. Signalling behavior of wild apes with special reference to vocalization. In Sebeok, T. (ed.), *How Animals Communicate*. Bloomington: Indiana University Press, pp. 965–1033, 1977.

Oller, D.K. The emergence of the sounds of speech in infancy. In Yeni-Komshian, G.H. et al. (eds.), *Child Phonology: Vol. 1, Production*. New York: Academic Press, pp. 93–112, 1980.

Oller, D.K. Infant vocalizations: Exploration and reflexivity. In Stark, R.E. (ed.), *Language Behavior in Infancy and Early Childhood*. New York: Elsevier, pp. 85–103, 1981.

Oller, D.K. (1986) Metaphonology and infant vocalizations. In Lindblom, B. & Zetterstrom, R. (eds.), *Precursors of Early Speech*. New York: Stockton Press, pp. 21–35, 1986.

Oller, D.K. Development of vocalizations in infancy. In Winitz H. (ed.), *Human Communication and its Disorders: A Review, Vol. 4*. Timonium, MD: York Press, Inc, pp.1–30, 1995.

Plooij, F.X. *The Behavioral Development of Free-living Chimpanzee Babies and Infants*. Norwood: Ablex, 1984.

Stark, R.E. Stages of speech development in the first year of life. In Yeni-Komshian, G.H. et al. (eds.), *Child Phonology: Vol. 1, Production*. New York: Academic Press, pp. 73–92, 1980.

Chapter 10

Arcadi, A.C. Phrase structure of wild chimpanzee pant hoots: Patterns of production and interpopulation variability. *Am. J. Primatol.*, 39: 159–178, 1996.

Bauer, H.R. & Philip, M.M. Facial and vocal individual recognition in the common chimpanzee. *Psychol. Rec.*, 33: 161–170, 1983.

Clark, A.P. Rank differences in the production of vocalization by wild chimpanzees as a function of social context. *Am. J. Primatol.*, 31: 159–179, 1993.

Clark, A.P. & Wrangham, R.W. Chimpanzee arrival pant-hoots: do they signify food or status ? *Int. J. Primatol.*, 15: 185–205, 1994.

Goodall, J. The behaviour of free-living chimpanzees in the Gombe Stream Reserve. *Anim. Behav. Monogr.*, 1: 161–311, 1968.

Goodall, J. *The Chimpanzees of Gombe*. Cambridge: Belknap, 1986.

Ghiglieri, M. *The Chimpanzees of the Kibale Forest*. New York: Columbia Univ. Press, 1984.

Hauser, M.D., Teixidor, P. Field, L. & Flaherty, R. Food-elicited calls in chimpanzees: effects of food quantity and divisibility. *Anim. Behav.*, 45: 817–819, 1993.

Hauser, M.D. & Wrangham, R.W. Manipulation of food calls in captive chimpanzees. *Folia Primatol.*, 48: 207–210, 1987.

Itani, J. Chimpanzees and Gorillas. Nikkei Science: special issue on *Animal Sociology; from Monkeys to Human Being* (in Japanese). pp. 92–105, 1976.

Marler, P & Hobbett, L. Individuality in a long-range vocalization of wild chimpanzees. *Zeitschr. Tierpsychol.*, 38: 97–109, 1975.

Marler, P. & Tenaza, R. Signaling behavior of apes with special reference to vocalization. In Sebeok, T. (ed.), *How Animals Communicate*. Bloomington, Indiana Univ. Press, pp. 965–1033, 1977.

Masataka, N. & Biben, M. Temporal rules regulating affiliative vocal exchanges of squirrel monkeys. *Behaviour*,101: 311–319, 1987.

Menzel, E.W.Jr. A group of young chimpanzees in a one-acre field. In Schrier, A.M. & Stollnitz, F. (eds.) *Behaviors of Nonhuman Primates*. New York: Academic Press, pp., 83–153, 1974.

Mitani, J.C. & Brandt, K.L. Social factors influence the acoustic variability in the long-distance calls of male chimpanzees. *Ethology*, 96: 233–252, 1994.

Mitani, J.C., Gros-Louis, J. & Macedonia, J.M. Selection for acoustic individuality within the vocal repertoire of wild chimpanzees. *Int. J. Primatol.*, 17: 569–583, 1996.

Mitani, J.C., Hasegawa, T., Gros-Louis, J., Marler, P. & Byrne, R. Dialects in wild chimpanzees ? *Am. J. Primatol.*, 27: 233–243, 1992.

Mitani, J.C. & Nishida, T. Contexts and social correlates of long-distance calling by male chimpanzees. *Anim. Behav.*, 45: 735–746, 1993.

Nishida, T. Social behavior and relationship among wild chimpanzees of the Mahale Mountains. *Primates,* 11: 47–87, 1970.

Nishida, T., Hiraiwa-Hasegawa, M., Hasegawa, T. & Takahata, Y. Group extinction and female transfer in wild chimpanzees in the Mahale National Park, Tanzania. *Zietschr. Tierpsychol.*, 67: 284–301, 1985.

Nishida, T., Uehara, S. & Nyundo, R. Predatory behavior among wild chimpanzees of the Mahale Mountains. *Primates,* 20: 1–20, 1979.

Oda, R. & Masataka,N. Interspecific responses of ringtail lemurs to playback of antipredator alarm calls given by Verreaux's sifakas. *Ethology,* 102: 441–453, 1996.

Okamoto, K., Agetsuma, N. & Kojima, S. Greeting behavior during party encounters in captive chimpanzees. *Primates*, 42:161–165, 2001.

Reynolds, V. & Reynolds, F. Chimpanzees of the Budongo Forest. In *Primate Behavior*, DeVor, I. (ed.), New York: Holt, Rhinechart, Winston, pp. 368–424, 1965.

Seyfarth, R.M. & Cheney, D.L. How monkeys see the world: A review of recent research on East African vervet monkeys. In Snowdon, C.T., Brown, C.H. & Petersen, M.R. (eds.) *Primate Communication*. Cambridge: Cambridge Univ. Press, pp.239–252, 1982.

Seyfarth, R.M. & Cheney, D.L. The ontogeny of vervet monkeys alarm calling behavior: a preliminary report. *Zeitschr. Tierpsychol.*, 54: 37–50, 1980.

Struhsaker, T.T. Auditory communication among vervet monkeys (*Cercopithecus aetiops*). In Altman, S.A. (ed.) Social Communication among Primates. Chicago: Univ. Chicago Press, pp.281–324, 1967.

Wrangham, R. Feeding behaviour of chimpanzees in Gombe National Park, Tanzania. In Clutton-Brock, T. (ed.) *Primate Ecology*. London: Academic Press, pp. 503–538, 1977.

Wrangham, R. & Smuts, B. Sex differences in the behavioral ecology of chimpanzees in the Gombe National Park, Tanzania. *J. Reprod. Fert. Suppl.*, 28: 13–31, 1980.

Chapter 11

Beck, C.H.M. & Barton, R.L. Deviation and laterality of hand preference in monkeys. *Cortex*, 8: 339–363, 1972.

Custance, D.M., Whiten, A. & Bard, K.A. Can young chimpanzees (*Pan *troglodytes*) imitate arbitrary actions? Hayes & Hayes (1952) revisited. *Behaviour*, 132: 838–859, 1995.

Fouts, R.S. Use of guidance in teaching sign language to a chimpanzee (*Pan troglodytes*). *J Comp. Physiol. Psychol.*, 80: 515–522, 1972.

Gallese, V., Fadiga, L., Fogassi, L. & Rizzolatti, G. Action recognition in the premotor cortex. *Brain*, 119: 593–609, 1996.

Gallup, G. G. Jr. Chimpanzees: Self-recognition. *Science*, 167: 86–87, 1970.

Gannon, P.J. Holloway, R.L. Broadfield, D.C. & Braun, A.R. Asymmetry of chimpanzee planum tempolare: Humanlike pattern of Wernicke's brain language homology. *Science*, 279: 220–222, 1998.

Gardner, R.A. & Gardner, B.T. Teaching sign language to a chimpanzee. *Science*, 165:664–672, 1969.

Goodall, J. (van Lawick-Goodall, J.) A preliminary report on expressive movements and communication in the Gombe Stream chimpanzees. In: *Primates: Studies in Adaptation and Variability*. Jay. P. (ed.), New York: Holt, Rinehart and Winston, pp.313–374, 1968.

Grafton, S.T., Arbib, M.A., Fadiga, L. & Rizzolatti, G. Localization of grasp representations in humans by positron emission tomography. 2. Observation compared with imagination. *Exp. Brain Res.*, 112: 103–111, 1996.

Hamilton, C.R. & Vermeire, B.A. Complementary hemispheric specialization in monkeys. *Science*, 242: 1691–1694, 1988.

Hayes, K. *The Ape in Our House*. New York:Harper, 1951.

Hayes, K.J. & Hayes, C. Imitation in a home-raised chimpanzee. *J. Comp. Physiol. Psychol.*, 45: 450–459, 1952.

Heffner, H.E. & Heffner, R.S. Temporal lobe lesions and perception of species-specific vocalizations by macaques. *Science*, 226:75–76, 1984.

Heilman, K.M. Valenstein, E. *Clinical Neuropsychology*. Oxford: Oxford Univ. Press, 1979.

Hopkins, W.D. Chimpanzee handedness revisited. *Psychon.Bull. Rev.*, 3: 449–457, 1996.

Iacoboni, M. Woods, R.P. Brass, M. Bekkering, H. Mazziotta, J.C. & Rizzolatti, G. Cortical mechanisms of human imitation. *Science*, 286: 2526–2528, 1999.

Kimura, D. & Archibald, Y. Motor functions of the left hemisphere. *Brain*, 97: 337–350, 1974.

Kolb, B. & Milner, B. Performance of complex arm and facial movements after focal brain lesions. *Neuropsychologia*, 19:491–503, 1981.

MacNeilage, P.F., Studdert-Kennedy, M.G. & Lindblom, B. Primate handedness reconsidered. *Behav. Brain Sci.*, 10: 247–303, 1987.

Nishitani, N. & Hari, R. Temporal dynamics of cortical representation for action. *Proc. Natl. Acad. Sci.*, 97: 913–918, 2000.

Povinelli, D. J., Rulf, A. B., Landau, K. R. & Bierschwale, D.T. Self-recognition in chimpanzees (*Pan troglodytes*): Distribution, ontogeny, and patterns of emergence. *J. Comp. Psychol.*, 107: 347–372, 1993.

Premack, D. Putting a face together. *Science*, 188: 228–236, 1975.

Premack, D. *Intelligence in Ape and Man.* Hillsdale: Lawrence Erlbaum Associates, 1976.

Rizzolatti, G. & Arbib, M. A. Language within our grasp. *Trends in Neurosci.*, 21: 188–194, 1998.

Rizzolatti, G., Fadiga, L., Matelli, M., Bettinardi, V., Paulesu, E., Perani, D. & Fzio, F. Localization of grasp representations in humans by PET: 1. Observation versus execution. *Exp. Brain Res.*, 111: 246–252, 1996.

Rizzolatti, G., Luppino, G. & Matelli, M. The organization of the cortical motor system: new concepts. *EEG. Clin. Neurophysiol.*, 106: 283–296, 1998.

Rumbaugh, D. *Language Learning by a Chimpanzee.* New York: Academic Press, 1977.

Schopler, E. & Reichler, R.J. *Psychoeducational profile, vol. 1, Individualized Assessment and Treatment for Autistic and Developmentally Disabled Children.* Baltimore: University Park Press, 1979.

Yeni-Komshian, G.H. & Benson, D.A. Anatomical study of cerebral asymmetry in the temporal lobe of humans, chimpanzees, and rhesus monkeys. *Science*, 192: 387–389, 1976.

Zatorre, R.J., Evans, A.C., Meyer, E. & Gjedde, A. Lateralization of phonetic and pitch discrimination in speech processing. *Science*, 256: 846–849, 1992.

Chapter 12

Iacoboni, M., Woods, R.P., Brass, M., Bekkering, H., Mazziotta, J.C. & Rizzolatti, G. Cortical mechanisms of human imitation. *Science*, 286: 2526–2528, 1999.

Kimura, D. Manual activity during speaking- I. Right-handers. *Neuropsychologia*, 11: 45–50, 1973.

Kimura, D. *Neuromotor Mechanisms in Human Communication.* New York: Oxford Univ. Press, 1993.

Nishitani, N. & Hari, R. Temporal dynamics of cortical representation for action. *Proc. Natl. Acad. Sci.*, 97: 913–918, 2000.

Rizzolatti, G., Fadiga, L., Matelli, M., Bettinardi, V., Paulesu, E., Perani, D. & Fzio, F. Loalization of grasp representations in humans by PET: 1. Observation versus execution. *Exp. Brain Res.*, 111: 246–252, 1996.

Index

ABR, 41
acoustical modification, 113
acquisition of audio-visual intermodal matching to sample, 94
action, 152
AP, 42
aphasia, 153
apparatus, 18
audio-visual intermodal matching to sample, 94
audio-visual matching to sample task, 25
audio-visual sample, 95
auditory cognition, 94
auditory evoked potentials, 41
auditory nervous system, 8
auditory ossicles, 7
auditory sample, 95
auditory sensitivity, 27
auditory system, 5
auditory working memory, 116, 121

basilar memb, 7
body image, 156

canonical babbling, 142
categorical perception, 15,, 64
chimpanzee name, 114
chimpanzee 'language' project, 1
CM, 42

cochlea, 7
consonant, 11
context effect, 17, 69
coo, 90
crying vocalization, 135

difference threshold, 31
digital filter, 23, 75
'duets' of pant hoot, 108, 110

early vocal development, 128
effort grunt, 137
encounter, 144
enculturation, 140
environmental sound, 101
expansion stage, 134
external auditory meatus, 5
external ear, 5
external ear canal, 5

face construction test, 168
filter, 113
fine motor skills, 173
first and second formant (F1-F2) plane, 10
formant, 10
forward and backward fading procedure, 121
French consonant, 58
frequency difference threshold, 31
fundamental frequency, F0; pitch, 10

fundamental tone, 9

generalized imitation, 156
gestural origin theory, 120
Go/No Go auditory delayed matching to sample task, 25
Goo, 142
Goo stages, 133
grunt, 72, 128

hair cell, 7
handedness, 152
harmonics, 10
hominization, 174

imitation, 154
incus, 7
infraphonological analysis, 133
inner ear, 7
intensity difference threshold, 34
internalization, 175

Japanese macaque, 39, 41, 70, 90, 121

language, 153
laterality, 154, 174
laughter, 128
loudness, 27
LPC, 23

magnet effect, 15, 57
malleu, 7
manner of articulation, 11
middle ear, 7
mirror system, 120, 170

natural French vowel, 49
natural Japanese vowel, 48
non-crying vocal behavior, 130

non-crying vocal sounds, 128

onomatopoeia, 115, 117
organ of Corti, 7
overlap of two successive vocalizations, 146

pant grunt, 107, 109
pant hoot, 107, 109, 143
perception of consonant, 58
perception of grunt, 75
perception of stop consonant, 61
PET, 117
phonation, 133, 142
phoneme boundary effect, 15, 64
pitch shift, 113
place of articulation, 11
production of grunt, 73
prototype effect, 15, 57

rate normalization, 17, 69
rCBF, 118
reaction time task, 23
recognition of chimpanzees by voice, 107
recognition of human individuals by voice, 104
resonance of the external auditory meatus, 37

scream, 109, 135
self-awareness, 158
self-recognition, 158
'semantic' communication, 151
sound spectrograph, 23
speaker identification, 106
species-specific vocal sound, 72
speech, 1
squeak, 83, 135
staccato, 128

stapes, 7
subject, 18
supralaryngeal vocal tract, 10
synthetic grunt, 77
synthetic Japanese vowel, 47
synthetic vowel, 23

task dependency, 97
transfer of audio-visual intermodal
    matching to sample, 98

understanding of spoken word,
    114

variegated babbling, 142
visual sample, 98
vocal communication, 143
vocal cords, 9
vocal imitation, 131
vocal interaction, 137, 143
vocal operant, 125
vocal self-recognition, 112
vocal system, 9
vocal tract normalization, 13, 52,
    70
voiced-voiceless distinction, 11
vowel, 9
vowel perception, 47

whimper, 83, 137